GET IN THE VAN

HENRY ROLLINS

ISBN 1-880985-24-1

Copyright ©1994 by Henry Rollins

Published by 2.13.61 Publications, Inc.

THIRD PRINTING

Design: Stan Fairbank / Endless Graphics
Original front cover design: Timothy Eames

Manufactured in Hong Kong through Palace Press International.

2.13.61
P.O. BOX 1910 · LOS ANGELES ·
CALIFORNIA · 90078 · USA

OTHER BOOKS FROM 2.13.61:

THANK YOU: Gail Perry, Richard Bishop, Lorraine Walters-Morse, Gary I., Stan Fairbank, Modi, Iris and Les Silverman, Hubert Selby Jr., Don Bajema never quits.

DEDICATED: To all the bands who know. All the shit that these bastards will put you through. The record companies who bullshit you, promoters who lie to you, waste your time and rip you off. The all night drives that leave you wasted and barely able to think straight when you have a long set and another all night drive ahead of you. Working harder than anyone you know and still not being able to pay the rent. Years of watching shitty, fake bands headline over you. The endless blank hours of waiting. The depression of all the beat down towns crowding your mind month after month. Few have your courage.

All the members of Black Flag and the crews. Ian MacKaye, Jill Heath, Mugger, The Sookey Bros., Dave and Brian of Rat Sound, Tom Troccoli, Davo, Joe Carducci, Raymond Pettibon, Merrill Ward, Byron Coley, Chris Morris, Robert Palmer, Deirdre O'Donoghue, Pat from Omaha, Paul Boswell, Sean Duffy, Randy Ellis, Dirk Dirksen, John Golden, The Ginn Family, Julie Lawrence, Ed Colver, Glen Friedman, Naomi Petersen, Staci Rolfe, Murray Kappel, Target Video, The Minutemen, The Misfits, Saccharine Trust, The Nig Heist, The October Faction, Dog, Flipper, Spittin' Teeth, The Big Boys, The Dicks, Minor Threat, The Oil Tasters, The Damned, Angst, The UK Subs, DOA, 7 Seconds, The Stains, The Bad Brains, The Sluts, Mitch Bury of Adams Mass.

Greg Ginn and Chuck Dukowski. Hardest working people I've ever met. Delivered under pressure at incredible odds. Heaviest people I've ever been onstage with. Guts, influence and inspiration beyond words.

This book was Joe Cole's idea. "Man, you gotta document this stuff. It's important."

JOE COLE 4.10.61 – 12.19.91

INTRODUCTION

I was in the band Black Flag from summer 1981 to summer 1986 when the band broke up. I kept a loose journal from 1983 to the end. What you've got here is all the journal entries from 1983 to 1986 and two chapters detailing events in 1981 and 1982 when I wasn't keeping a journal. I took the tour dates from these years and if I remembered anything worth writing about, I put it in.

There are several entries in the journals that say "Shed." The Shed was a small tool shed that I lived in for a couple of years. I did a lot of writing in there.

I did the best I could to include a lot of pictures. I contacted the main photographers of the band — Glen Friedman, Ed Colver and Naomi Petersen — they supplied me with some great stuff. We took some of more well-known lineup shots and included alternate shots off the same roll. In addition to this, I selected a lot of photos from my files that I thought told the story well. Some of these photos have no credits. These were pictures sent to me in the mail or given to me at shows and I never got the name. If you see a picture you took and don't see your name, no offense is intended.

I hope you have a good time with this book. We started work on this in 1990. I have never been so happy to see a file leave my computer.

H. ROLLINS
JUNE 1994

WASHINGTON, DC / 10.31.80 *(JAY RABINOWITZ)*

SPRING: I was living in an apartment in Arlington, Virginia, which is right over the DC line. I walked to work every day which was at an ice cream store at the time. I was the store manager and was there 40 - 60 hours a week making the deposit, hiring, firing, inventory, scooping, etc.

I was in a band at the time. Nothing much musically speaking, four of us with fucked up equipment. But we had fun playing and practicing.

A guy named Mitch Parker gave my friend Ian MacKaye and me a copy of Black Flag's *Nervous Breakdown* EP. We played it all the time. It was heavy. The record's cover said it all. A man baring his fists with his back to a wall. In front of him, another man fending him off with a chair. I felt like the guy with his fists up every day of my life.

Black Flag soon became my favorite band. Stories of their

w/ IAN MACKAYE / 1980 *(SUZIE JOSEPHSON)*

shows in Los Angeles were legendary on the East Coast. They had their own record company called SST and they took no shit.

Ian called SST and talked to their bass player Chuck Dukowski. He told Ian about the tour coming up and gave him the dates for the East Coast. They had dates booked for New York and DC. *We were going to see the mighty Black Flag.* A group of us went up to NYC to see the band play because we couldn't wait to see them in DC and we figured the more we saw them, the better.

So we drove up to NYC and saw them at the Peppermint Lounge. I will never forget how excited I was when they came on the stage. Chuck Dukowski was out there walking around in circles pounding his bass making all this fucked up noise and screaming at the crowd. They hadn't even started playing yet and it was already a trip. I think they opened with "I've Heard It Before" and the place exploded. All the songs were abrupt and crushing. Short bursts of unbelievable intensity. I had never seen anyone play like that before. It was like they were trying to break themselves into pieces with the music. It was one of the mos powerful things I've ever seen. There was not a second wasted onstage. The songs were devoid of filler. The urgency of the music and the playing was unsettling. Made me wonder what planet they came from. I wanted to move there immediately.

After the show, we hung out with the band for a little while and they were really cool to us. It meant a lot. I respected and liked them.

S.O.A.

A few days later, they came down to DC to play at the 9:30 Club. Again they were good and the place went off when they played. I liked the DC show better because they played two sets and I got to hear all of their songs.

They stayed at Ian's house after the show and left the next morning. I remember watching their van pull away up the street and wanting to be in it. It was amazing to me how they pulled in, played, hung out with the locals and then took off on the next adventure. I had to hurry up and get to work. As I walked down the hill toward a long night at the work-place, I started getting depressed. Black Flag was a bunch of guys who were out there winging it and trying to do something with their lives. They had no fixed income and they lived like dogs, but they were living life with a lot more guts than I was by a long shot. I had a steady income and an apartment and money in the bank. But I also had a job where I got yelled at when things didn't go right. I had to be there all the time. I saw the same streets and the same people every day. My job took over a lot of my waking hours.

After I had hung out with the Flag guys, I saw that there was a lot more out there to be seen and done and I didn't think I was ever going to do any of it. That night at work, everything in my life felt meaningless. I knew that somehow I was blowing it. I had a low level panic attack. I got a glimpse of something that made it impossible to bullshit myself. I wished it didn't open my eyes so much and make me see so clearly. I saw my life stretching out in front of me. Same town, same people, same everything. It felt as if I was getting tied down and beaten by life. They had guts. The way they were living went against all the things I had been taught to believe were right. If I had listened to my father, I would have joined the Navy, served and gone into the straight world without a whimper. I'm not putting that down. But it's not the life for everyone.

Chuck Dukowski had given me a demo tape of unreleased Black Flag music. Every morning before I would go to work, I would play that tape: "Damaged I", "Police Story", "No More" and their version of "Louie, Louie". I loved and hated that tape. I loved it because the tunes were great and the words said what I was feeling. I hated it because I wanted to be the singer. Dez, who was the singer at the time, was great. But I still imagined myself up there doing it.

Black Flag came east again in June. They played New York on June 27 at the Irving Plaza. The Bad Brains and UXA played as well. I went up to see them. I got up there early and met up with Greg and Chuck. I hung out most of the afternoon. They were great that night. After the show, the band went down the street to a small club called 7A to play some more. I went along.

The sun was coming up and I had to be at work in six hours. I had a five hour drive. Time to leave. I went up to the stage and asked them to play "Clocked In" to send me on my way. Dez said, "This is called 'Clocked In'. It's for Hank because he's got to go to work now."

The band laid into the song. I got onstage, took the microphone and sang the song. I don't know what compelled me to do that. Sure was fun and Dez didn't seem to mind. I left the club to drive home. I went right into work with no sleep. I didn't need it. I was still pumped from singing with Black Flag. The fact that I had been onstage and had a taste of what it was like to be in the band was good enough for me.

Days later, I'm working at the store and I get a phone call. It's Dez. The band is up in New York taking a few days off and they want to know if I want to come up and jam with them. I didn't understand what they meant, but it was the Flag talking so I hopped to it. I went back to the apartment and called Ian and explained that I thought I was being asked to audition for Black Flag. After that, my roommate came in and asked what was up and I told him that I had to go to New York because I might be asked to join Black Flag. He thought I was talking some shit. It sure sounded like a load. I walked all the way to the train station because I didn't feel like getting a cab. It was a long walk and it was a good chance to think about the whole thing. I thought it best not to get my hopes up. I got on an early train and fell asleep.

The next morning we all met at Odessa's, a restaurant in the East Village. I ask them what the deal is. Greg tells me that Dez wants to play guitar and they are looking for a singer since Dez is moving over. Would I want to try out? I couldn't believe what I was hearing.

We went to Mi Casa rehearsal studios and set up. All of a sudden, I'm standing there in front of them with a mic in my hand. Greg asked me what song I wanted to play first. I thought I must be dreaming. For a second, I didn't think that I was there at all. I told him "Police Story". It was as if I had flipped the switch on some kind of angry machine. The entire band kind of reared back and lurched forward and I heard the classic Ginn feedback, and all of a sudden, we were into the song. We played all of their material. What words I knew, I sang. The ones I didn't, I made up. We did two sets. At the end, we all kind of looked at each other. The band went out in back to talk it over and I sat on the floor of the practice room and waited it out.

They came back in and Chuck said, "Well?"

I said, "Well what?"

"Are you going to join or not?"

I was in. That's pretty much how I joined Black Flag.

I took the train back to DC and spent the trip looking over the lyrics that the band had given me to learn. It was all the material that would later comprise the *Damaged* album — "Padded Cell", "Damaged II", "Room 13", etc. It was heavy stuff. I became so absorbed, I barely noticed when we hit DC.

In a couple of days, I packed up, quit my job, sold my car and left Washington DC. I had no idea what was going to happen. But this is what I wanted so off I went. It was great telling my boss that I was quitting. He offered me more money. I told him it wasn't a money issue. I told him that I was off to do this thing and I didn't know how it was going to go, but I had to go for it. He told me it was a crazy idea and I should get back to work. He laid into me hard and it got to me a little. Luckily for me, Ian MacKaye was really behind me and told me that he knew this was going to be great and to go for it. I respected everything he said and still do. He gave me the extra shove out the door that I needed. For me, it was a chance to live. Ian took me to the Greyhound station and wished me good luck. I left my hometown like a guy making a jailbreak.

I caught up with the band in Detroit. Dez wanted to finish the tour on vocals and there was no way I was ready. I worked stage and sometimes did the encores. Soundcheck was used to teach me the songs and to make rhythm guitar parts for Dez to play.

We played Chicago, Minneapolis, Madison and Salt Lake City before we hit LA. The Chicago show was intense. The Effigies opened and they were great. Flag went on next. A few songs into the set, a girl was getting roughed up by one of the bouncers. The guys in this place were out of line. Chuck knocked the guy on the head with the end of his bass. The guy started to bleed. He got taken to the hospital to get stitches. After the show, we're packing the gear out and we can't find some of the drums. The drums were big, it's not as if they were misplaced. We knew something was up. One of the shithead bouncers came out and

BLACK FLAG, 1981. L-R: HENRY ROLLINS, GREG GINN, DEZ CADENA, ROBO, CHUCK DUKOWSKI *(GLEN E. FRIEDMAN)*

asked us if we wanted the drums back. Mugger and I went into the manager's office and the kick drum was sitting on a desk. The guy who ran the place was sitting there surrounded by bouncers. He started giving us shit about what fuckups we were and all this other shit. I have no idea how we managed to get the gear out of there and not get our asses kicked, but we did. We found out later that the club owner called ahead to our other shows and told them that we were bad people and not to pay us. This was a normal thing back in those days.

We played in Madison, Wisconsin around this time, maybe after the Chicago show. I liked Madison, a cool town. The place we played was called Merlin's. After the show, people were out skating and hanging around. We stayed with some skaters that night.

I do remember anything special about the Madison show or the Minneapolis one either. In those days, if there wasn't some kind of outbreak or police intervention then it wasn't all that memorable.

The show in Salt Lake was interesting. I met a kid who was cuffed to the door handle of a police car outside the gig. He was there early to catch soundcheck and the cop busted him for drinking a beer in the parking lot. I hung out with the guy and gave him some water. It was strange to be talking with this guy who was standing in the sun tied to a car. I guess the pig figured he was teaching him a lesson. That taught me plenty.

We got to LA days later and we had nowhere to stay. SST, which was located in Torrance at this time, had been shut down by the cops. Black Flag was told to leave or else.

We crashed at a house in Hollywood. It was a bunch of people living together and I guess Chuck and Greg knew some of them. All of a sudden their place was overrun by us. I didn't know any of them and kept to myself. I didn't like them and they didn't like me. I'm sure I didn't act very friendly toward them and they had a right to hate me. I couldn't help myself though. For the most part they were lazy, slacker hippie punkers. I thought they were full of shit and I'm sure they thought the same thing about me. They sure were cool to let us stay all that time with them.

We found a space to live on Santa Monica Boulevard. It was an office space above the studio where we recorded the *Damaged* album. We all slept on the floor. Eventually, we got a practice space in the building and more space for sleep.

On any given night, you could look out the window to the back parking lot and see an unmarked police car. They were watching us. I remember that really scaring me. One morning, we came out and all the doors of the van were open, but nothing was missing. I wondered if it were the pigs fucking with us. It was at this time that it became my understanding that the police were fucked.

At one point, a woman in the neighborhood called the police and told them that one of us had tried to rob her with a shotgun. That's all we needed.

I was learning a lot of things fast. Everything was different. Just a few weeks before, I was working a straight job and money and food weren't a problem. Now the next meal was not always a thing you could count on. Money was hard to come by. It was a lot to get used to, but it was great. At that point, I didn't feel fully integrated into the band and at times, I felt like I was a visitor. The way we were living was foreign to me. Slowly I came to realize that this was it and there was no place I'd rather be. As much as it sucked for all of us to be living on the floor on top of each other, it still was better than the job I had left in DC.

During the next five years, I was to learn what hard work was all about. Black Flag/SST was on a work ethic that I had never experienced and have never seen since. Greg, Chuck and their nonstop roadie Mugger were the hardest working people I had ever seen. They went into whatever it was that we had to do without questioning the time it took, the lack of sleep or food. They just went for it. No one had time for anyone else's complaining. If you ever made a noise about anything, Mugger would just start laughing and say something like, "This isn't Van Halen! Get it happening!"

A U G U S T

I found it hard to get exact dates on the first few shows. I found a review of what was supposed to be the first show I did with the band, but it said that the show was on the 25th and I don't think that's correct. I do know that we did this back-to-back Huntington Beach to Boston trip and I know that it was not the first show that the band did with me in Huntington Beach.

One of my first shows with Black Flag — Cuckoo's Nest, Huntington Beach, CA / August 1981 *(Glen E. Friedman)*

HUNTINGTON BEACH CA: After all the weeks of practice, I felt ready to play. It was interesting to hang out in the club and walk amongst the people. None of them knew what the new singer in the band looked like yet. Later, a few girls had found out that I was that guy and started talking to me. This was a new experience for me. I was not used to women giving me the time of day. Eventually the conversation came to the bottom line of what they really wanted: guest list for their friends stranded outside. After the opening bands played, we hit stage like a bomb. All the crazy motherfuckers up front were yelling at me that I had better be good or they were going to kick my ass. I think we opened with "Revenge" and the place exploded.

It was that kind of music. Greg and Chuck had created the ultimate soundtrack for a full-scale riot. This era of the band was like nothing before or since. No band made people react like that. I had seen the Circle Jerks make some people lose their shit, but not like the Flag. Every song was the most direct line to what the fuck it was about. In my opinion, the finest Black Flag record is *The First Four Years* compilation. It's all the singles and compilation cuts that the band made before I joined. The record spans the work of the three singers that came before me. It's 34 minutes and it's about three full-length album's worth of anyone else's music. It is the densest batch of jams I have ever heard on one record besides *Fun House* by the Stooges. When you put it up against what's out there today, it's hilarious. These bands would have been eaten alive at a Black Flag show. Music has mellowed out to the point to where most of it doesn't interest me anymore. I'm not a snob either. I just can't forget what I know.

HUNTINGTON BEACH, CA / 1981 *(GLEN E. FRIEDMAN)*

Anyway, the gig was great and the crowd liked me enough that they didn't beat the shit out of me.

GREG GINN, DEVONSHIRE DOWNS / 9.11.81 *(ED COLVER)*

22 BOSTON MA: Flew out and played. Didn't sleep and flew right back to LA. First time I met Mitch Bury. The guy is awesome. He gets better with age.

SAN DIEGO CA: This was a great show. Played the first few songs and saw this girl trying to grab me. I move away from her. Her boyfriend and his two friends were apparently on angel dust and see this as a great opportunity to drag me offstage and beat the shit out of me. It was funny. I was held down as this fist kept bashing me in the face. I yelled for Mugger between fists. Eventually the guy was pulled off of me. I finished the set and then went to the men's room to straighten my nose. I did a pretty good job. It only goes slightly to the right. The best part was the ride to the gig. We were stuck in traffic near San Diego and we had been cut off by a woman driving a large car. Mugger had enough of her bullshit and hopped out of the van and dumped his yogurt on her through her window. Of course, we got busted and Greg had to do all the talking. I don't know how we got out of it, but we did. San Diego is a tough town.

SEPTEMBER

11 DEVONSHIRE DOWNS, NORTHRIDGE CA: I learned what hard work was with Black Flag. I thought I had worked my ass off before, doing minimum wage work. For this show, we put up flyers for days on end. Start in the morning and come back at sundown. One day, Greg and I went out to put some up on telephone poles around La Cienega and Sunset Boulevard. We were across the street from the 7-11 on La Cienega between Santa Monica and Sunset. Greg was telling me about the pigs in the area and how the last thing you wanted was to get caught. Right after he said that, we got nailed. The pig gave us so much shit. For some reason, he let us go.

I ended up going out on flyer patrol with Mugger. We would make a combination of white glue and wheat paste. One guy on lookout, the other guy slapping up the paste. One layer on the pole, put the flyer

HENRY ROLLINS, DEVONSHIRE DOWNS / 9.11.81 (GLEN F.

on and then another coat of paste. After that, all you had to do was let the sun do the work. These flyers would stay for up to a year. They would not come off, much to the town's dismay. We would pick a main street and put up flyers for miles. We went to UCLA, the Valley — everywhere. This was just for one gig.

One day we were putting up flyers in Hollywood and we walked through a supermarket parking lot. We saw this guy putting his groceries into a gray Mercedes. Someone had spray painted a big swastika on the guy's hood. I just kind of stared at it. Mugger went off and started laughing his ass off. The man shook his fist at us and drove away. Mugger and I had no hair on our heads. He probably thought we were skinheads getting off on the artwork.

I learned a lot from Mugger. We went flyering up around Westwood. We were hungry all the time and never had much money besides bus fare. We went to a Carl's Jr. and each got a small salad plate. The place had one of those deals where you get to fill the plate, but you don't get to go back for seconds. I followed Mugger's lead. He put the plate on the tray and proceeded to make the entire tray into his salad plate. It was a mountain of food. Awesome. I did the same. The manager saw us and he didn't like it, but I could see immediately that he

HUNTINGTON BEACH, CA / 1981 (ED COLVER)

wasn't going to do shit about it. We were too fucked up looking — covered with paste and dirt and sunburnt with our bucket of paste and backpack of supplies. Forget it, not worth it. I learned that you can get away with a lot of shit if you just do it like it's all you knew how to do. Mugger told me about times he was living on the streets and was reduced to eating dog food out of cans put on white bread. He said you balled it up and ate it as fast as you could and tried not to taste it. All this was new to me.

Finally the gig came. I hoped all the flyering was worth it. It was a great bill — Fear, the Stains and Black Flag. I can't remember who was onstage at the time, but at one point, someone shot tear gas or mace into the crowd. People were on the ground holding their faces and screaming. I carried a few people to the bathroom and got them under the sink. Finally, we got to play. A few songs in, I looked out and saw this brown shape in front of me. I was thinking to myself how strange it looked and what was it doing suspended in the air like that. A one quart Budweiser bottle bounced off my hand and went under the drum riser. Tough crowd. The PA company normally did country and western gigs. There was no way they were ready for this audience. I broke one mic and went to get another one. The PA man gave me one and gave me a look. A kid landed on one of the monitors and stomped on it on his way offstage. The PA man came out and s⸺ed lli g at the crowd and looking over his monitor. He was immediately showered in oaths,

spit and cups. He looked at me and said he was going to turn off the PA. Chuck told him that his PA would be destroyed and he would get his ass kicked by the crowd. All this was true. He looked at us and called us every name in the book and went back behind the monitor board and remained there, glaring at us for the rest of the gig.

O C T O B E R

10 / 09 SAN DIEGO CA: I'm not exactly sure, but I think this one was a bust. I think we got a few songs done before the pigs came busting in. It was one of those nights where they say they're going to impound the equipment. I grew to hate police quickly. All the bullshit they got up to was so out of line. They did what

they wanted with punk rockers. They did stuff at our shows that they could have gone to jail for. It was an eye-opening experience for me. I grew up in a neighborhood where cops went after "bad guys", not kids standing there with their hands on their heads saying, "I'm not resisting you!" over and over again as these pigs called them every name in the book and beat the shit out of them. I understood that I had no rights at all and whatever went down would be up to the pig in charge. The California pigs would come on so hard and heavy. It was like being bossed around by a child twice your body weight. It was always funny when the pig would take the mic from me and start talking. I would have to stand next to him and watch the crowd bum out.

10 / 11 SAN FRANCISCO CA: This was the first time I played the Mabuhay Gardens. I had been there before when the Teen Idles went there in 1980. I'll never forget that. We went there to see a show on a night we weren't playing. It was The Circle Jerks (before they had a record out), followed by Flipper and then the Dead Kennedys. The place was packed. The crowds in SF were not violent in those times like the crowds in the beach cities of Southern Cal. They weren't ready for the guys the Jerks brought with them — some of Huntington Beach's hardest. As soon as the Jerks started playing, they immediately took over the entire place. They got into an altercation with the bouncers and beat the shit out of them. I had never seen anything like it. For some reason, they liked us DC guys which was a good thing. We hung out with them for a few days and had our minds blown minute by minute by the intensity of these guys. I had never seen so much violence entertained by such a small group of people. They were in some shit every hour wherever they went. I know it sounds like I'm exaggerating, but I'm not. If you were there then you know what I mean. We couldn't believe how these guys were going to survive themselves. A few days after our first encounter with them, the Teen Idles played the Mab. They all showed up and soon there was blood and fights. One of the HB's got sliced open by a guy wielding a broken bottle. He got dismantled. The most vivid memory I have of them is getting on a public bus with them. We DC guys paid and sat down. The HB's all filed past the driver. The last one in line put a nickel in the box and sat down. When the driver asked about the rest of the money, one of them said, "We're students." The driver wisely didn't do shit. The HB's terrorized everyone on the bus. Anyone who looked their way got spat at. Like I said, I never saw anything like those guys in my life.

The best part about playing the Mab was the guy who ran the place, Dirk Dirksen. He was a real character. He would insult you on the way in, and between bands he would get onstage and rip on the crowd and the band that was just on and the band about to come on. He would crack people up. He was a good friend of Black Flag's and was always cool to us. He later ran the club on top of the Mab called the On Broadway. We played many shows there.

The backstage area was where I spoke with Will Shatter from Flipper for the last time. He was on something and talking real slowly, a few inches from my face. "Have a really, really good show. Have a beautiful show…" He knew he was tripping me out and he was liking it.

I remember the first set at the Mab. I jumped offstage and bounced off the piano and landed hard on some guy and pinned him to the floor. I looked down. It was Jello. Sorry about that, Chief.

20 SAN PEDRO CA: We played at lunch time on the front steps of San Pedro High. I don't know how it sounded out front, but it was a good enough time. I remember people throwing food and Dukowski picking it up to eat later. People threw money too. I ran all over the steps between songs picking up the coins. I don't think anyone was into it besides us and the three people or so who knew who we were.

21 HUNTINGTON BEACH CA: This was great. Dukowski is walking back from a hamburger place across the street from the club. He jaywalked and got hassled by the police. They run a warrant check and find out that he has an outstanding parking ticket or some shit so they take him away. Greg and I went down to pay the ticket and get him out so we can play. They ran warrant checks on both of us and nailed Greg on an outstanding ticket. I drove the van back to the club and borrowed money from Jerry the owner. I drove back to the police station with Robo, and I paid the tickets and the guys were released and we got to play. We opened the set with "Police Story".

L-R: ROBO, DEZ, C

We were supposed to play a show at the Breiner Hall in San Jose on October 23. We loaded up the van and got about as far as the Grapevine (a stretch of road outside of LA) and the van made a bad sound and the engine kind of melted. We pushed it backwards down the highway and into a truck stop. We were there most of the night. The promoter drove down from San Jose to pick us up even though we had missed the show. The band went home. Mugger and I went up with the equipment. We did the drive in the back of a pickup truck. It was so cold. By the time we got to San Jose hours later, we were stiff. We crashed at someone's house and I don't remember what we did the next day.

This is the great part. We tried to play the same hall again on the 29th. We loaded in and soundchecked. We felt good that we were going to be able to make the date up and not look like idiots. After soundcheck, Greg, Chuck and I drove to San Francisco to do an interview at some radio station. We would go to any length to do press. The interview was a waste of time. Most of the press stuff we did at the time was. We started driving back to the venue to play and the van ran out of gas several miles from SJ in the middle of nowhere. Greg had to run a few miles to find a gas station to make a call. Getting gas was not an option — we had no money. Greg managed to contact the promoter. He came with a gas can. We finally got to the gig to find a bunch of people standing around outside. The pigs had shut down the show. I remember seeing Dez looking at us totally disgusted. People were coming up to us saying that we sucked. I couldn't disagree.

ROBO, RIVERSIDE, CA / 11.21.81 *(ED COLVER)*

31 SAN FRANCISCO CA: Mugger and I went into SF early to put up flyers for the show. We were on the scam from day one. I learned a lot. I was asking him stupid questions like where were we going to sleep and when do we eat. He laughed at me and said that we were going to have to make it up as we went along. We stood out in front of the Mabuhay Gardens after a day of putting up flyers and got some money from some friends of Mugger's who were selling fake joints on the street. We met some guy who had seen Black Flag play before in SF and he said that he would put us up in his parents' house, but they couldn't find out. We went there and the parents were actually in the house and we had to sneak around them. The next day, we were back out there on flyer patrol. We saw Jello Biafra in a restaurant. We went in and sat down at his table and immediately started eating his food. He didn't seem to mind. I did my part by going to the back and talking to the waitress, telling her that we were here early to put up the flyers and we had no money and could she help us out even though we were filthy and crazy looking. She gave us some food and I put her on the guest list. We did this kind of thing for a couple of more days until the rest of the band came up. I think the show got shut down by the police partway through.

In the fall of this year we recorded the **Damaged** *album. The building where we did the sessions is now gone.*

The guys did the songs without me and I did the vocals later on. It was amazing to watch Ginn in the studio. He was relentless — so much energy. He would tape the headphones to his head for over-dubs so they wouldn't fly off. Robo always wore these bracelets on his left wrist and the drum mics would pick them up. It became part of the sound. You can hear it on the record.

Chuck and Greg coached me on the vo-cals. I needed all the help I could get. I would sing as hard as I could every time. I didn't know anything about pacing myself. Chuck walked me through the breakdown section in the song "What I See" because I couldn't come up with anything. It must have been funny to see me work hard instead of smart. We did a version of

UNICORN RECORDS BOSS, DAPHNA EDWARDS w/ BLACK FLAG / 1981 *(ED COLVER)*

"Louie, Louie" that was never used. The guys did a strange jam at the end of it until the tape ran out. I heard it back once and never heard it again. I don't think it was even mixed down. I did the vocal for "Damaged 1" in two takes. It was just me winging it like I did it live. After the 2nd take, Spot told me the first one was the one and I was finished. We used a different version of "Rise Above" than the one we recorded for the album — we used one from a previous session. Several weeks before, we had gone into a studio to record what was going to be a single. "Depression" and "Rise Above" were the two songs. We never released the single. I guess Greg liked the version of "Rise Above" from this session better so we used it.

THIS IS THE ROOM WHERE THE DAMAGED ALBUM WAS RECORDED—UNICORN STUDIOS, HOLLYWOOD, CA / FALL 1981 *(GLEN E. FRIEDMAN)*

THIS STICKER WAS PUT ON THE FIRST 25,000 COPIES OF DAMAGED. QUOTE IS BY AL BERGARNO OF MCA.

We did the record fairly quickly. I remember the vocals for "TV Party" taking a long time because there were so many parts to do.

It was fun to work with Spot at this time. Spot was the band's producer and soundman. He produced several records for SST. He was one of a kind. He would go in and play Greg's guitar so Greg could hear it at the mixing board. He could play any Black Flag song, no problem.

I never thought Spot liked me. I got that feeling as soon as I joined the band. I had a feeling that I was intruding on some imagined territory. It was just bullshit. Years after the band had broken up, I wrote him and asked him what was up and he told me that in his opinion, I had ruined the band. Whatever. Listening back to the records he produced, I think he ruined them. It doesn't matter at this point.

It was the best time I ever had doing a Black Flag album. The rest were hard to get through for a number of reasons. Financial stress was a 24-hour a day reality for the band. We were up against it for the entire time the band was together. There never was any "sellout" or any "rock star" bullshit. People would sometimes talk that shit and it was always so funny to us.

HENRY, SPOT, GREG AND CHUCK, KUCR-FM / OCTOBER 1981 *(JIM ACOMB)*

Soon after the recording was done, we set out on the first tour with me singing. It was amazing to me. A few months before, I was working behind the counter at a straight job and now I was hitting the road with the baddest band in the land. What follows is what I remember from the dates.

N O V E M B E R

06 TUCSON AZ: I think we played this small bar where we ended up playing a few times over the years. It eventually burned down. One time, we were there playing away and there were these filthy guys in trench coats on Dez's side going off. Dez had put all the local bums outside on the guest list. Dez was always into great music and turned me on to a lot of stuff that I still play to this day. I first heard the Pink Fairies song "Do It" from Dez. He was the one who turned me on to Hawkwind, Lightnin' Hopkins, Mountain, all kinds of good stuff.

07 PHOENIX AZ: For the first few visits to Phoenix, we played this place called the Madison Square Gardens. It was an old boxing/wrestling ring. Really small. It had a chainlink fence up in front of the stage which was pretty strange. We played there with this really weak band who had a singer named Frank Discussi n. They're playing their set before us, and at one point, Frank pulls out a lab rat and a hammer and tells the crowd that he's going to kill the rat with the hammer if someone doesn't stop him. People just stood there. I only heard the last few words of his sentence because I was backstage. I went running out to save the rat only in time to watch it get hammered. I thought it sucked. When he came backstage after the show, I threw the cage at his head. I don't think he ever understood why I was mad.

14 WESTCHESTER CA: I was hanging out with a very intense woman the week we played this show. She was a drunk. She came with us when we went to the university to play. We played on a landing near a set of stairs. A few bored, drunk dorm dwellers watched us and talked all the way though. It was one of those deals where one guy got the band to come and play and he was the only person in the school that was interested in the band at all. After the set was over, I went looking for the wild woman. I found out that she had gone off with some guy to his room because he promised her a drink. She went into the room and was assaulted by the guy. She was crying and freaking out and would not tell us who the guy was or where his room was. She was apologizing for the fact that she had gone with him. I guess that's how a lot of those guys get away with that kind of thing. I never saw her again after that. She probably thought I was lightweight.

15 HEMET CA (PARTY): We were playing in a kitchen and all was well when for no reason, people started clearing out fast. I looked over and saw police running down the hall of the house. I said something about pigs and they started after me. Earl from the band Saccharine Trust grabbed me and we ran out the back.

9:30 CLUB, WASHINGTON, DC / 12.3.81 *(TIFFANY)*

I hid in a girl's car. By this time, fire engines were there and more police were pulling up. I sat in the back of the car and waited it out. Eventually, the girls took me up the street and I sat in the bushes by the side of the road. At some point, the van came up the street and I flagged them down and we got out of there.

The next morning we heard some bad news. Earl had to run from the pigs. He saw a retaining wall and jumped over it hoping for the best. His foot caught on a piece of wire that was going across the top of the wall. The front of his body smashed hard on the wall and he fell to the ground — his leg bone sticking out and all of his front teeth smashed out.

19 / 20 San Francisco CA: We got to the Mab and I went to the dressing room and tried to find a place to sleep for a little while before soundcheck. I heard a Misfits song seeping in from the club upstairs. I figured that someone was playing a tape through the sound system. The song came to an end and then I heard someone tuning up. Okay, some band playing a Misfits song at their soundcheck. The band played another Misfits song and then another one. I walked up there to watch this band that seemed so bent on playing Misfits covers. I came through the door and looked at the stage. It was the Misfits. I didn't know they were playing that night. I only knew one person that had seen them play as they usually only played on Halloween. I recognized Glenn Danzig immediately. It was amazing to hear them live after years of playing the singles endlessly. They all came up to the edge of the stage and shook my hand. They were great people. They asked me what song I wanted to hear and I asked them to play "Horror Business" and they did. Later on that night, they played their set. Luckily for me, they went on before we did and I got to see the whole thing. They were great. Walking into the On Broadway in the late afternoon and encountering them will be something that I'll never forget.

On one of these early SF trips, we went to Jello's wedding reception at Target Video. Some of the Flipper guys and some of the Flag guys played together on the Target stage. It was intense. I didn't sing. I was kind of scared of the Flipper guys. They were scary. Their bass player, Ted Falconi, was heavy. They never relented — ever. I would try to talk to them and they would always give me the Flipper treatment. I never knew if one of them was going to pull some shit. It's not that they were rock stars or anything. They were just heavy. Heavier than you, heavier than anything. They didn't care. That's just the way they were. I didn't mind. When they played, they were amazing. Even when they weren't, they were. They really couldn't miss.

21 Riverside CA: This was one of Greg's bad equipment nights. He would often have problems with his gear — amps smoking and shorting out. His shit started frying during the middle of the set

Greg takes the mic — Riverside, CA / 11.21.81 (Ed Colver)

on this night. He sat down on the stage with a soldering iron and started to work while the rest of us kept going. We were doing what we called the "Trudge Riff" at the time. It didn't have any lyrics. I looked over at Chuck for some advice as to what to do. He said, "Just scream!" So I started screaming. Greg wrote real lyrics to the song later on and the song title was changed to "Scream".

27 HOUSTON TX: We played a place called the Island. I remember the size of the roaches that ran out from underneath the drum riser. Towards end of the gig, I was getting shocked by the mic and the lights were flickering. The guy who ran the place was cool though. He gave us some turkey for dinner.

AUSTIN, TX / 1981

28 AUSTIN TX: We hung out with the Big Boys and the Dicks. Both bands played on the bill with us and were great.

D E C E M B E R

01 GREENSBORO NC: At one point during the set, I turned around quickly and my elbow and Dukowski's broken bass peg collided. The peg punctured my arm pretty deep. The next morning, we were pulling into DC, and I woke up in the van and I had this near lemon-size lump on my arm. It stayed that way for weeks.

03 WASHINGTON DC (2 SETS): The 9:30 Club. It was cool to play at the same club I had seen Black Flag several months before. I saw a lot of people that I knew. I learned something that night that stuck with me. I got shit from some of the people I knew. They told me that I had become some kind of rock star. The fact that I left Washington DC and come back in this "big" band was a sellout. Some people I had known for years treated me strangely. It hurt at first, then I realized something. You're going to do what you're going to do and that's all there is. That's all you got and that's that. From that night on, I figured they can go get fucked. From then on, I treated DC like any other city on the tour. When I played there, I did the same thing that I did in the city the night before and the night after. I played my guts out and loaded the gear back into the van. Most of the people I knew were glad to see me and that was good. I was very young and had a lot to learn about how people were and how the real world worked. I found out big time. Often in large doses I might have been unready for. I did the best I could.

LONDON, UK 1981

U . K . T O U R

After our gig in Washington DC, we set out for England. I had been there once with my mother several years earlier. I remember being very excited about going out of the country with the band. It was a great adventure for me. Ian MacKaye came out with us for the tour. He wanted to check it out so he bought himself a ticket and off we went.

Our first show was with the Damned at a place called the Lyceum. I was excited about this. The Damned were one of my favorite bands.

We loaded in the gear in the early afternoon. It was cold and the place smelled old. I was to learn soon enough that a lot of the places in England were cold, old and stank.

I don't remember what we did until gig time. I remember Captain Sensible of the Damned coming to our dressing room and telling us that he liked our band a lot and he was looking forward to seeing us play. He was incredibly cool. I told him that I had been listening to his band for years and it meant a lot to be playing with them. He told me that the audience would probably hate us, but not to worry about it, just play and everything would be okay.

Half hour before we went on, a man came to interview us for Sounds. I was flying around the room, unable to sit still because I was so excited to be playing. We were going to go on first, then a band called the Anti-Nowhere League would play and finally, the Damned.

When we were told it was gig time, I went running down the steep stairs toward the stage. I wasn't thinking about anything besides getting out there. I turned a corner and ran full on into Dave Vanian, the Damned's singer. He was dressed to the hilt in his vampire gear. I nearly knocked him over. I felt like such a jerk. He was cool though. He extended his hand and said hello. I was tripping out on that as I went down the rest of the stairs. A guy whose records I had listened to for years and all I could do was nearly send him flying down a flight of stairs. Off to a great start.

We hit stage. I probably blew my voice out on the first song. I was going for it so hard. I don't know how long our set was, perhaps a half hour or so. I remember finishing that last song and the audience looking at us blankly. They were much too cool to acknowledge us at all. I looked out at them with all their punk rock clothes and the haircuts two feet above their heads. I knew then that they were just a bunch of weak punkers and I shouldn't take them seriously.

The ANL sucked. They were just stupid. They couldn't play and made no bones about it. They did pose out though and the audience loved them. I thought they were weak. Ian and I were told that it wouldn't be a good idea if we went into the crowd when the Damned played. Like we might get hurt or something. So we went way up in the nosebleed seats and watched them from there. They were great.

Journal entry found in an old notebook — 12.6.81 London UK: No soundcheck. Hung out in the fucking Lyceum for hours. We played. Lots of spit on me. Lame stage sound. Lots of insults from the crowd. No applause.

We found a place to stay with these two American girls who were over there hanging out. We put the entire lot of us in their tiny single room. I don't know how they stood us, but they did and they saved our asses from the cold. We were miserable. There was not a lot of money for food and we were hungry and cold all the time. We all sat on the floor and watched Greg practice scales for hours. Time passed slowly and it was depressing as hell. It was the first time I had to deal with the downtime that comes with touring. It's the endless hours of nothing that can crush you harder than the rigors of playing.

These two girls were friends of Jimmy Pursey, singer of the legendary band Sham 69. They told us that we might be able to meet him if he had time. This didn't mean anything to the guys, but it meant a lot to Ian and myself. We had met him briefly years before when Sham had played in New York. He was cool to us and we were into checking him out.

They called him and he said we could come out and visit him. All of us got on a train and went way out of London. I forget where we got out, but we didn't have any money so we faked like we didn't know what the deal was and just bolted out of there. People from the station came out and nailed us. I think the girls had some money and paid our way. We took a cab out to his place, a small house in a wooded area.

He remembered me and Ian. We played him tapes of all the new stuff coming out on SST like the Minutemen, Saccharine Trust and the Stains. He didn't like any of it. He played us one of his solo albums and we thought it sucked. I don't think any of us told him that. We talked about all kinds of stuff and I forget what most of it was about because it was so tripped out. It started to occur to me that this guy had a screw loose. He insisted that we watch *Oh Lucky Man* with him. He had it on video. We sat up most of the night and checked it out. Cool movie. He seemed to read deeply into it.

After that, he asked if we needed any clothes. He had this big suitcase that he opened up explaining

LONDON, UK 1981 *(SPOT)*

that it was his tour clothes and he didn't need them anymore. He pulled out stuff and put it on the floor. All the guys took something because we really hadn't dressed correctly for the cold. He pulled out a pair of pants that I recognized from photos of him. He told me that they were his "Sham Pants" or something. He wanted me to have them to carry on some cause or whatever. I took them. I eventually gave them to a Brit named Mike Heath because they fit him.

At some point in the morning, we all got on the train and headed for London. Jimmy didn't have any money and borrowed some from Ian. He tried to be funny about it like Ian was really ever going to see the five pound note again. He bought some cigarettes, a paper and a ticket and just kind of grinned and stood around laughing. I think it was then that he started to get on my nerves.

When we got to London, he got off the train and said goodbye and split really fast. It was a strange night.

For some strange reason, we were supposed to do dates with Bow Wow Wow and the Exploited. The next few days were spent spinning our wheels because BWW kept canceling. Finally, we got to go play in Manchester.

That morning, we drove our rented van from London north to Manchester. We spent all of our remaining dough on petrol to make the drive. So we get to Manchester Polytech and we find out that we're playing with Chelsea, a well-known English punk rock band. For some reason, Black Flag was headlining. I smelled trouble immediately. We didn't even have an album out there yet. Just the "Six Pack" single and we were headlining? Someone somewhere was going to be pissed off.

We loaded in the equipment and went upstairs to the dressing room to try to find some food. The dressing room was huge and was to be used by all the bands on the bill that night. I fell asleep on the floor next to the wall, out of the way of everything and everyone. Fine.

I'm woken up by a boot in my ribs. I grabbed my side, looked up and there's Gene October, the singer in Chelsea. "Excuse me Los Angeles! Sorry about that. I just tripped over you." Yeah right. I

PRESTON, UK / 1981

go back to sleep. I get woken up again by the same boot. "Oh Los Angeles, so sorry." I remain cool, being the only Flag member in the room which is now full of Chelsea and crew. The prick starts talking to me. "You really don't have any good music in America do you Los Angeles? The Dickies and the Ramones! I mean they are a load of shit aren't they Los Angeles?" What a drag. I had two Chelsea records at home. I just stared and nodded my head. I was hoping that I would get to talk to the guy about all the bands that he's played with over the years and what his band is up to as I was a bit of a fan. It was a bit hard to take.

Hours later, Chelsea is onstage. Gene is talking to the crowd between songs, "There are some short-haired hippies from Los Angeles in the crowd tonight. It's Black Flag. I want you to get them." The crowd cheers. Ian and I walked into the crowd smiling and waving, saying, "Here we are motherfuckers! Come and get us!" No one came and got us. Personally, I was kind of hoping one or five of them would have so I could have had the pleasure of taking nine days of misery out on their faces. Finally, we got to play. The kids in the crowd were real cool. I thought we were doing okay.

This one boy kept spitting on me for the whole set. I didn't do anything about it. I was trying to be cool with these people. The spitting thing was too much for old Ian. He walked up and smacked the guy upside his head. After that, the entire audience took a few steps back. I apologized for Ian's actions even though I thought what he did was right on. Now as I write this, I have to put my pen down because I am laughing so hard. The look on that guy's face was worth the entire trip.

Of course, we had no place to stay, no blankets — nothing. We met these two girls who agreed to put us up in their flat. "Don't get your hopes up, we're on the dole," said one girl. Fine. We get to the flat. I was expecting a hovel. It's a split level apartment. The place is nicer than any place I have lived in since I lived with my Mom. This place was a little different — no heat, no hot water, no food. I wiped the spit off my hair, face and chest as best I could with a washcloth and went to sleep on the floor in my coat. I kept waking up because of the cold and dampness. Finally morning came. We drank all the hot tea that these girls would let us have and then we got in the truck and left for the next show.

We went to London and played at a place called the Rainbow. This was the first gig with the Exploited. I remember going to the dressing room and seeing one of the roadies from the Exploited walking out with our small box of food. He looked at us and told us to come and get it if we dared. None of us thought it was a good idea. We went into the room and there was a newly punched out hole in the window. The cold air was coming through big time and we stuffed some piece of clothing into the hole. We did get a soundcheck though and it didn't sound so bad in there.

Honey Bane went out and opened the show in a raincoat and umbrella to protect herself from all the spit flying at the stage. Their bass player was the guy from the Lurkers, a favorite band of mine and Ian's. I think we scared him a bit when we came up to him because we had no hair and we were excited. He cooled out when we explained that we had all of his records. It was funny as hell to see Honey take the spit-covered raincoat off and say, "Thankyougoodnight" and walk offstage without getting spit any on her.

So finally we go on. The Exploited fans are probably the most thickheaded, moronic, capable of kicking the shit out of you bunch I have ever encountered. They immediately started giving us the Nazi salute and waving their football scarves. I was beyond caring at that point. We just kept out of the way of the spit and did our thing. At one point, I accidentally elbowed Chuck in the head. I opened up a cut on his forehead that took seven stitches to close. There was blood everywhere. I think this actually made the skinheads like us a little. The next song, Chuck swung his bass around and one of the tuning pegs slashed into me, so now I was bleeding too. It was a blood festival. Chuck is pouring a soda on his bass to get the blood off the strings and we kept on playing like nothing happened.

So we finish the set and Chuck goes off to the hospital to get stitched up. Ian and I go check out the Exploited and their singer, Wattie. They sucked. The skinheads knew every word and sang along. Finally at the end of the set, Wattie told the crowd that the Jam show had just let out up the street and they should go out and beat their fans up as they went to the tube. The band played "Fuck The Mods" and the skins tore out of that place. We later found out that they indeed caught up to the people going home and beat some up pretty bad. One paper had it down as "Black Flag Violence."

Funny how that used to happen often. We would do a show and things would be fine. The pigs would show up and start shit with kids and then a riot would happen. They always blamed the youth and "punk rock" for all of it. There was never a riot until the pigs came and started pushing people to the ground, threatening them, etc. That's why I don't like pigs. I've seen what they do and there's no way any of them can tell me that we were the cause of violence. After the show, we went back to the girl's place and called it a night.

Show at the 100 Club. We were burning out at the girl's place in London and we got a call to play at

HENRY ROLLINS, CUCKOO'S NEST / HUNTINGTON BEACH, CA / AUGUST 1981 (GLEN E. FRIEDMAN)

the 100 Club opening for a band called Chron-Gen. It was a gig and we took it. We went and loaded in through the snow.

We played two sets since there was no one else playing and no one seemed to notice our presence anyway. After we got off, CG played. A skinhead girl came up to me and kissed me on the cheek. I think I said something funny like, "Why thank you ma'am," and thought nothing more of it. The next thing I knew

I was on the ground. Someone had punched me in the back of my head real hard. I got up wondering what fucking time zone I was in and saw the guy who delivered the sucker punch. It was this big skinhead motherfucker who was rolling up his sleeves to show me his swastika tattoos. I didn't know what I had done to deserve this beating. I kind of stood there trying to get my balance back. A roadie from the UK Subs came over and talked the piece of shit skinhead out of killing me. Charlie Harper of the Subs got me out of there and took me to this room in the back. He told me that the guy used to be a bouncer there, but got fired for breaking a chair over another bouncer's head. My head felt like it was going to explode.

I figured out that I had been set up by the skinhead girl. It was par for the course. That's the way these pieces of shit are. This was a shitty tour and all the worst things in the world would come our way. Next stop Wales.

We drove the box truck up to Colwyn Bay, Wales. Most of us had to ride in the back of the truck with the equipment. We couldn't see out and it was freezing back there, but that was the deal. It was not an assuring thought of Dukowski up front driving on the wrong side of the road. If any bad was to befall us, at least we would never see it coming.

We loaded into this freezing hall that was on the end of a dock overlooking some depressing gray body of freezing water. We soundchecked and were fed some shitty fried fish. I wondered what was going to happen to us this time. Bombs? Poisonous snakes?

The Nig Heist went on first. This was the band that was made up of BF types and road crew. Mugger was the frontman. This evening's lineup included Ian on bass and Spot on guitar. I think Dez played drums. They played and people loved them and covered them with spit and beer. Poor Mugger. He had just scored a nice sweater from somewhere and made the mistake of playing in it. By the time their short set was over, the sweater was covered with saliva and beer. I think he left it behind.

So finally we got to play. We're having a great old time and the audience was great. We were right in the middle of "Padded Cell" and the song just kind of falls over. I look to Greg to see what's going on and he's holding his head and there's blood streaming down his face. I ask him what the hell happened and he says that he has been hit with a bullet. Greg was shot?! No — someone threw a bullet at him and opened him up. I looked up right in time to see a pint mug smash against the wall right over the drum riser. Time to leave. End of show.

After that, we're sitting backstage wondering what the fuck we're going to do. This kid named Fred comes backstage to talk to us. I ask him why someone threw the bullet at Greg. He said that it was some skinheads that had come to the show just to break it up. They didn't know who we were. All they knew was that we were Americans and we had to be beaten up.

We had no place to stay of course and Fred said that we could stay with him. We drive the truck up to his parents' place and find it's a small house. Mugger quickly scams on the guy's sister — he's in. A few of the others quickly run in. There's no more room.

I went out to the truck with Chuck. I tried to sleep in the back of this truck with my trench coat as a blanket. At some point, I did fall asleep. I remember getting up in the morning and seeing frozen condensation drops on the ceiling of the truck and Duke sleeping away in his sleeping bag that he had been smart enough to bring. He looked so peaceful and happy sleeping there that I wanted to slug him. Eventually we got up and left for Preston.

So we get to Preston and find that it's depressing and freezing. The place wasn't open when we get there so a few of us stood in a phone booth to stay warm. I walked up to the booth to talk to one of the guys inside. There is a line of people waiting outside, thinking that they were using the phone. When the people in line found out that they weren't, they started yelling at us.

Hours later, we're playing in this small freezing dump. The nightly skinhead confrontation happened. They came onstage and tried to fuck us up. I remember Dukowski knocking one of them hard with his bass and Ian dealing on one. I think I got a shot in as well. They were thrown out by the security, a single black man with a heavy accent. We kept playing and finished the set.

After the set, we had to stay inside because the skinheads were outside waiting for us. We figured that since we had no place to go we might as well stay inside and let them freeze. I was hoping that they would be so stupid that they would freeze to death and that would be the end of it. We hung out with this old man who was very drunk. He sang songs and we all sang along with him even though we didn't know any of the words. Finally, the skinheads left, but they ripped the mirrors off the truck and kicked in the sides. Hey, it was a rental so who gives a fuck.

I think we drove back down to London. We didn't have any other place to go. I guess we crashed at the girl's place again.

A few days later, we were to drive to Leeds to play at the Christmas On Earth Festival. It was a ton of bands with the headliners being the Damned. We got there early and had nothing to do all day except hang out and watch the endless run of shitty bands. Ian and I had a brief food fight with Captain Sensible. A lot of the bands were showing up without equipment. Stupidly, we lent our rented gear to them. GBH used our stuff and later slagged us off in the press. The Anti-Nowhere League used our gear as well.

Somewhere in there, we got to play. The stage hands were yelling at us to hurry up. We got out there with no soundcheck and the first note Chuck hit, he broke his big string. Somehow we got it together and played the set. I don't remember much except that Ian came onstage and said, "Hey man, don't take the brown acid! It's a bummer man! There's been a baby born out there! I think we're going to name it Sid. Far out!" a la Woodstock. I don't know how many of these stupid punkers got it, but we were laughing our asses off looking at the three thousand clones out there. We finished the last song and no one did anything. They didn't even hurl abuse. I swear I could hear leather jackets being zipped up all the way at the back.

After our set was over, it was time for the punk rockstar bands to play. The ones that people had traveled on a train from who the fuck knows where and stood in piss and water for hours to see. Vice Squad, the band fronted by Bekki Bondage played. They played their single two times. This band was pathetic. Chelsea were out there milking it for it was worth. It was high comedy to listen to the ridiculous shit that Gene was saying. "This is the greatest thing since '77!" Incredible. The UK Subs on the other hand were great. They rocked the place. I didn't see how a crowd like that would be into something with that much energy.

Before the Damned went on, I walked back through the audience towards the toilets. It was a mess. People passed out, asleep in three inches of water. The men's room was trashed with a few inches of piss and water on the floor. It looked like a war zone. People were all over the place all fucked up. Puke everywhere. Punk Rock! Excellent!

The Damned played and they were great. I knew they would be anyway. This is where the story gets good. The truck rental company came and repossessed our truck from the parking lot. We were left with no way to get the rental gear back down to London. We were also supposed to be leaving the next day.

We went from band to band and asked for help. None of them would even talk to us. We didn't even think to ask the Subs or the Damned. They were the headliners. As soon as they found out that we were stuck, they immediately came to our aid. The Subs had their crew load our gear into their truck and they said they would take it to the rental place. The Damned had a coach with a lot of extra seats and they said we could all get on and ride back to London no problem. How cool were these guys?

So I walked onto the bus thinking that this is the coolest thing — to be riding in the bus with the Damned. I got on and the bus driver says it's full and he won't take anymore people because it's the law. Mugger and I are left to get down to London on our own somehow with no money. Typical.

> **But the failure of nine-tenths of Black Flag's material — and most other hardcore music as well — is that it is not really emotional or politically extreme.**

We got to the train station and it's full of punkers waiting to get home. We met up with some kid who had some passes or something and we scammed on the train and got down to London. We get out of the train and we had enough money to get back to the girl's house. They weren't home and it's dawn and it's freezing so we said fuck it and broke into the damn place. We beat the rest of them back by hours.

I'm in a great mood because we're going to leave and go back to America. We get our gear together, hump it to the train and go out to the airport. We are, of course, too late and are denied access. We will have to wait another day.

We humped all this gear back to the girl's house and at this point they're getting pretty pissed off at us, but they were so cool to us anyway. We spent the day sitting around doing nothing in this cramped space.

The next day, Ian got up really early and said he's leaving to the airport. I said that he has hours to go. He said he's not going to miss it again. Off he goes. Hours later, we're out there again running down the street with our luggage and assorted pieces of equipment. We get to the airport and check in. We get yelled at because we're so late. They had to hold up the flight several minutes for us. The entire flight was boarded. They didn't even bother to look at our passports. The lady at the gate was furious. I was so glad to be leaving I didn't care. I have never been so happy to be on a flight in my life. I will never forget walking to my seat with all these people giving us the eye because they knew full well that we were the reason that they had been sitting. I saw Ian grinning at me and shaking his head.

Due to visa problems, Robo was detained in the UK. The show in Leeds UK ended up being Robo's last show with Black Flag.

We flew in to Dulles Airport near Washington DC. I spent the evening hanging out with some friends in town. I took a bath at this guy's house. First time I had bathed in several days. As I sunk under the water, a few hunks of spit re-constituted and floated to the surface. I decided that the next time I went back there, I would handle myself and the audiences differently.

23 NEW YORK NY: We were in the shits because we had no drummer. We called Bill from the Descendents and asked him to fly in and play. He knew all the songs well enough. He flew right in and the tour resumed. It was a great gig. The tension of seeing if we could pull it off only added to the excitement. Bill played great. We were happy to be back in the States with an audience that was into us and not trying to attack us and spit on us. It was a great homecoming.

25 PASSIAC NJ: We were in NYC hanging out. I think we were staying in the place where the Bad Brains had recorded their ROIR sessions. The Necros were in town and told us they were going to Lodi, NJ to hang out with the Misfits and play with them in Passiac, NJ on Christmas. We went along to see the show. We ended up being the opening band. It was so cool. The Misfits were so great that night. So were the Necros. It was one of those nights that you know you're going to remember for a long time.

26 BOSTON MA (2 SETS): Another great night. The Boston crowd always rocks hard. To this day, Boston is one of the

PASSIAC, NJ / 12.25.81

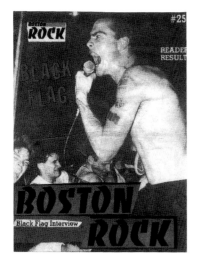

greatest cities to play in the world. It was two sets of people going apeshit and it was a great night. I've had so many great nights in this city it's not even funny.

27 NEW YORK NY: The Peppermint Lounge. It was cool to play on the stage where I first saw Black Flag play. They made us go on at some obscene hour of the morning. I think when we loaded out, the sun was coming up.

28 PITTSBURGH PA: The first of many visits to the Electric Banana, a small club in Pittsburgh. Played every year with Black Flag except for 1986 when we played a roller rink or something. One of the first places the Rollins Band ever played.

29 CHICAGO IL (2 SETS): We played two sets with Hüsker Dü. They were pretty amazing as you would expect. It was a good night. It was so cold outside when we loaded out after the show. Most of us were still wet from playing. The best was yet to come. We had a show in LA in less than two days. We hauled ass across the country. Sometimes not even stopping to use the bathroom. You went right out the window. We would stop at gas stations and get food in the small stores and get back in the van and go. We really had to make time.

PEPPERMINT LOUNGE, NEW YORK, NY / 1981 *(VICKI HAAS)*

31 LOS ANGELES CA: I don't know how we did it, but we did. We pulled into Olympic Auditorium in time for a late soundcheck. It was a wild show. The Blasters played before us. In my mind, they were a great band that not enough people found out about. Bill Bateman is one of the best drummers there is, and then of course, there are the Alvin brothers. A lot of talent for one band. I thought we played well. It was a great feeling to have gone all over the place and made it back. I felt more legitimate with a real tour under my belt. What I didn't know was the real heavy shit was yet to come.

Hours after the gig, I was on the floor of SST trying to get to sleep. I was glad it was over, but when I found out that Bill had a Descendents gig up in SF the next night, I remember feeling jealous that he was getting to play and I wasn't. I was hooked.

GLEN DIDN'T KNOW IT BUT HE CAPTURED THE ESSENCE OF BLACK FLAG RIGHT HERE — ENDLESSLY PUSHING ON ONE OF OUR BROKEN VANS—
REDONDO BEACH, CA / 1982. TOP TO BOTTOM: CHUCK, GREG, CHUCK BISCUITS, DEZ, HENRY, DAVO. *(GLEN E. FRIEDMAN)*

M A Y

08 AUSTIN TX: I think we played with the Dicks and the Big Boys or maybe one of the bands. I don't remember. Always a good time with those bands.

10 OKLAHOMA CITY OK: We played this bar where people in the parking lot were looking at us funny when we were pulling in. We loaded in and soon after, we were getting ready to play. I wondered when all the people were going to turn up. There was no one there. Finally, we start playing and I think there were about five people there at the most. They stood all the way back at the bar in the darkness and observed us. It made me mad, but I played anyway. After the show, Dukowski took me out to the parking lot and straightened me out on a few things. He told me that even though there were only a few people there, it didn't matter. They were there to see us and that was good enough. He said that you never pull a bullshit attitude onstage and you always play your ass off or don't play at all. He taught me a lot.

11 TULSA OK: It was some kind of cowboy bar. We played and there was this couple sitting there watching us like we were from another planet. Dukowski threw his bass on their table. It was still plugged in. It sent their beer pitcher's contents all over them. I jumped on the table and sang to them. It was a great night.

12 Dallas TX / 14 & 15 Houston TX / 16 & 15 New Orleans LA / 18 Atlanta GA / 19 Orlando FL / 20 Miami FL / 21 Tampa FL / 22 Daytona Beach FL / 23 Chapel Hill NC / 25 Raleigh NC / 26 Richmond VA: I don't remember much from the above shows. We got a bag of plastic beads when we were in New Orleans. I guess we got them from someone that had them left over from Mardi Gras. We would wear them and give them to girls and say shit like, "Peace. I love you!" and flash them

the peace sign. It really made the guys mad when we passed beads to them. None of us had shaved or cut our hair for a long time and it was a blast to have punkers get mad at us and call us hippies. The madder they got, the more we knew how lightweight they were. In Richmond, I got a hold of an empty Jack Daniels bottle. I went to the 7-11 and bought some ice tea and filled the bottle. I came out onstage with the bottle just like David Lee Roth and we started playing. I figured people would get the joke, but all the people up front were begging for some every time I took a sip. I gave the bottle to one guy and he took a drink and was mad that it was just tea. Great crowd. Oh yeah, at one of the gigs in FL, the sound onstage was so bad that I couldn't tell what songs we were playing a few times. I remember singing the words to "Fix Me" to the music of "Clocked In".

27 Asbury Park NJ: One long day. We got pulled over by the police on the way into Asbury Park. The pigs made us pull the van into the grass median strip. We were ordered to stand outside and not move. In our hurry to get out of the van and do what the fuckheads wanted us to do, no one woke up Emil who was still asleep in the back of the van. They were crawling through the van and I guess they stepped on him or something, but they scared the hell out of him and vice-versa. They freaked out on him. The poor guy wakes up to NJ highway pigs screaming in his face. We finally get to the place. I sat out front and watched three fistfights take place in front of me. Hours later, we're about to play and I have to run out and get something out of the van. I get can't back in because the door guy doesn't believe that I'm in the band. I can hear the band on the stage. He let me in and said that if he didn't see me onstage, he was going to take me out and beat me up. A few songs into the set, I saw him come in and check. I love this town.

28 Hartford CT / 29 Providence RI: At one of these shows, there was this guy fucking around with our stuff backstage before the show and we nearly had to throw him out. He came back in a few times and started pulling more shit. I guess he was drunk. A few songs into the set, he got onstage and jumped off. He landed on his head and an ambulance came and took him away. Never saw him again. Hope he's okay. He probably doesn't remember any of it.

30 Mt. Vernon NY: We played with the Angelic Upstarts. I hung out with Mensi, the singer, for a while. I remember he said he had a sore throat so I gave him this stuff that I used to gargle with. I thought he was a pretty cool guy. I got up to Canada and was told that he was interviewed and said how much he hated me and the band. I never got a chance to find out if it was true or not, but it bummed me out at the time.

31 LONG ISLAND NY: I sang "No Values" with my pants down. It bummed out some of the people up front. We bummed out a lot of people on this tour.

01 PASSIAC NJ: Some kids broke into a part of the club, ripped off some bottles of liquor and brought them to the dressing room. I saw the pouring spouts on the tops of the bottles and knew what they had done and told them to take them out. I knew that we would get blamed for it. Trouble was one thing we didn't need. We finished the show and the bouncers had broken some windows out of our van. Stuff like this happened to small touring bands all the time. Every band has a million stories like this one.

02 ALBANY NY: A typical night in a club where they weren't ready for a band like us.

HALLANDAH, FL / MAY 1982 *(LESLIE WIMMER)*

It happened often. A lot of places didn't know what they were getting themselves into. Sometimes the patrons were a bit surprised and dismayed by the small, but fierce, group of people that would show up to see us. When I walked onstage to play, the bouncer threw me off. It took a few minutes to convince him that I was the singer.

03 WORCESTER MA: Cops came and closed the show. I don't remember why. We were locked inside the place. I watched a cop slam a young guy's head against the back of the squad car as he threw him in.

04 PHILADELPHIA PA: I remember some guy punching me in the face and I was stupid enough to let him do it. It was videotaped and I actually saw it once. I've done some pretty stupid shit.

06 BALTIMORE MD: During the last song of the set, I punched out a mirror that was on the side of the stage and had to get stitched up. I was sitting on this bed with a guy stitching me up and next to me was this crazy street guy who had been outside the gig all night yelling and carrying on. He had broken all this glass on the sidewalk and ripped himself up with it and was bleeding all over. They must have put a lot of stitches in him. They had him tied down to the bed to work on him. It was a strange sight.

07 TRENTON NJ: The first time I ever played City Gardens, a place I have come to really like. I have played there many times ever since. Randy Ellis books the shows. He booked the first Rollins Band tour and has helped me a lot over many years. One of the good guys.

94 The Toronto Sun, Friday June 18, 1982

Black Flag didn't kill 'em, they *bored* them to death

TORONTO / 1982 *(FRED THORNHILL)*

08 / 09 PITTSBURGH PA: Two nights at the Electric Banana. Emil painted Robo's clear drums with spray paint. Too bad. I always thought those drums looked great the way they were. It was kind of the Black Flag look. Greg's clear guitar and the clear drums.

10 BUFFALO NY: The club owner said that we had to play three sets. We played for most of the night and did every song we knew and just took breaks every 35 minutes or so. It was pretty much like a regular night. I got pulled into the crowd at one point and some guy was trying to kick me in the skull. A road crew guy took him off me. After the show, the guy was hanging around the parking lot and some guy walked right up to him, stabbed him in the stomach and walked away. At first, no one knew he was stabbed, including him. He was so fucked up. Finally his shirt began to turn red and blood started going down his pants. He got in his car and drove away. It was a strange sight.

12 & 13 OTTAWA / 14 QUEBEC / 15 MONTREAL / 16 TORONTO CANADA: It was the first time I had ever been to Canada. The people were great to us every night. We got showers. We ate good food. It was a good break. I made a friend of Jill Heath who booked shows for Black Flag and eventually road managed the Rollins Band for several tours.

17 DETROIT MI (2 SETS) / 18 KALAMAZOO MI (2 SETS) / 19 CHICAGO IL (2 SETS): Dukowski and Emil were sick as dogs. They had been since Canada. They had some kind of bad flu and could hardly move. I don't know how they got through six sets in three days, but they did. I remember in Kalamazoo, Dukowski finished the set and walked right outside and threw up. He finished the set first though. Nowadays, when bands delay shows in major arenas because the singer is talking with his shrink, it makes me think of times like these for perspective. No matter what, we kept on playing.

MADISON, WI / 6.21.82

20 MILWAUKEE WI: All I remember was the gig was really hot and I was rolling all over the stage damaging myself.

21 MADISON WI: One of the punkers that we were staying with, tried to break into the van to get the scripts for the medicine that Duke and Emil were taking. They were on what I gathered was strong stuff. Anyway, the punker didn't know that Duke was crashed out in the back of the van and he busted the guy upon his entrance.

24 SALT LAKE CITY UT: They had us play on a stage made of scaffolding. When we moved, the entire structure bounced and swayed. I did a good part of the gig on my knees for a lower center of gravity. I nearly fell off a few times.

25 LAWRENCE KS: I learned a powerful lesson that day. We were pulling into town and we smelled smoke. The bottom of the van was on fire. We all got out and backed away from the van and watched it burn while backing slowly away. There's no gas cap on the van and we knew that it could go up any second. Dukowski grabbed a towel and got underneath the van and started trying to put the fire out. He yelled for us to help him. All I could do was watch. Mugger ran across the street to a gas station and got a fire extinguisher to help put it out. Dukowski's forearms had burning oil on them. He must have been scared shitless, but he saved the

DENVER, CO / JUNE 1982

van and our equipment. He could have been killed. All I did was stand there. I felt bad. Later that night, a pig came into the gig and told us to turn it down. He looked like Don Knotts and we didn't turn down and we kept on playing and nothing happened.

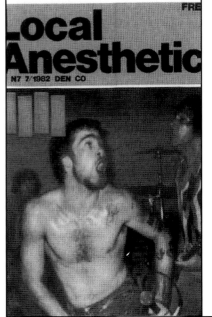

28 / 29 DENVER CO (2 SETS): This was a good stay. The owner of the Mercury Cafe where we played is a woman named Marilyn. She took good care of us for the time that we were there. We played well and had a great time. I still see her every once in a while.

30 PORTLAND OR: There were some belligerent motherfuckers at this show. I nearly got into it for no reason with someone in the front. It seemed like the whole front row was looking to fight someone and it didn't matter. I remember seeing a guy with a length of pipe in his hand.

01 VICTORIA BC / 03 VANCOUVER CANADA: In Vancouver, we played in this fucked up hockey rink. I remember the stage shaking and people giving me a lot of shit. I don't know why. I have never had a good time in Vancouver. Actually, one time was good. We played there in 1984 with St. Vitus and the idiots didn't like them. We were very hostile with the audience when they would try to pull the bullshit. I remember that it felt good. I have not played there since 1985.

04 SEATTLE WA: We were backstage after the show. I was still shook up from playing. A girl came in and started talking to no one in particular. No one knew her and no one wanted her back there. We could be pretty unsociable at times. I remember sitting back there trying to get my mind back from the music. She looked at me and told me to cheer up. I threw a folding chair at her. I barely remember doing it.

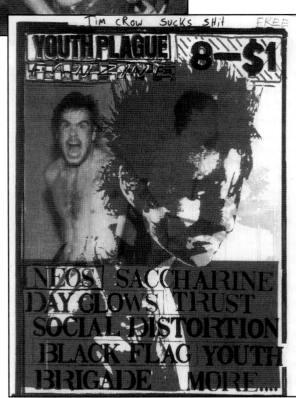

DENVER, CO – VICTORIA, BC / JUNE – JULY 1982 (*GREGOR SCHMIDT*)

06 SAN LUIS OBISPO CA: Before the show, some guy was fucking with Emil. Emil was dealing on him and the guy's brother rushed Emil. I ran up and took the guy off. I punched him in the nose and broke it real bad. I remember it breaking under my fist. I was so impressed with what a great punch it was

HOLLYWOOD, CA. L-R: CHUCK, HENRY, GREG, DEZ, EMIL.
(*GLEN E. FRIEDMAN*)

that I helped the guy to his feet and said something like, "You've got to admit, that was a great shot!" I was all bent out of shape at the end of the set and cut myself open with some glass on the right side of my chest. I bled all over the place. Minor Threat was on tour at the time and Ian was at the show. I remember that bummed him out so badly that he cried. It was my first experience with roadburn. It would not be my last or my worst.

09 MONTEREY CA: It was the last show with Emil. I don't remember anything special about the show. Emil was an excellent drummer. He could learn a song in minutes — a total natural.

EMIL / SUMMER 1982

CHUCK BISCUITS / 12.10.82 (*GLEN E. FRIEDMAN*)

Chuck Biscuits was recruited as the new drummer. We booked a short tour and after a few weeks of practice, we went out on a short tour of America and Canada.

30 SAN PEDRO CA: I stood in the parking lot and watched the security team arrive in the back of a pickup truck. They were given their shirts and they took their pick of assorted weapons out of a bag that was passed around.

31 HEMET CA: It was a party. The gig was actually more together than a lot of shows we played at the time. We were always a soft touch for parties. Kids would call us up, tell us that their parents were out of town and that the house was big enough. We would actually show up and play these places sometimes. It was always interesting. Usually not many songs were played before the show got shut down. It would be the kid cowering in some corner, the police threatening to impound our equipment and Greg would almost always have the bad luck to have to take the threats and lectures from the pigs. A great deal of the parties came off though. Some houses were so good that we came back and played again a few other times.

A U G U S T

19 SAN ANTONIO TX: The owner of the club didn't like us and called in the ritual noise complaint to the police himself and tried to find a way to not pay us. By this time, I was used to the occasional show being shut down by the police routine. It was always strange to be playing hard and to all of a sudden hear the band sag like the batteries had all of a sudden run out. I was always the last to know. I would look up and see the pig standing there and I would stop and give him the microphone. The pigs always liked to get on the mic. They loved that shit. Anyway, I took the 13-ball off the pool table from this shitty club and I have had it ever since.

21 HOUSTON TX: We played the Lawndale Art Annex. I remember finishing the show and walking back to the dressing room which I think was the kitchen. I heard this voice behind me say, "Hey faggot." I thought nothing of it and kept walking. I heard it again and turned around and there was this guy standing there. I asked him if he was talking to me and he said yes and just kind of stood there. I was still heated up from

IAN MACKAYE AND HENRY ROLLINS, SANTA MONICA, CA / JULY 1982 *(NAOMI PETERSEN)*

playing so I jumped on him and started banging his head on the floor. All of a sudden, I was in the air. Two cops had pulled me off of him. They had a hold of my neck and were restraining me. One of them asked why I was attacking the guy. I told him that the guy had called me a faggot. The two cops immediately let go of me and apologized as if they had made a grave error. In fact, they gave the guy more shit than they gave me.

22 NEW ORLEANS LA: This was the night that we played out in the middle of nowhere at a small bar. The Sluts opened. The singer, Dave Slut, had this really long mic cord and he was running all over the club attacking people while he sang. He was known for this. He was the crazy guy with the long mic cord. When it was our turn to play, I borrowed the cord and did some songs out on the street. It was fun. I sang "Jealous Again" to a group of bums hanging out front. These guys liked me because before the gig, I pulled a green treefrog off the glass of the front of the club and ate it. They flipped. "He ate a frog!" One guy ran off and came back with another frog and a cricket, and said if I was still hungry I could eat these. It was a fun show. New Orleans is always good.

25 / 26 MEMPHIS TN: Two nights at the Antenna Club. The guy who ran it was really cool, but the place was and probably still is a pretty depressing place to spend two nights. We did it though. Some of the guys went and checked out Graceland. I don't remember what I did with myself. Some stretches of these tours, it was all I could do to keep myself together. Sometimes there was nothing to do and a lot of hours to do it

in. You could sit in the van in a parking lot waiting to go on or look for a toilet that worked. Most of the toilets in the club didn't work. It was on these tours that I understood why people in bands take a lot of drugs and drink like fish. The boredom and depression can be immense. It's nothing new. Any touring band will be able to tell you about this.

30 RICHMOND VA: I remember rolling on the bar of the place screaming at people while the band played. I think there were a few Marines sitting at the bar that were getting a little tired of me knocking over their beer. They didn't pound the snot out of me for some reason.

BRIDGEPORT, CT / 9.11.82 (*JAMIE KEEVER*)

FALL 1982. L-R: CHUCK, HENRY, GREG, CHUCK BISCUITS, DEZ. *(GLEN E. FRIEDMAN)*

FALL 1982: THE NIG HEIST. L-R: MERRILL WARD, MUGGER, DEZ, CHUCK BISCUITS. *(NAOMI PETERSEN)*

SEPTEMBER

01 NEW YORK NY: At this gig, some huge guy jumped off the stage and I watched him land on top of this girl. From where I was, it looked bad. I met her a year or so later. I remembered her. I asked her if it hurt when that fat piece of shit landed on her. She showed me her glass eye. The guy took her eye out with his boot. I didn't know what to say. What do you say? "Sorry about that. How about a free shirt?" She said not to worry about it and walked away.

03 DETROIT MI: During the show, this girl in the front row had her fist up and was punching the air in a non-threatening way. I took her fist and started punching myself in the face with it. I don't know why. Strange mood I guess. She flipped out when she saw that I was pummeling my face with her hand.

09 ST LOUIS MO: This place had some kind of barrier so the underage non-drinkers couldn't get near the bar. I think it was some kind of chainlink fence or small retaining wall. It was such a joke.

12 MONTREAL CANADA: We played with Discharge and Vice Squad, two big punk rock bands from England. I remembered the singer of VS from the show in Leeds back in '81. It was good to see them opening. The Discharge guys were cool. We played hard and my right knee which had been giving me trouble for the last few weeks finally gave out. I had a piece of cartilage floating on the side of my knee that I had to keep shoving back into place with my hand during songs. We had to cancel the rest of the dates.

The next few days sucked. Our van broke down somewhere in Canada. We camped out in a gas station waiting for it to get fixed. The attendants must have thought we were crazy. We slept in the van and hung out in the parking lot for close to three days. My knee was fucked up and I couldn't go anywhere. The record company which we were dealing with at the time eventually sent us some money and we managed to sell our van and buy another used one. We rented a U-Haul trailer to put the backline into. We set out for LA.

SACCHARINE TRUST. L-R: EARL LIBERTY, JACK BREWER, JOE BAIZA, ROB HOLTZMAN / 7.27.82 *(ED COLVER)*

It was good in the back of the van. There was room for everyone. We had never had so much room. It was cool until we hit Des Moines. It was raining in sheets like some movie scene. I was looking out the back at the gray sky and all that rain. All of a sudden, the U-Haul became smaller and smaller. The trailer did a spectacular flip over the railing, flew through the air and disappeared. It nearly took out a car on its way. We pulled over and backed up. The damn thing was way down in a ditch partially submerged in water. My knee made it

HENRY, LOS ANGELES, CA / 7.17.82 *(ED COLVER)*

impossible for me to do anything. The rest of the guys slid down the grassy bank and opened up the little doors at the back and started to pull the cabs out. They tried to drag them up, but slid back down. All the while, the rain was relentless. Some of the cabs were too damaged so we left them. We left the U-Haul down there as well. We loaded all the wet gear into the van and went to some roadside place. We called U-Haul and told them that their shitty hitch had cost them a trailer and we gave them the approximate location of the thing and that was that.

The van that we took on the tour and ditched in Canada didn't belong to us. It belonged to Saccharine Trust and they had lent it to us. We had some pretty bad news for them when we got back to LA a few days later. Another tour over. I had surgery done to my knee.

HUNTINGTON BEACH / 1982. L-R: CHUCK, CHUCK BISCUITS, GREG, DEZ, HENRY. *(ED COLVER)*

O C T O B E R

23 REDONDO BEACH CA (PARTY): This was fucked up. We got the call to play this place near where we lived. It looked like an old recording studio. None of us knew the guy or any of his friends. We just showed up with some of our friends. The setup was good though and it looked like it was going to be a good night. The guy pulled out a large bag of cocaine and threw it on a table. It was a lot of damned dope. We just kind of looked at these people doing drugs and we just kept playing. A few songs later, the police came busting in and all these people just kind of disappeared. In about a minute's time, it was just us, the police and this big bag of coke. One pig comes up to me and asked why I'm sweating and out of breath. I told him that I've been playing. He shined his light in my eyes and looked at me all hard while his buddy pounded his stick

REDONDO BEACH, CA / FALL 1982 *(GLEN E. FRIEDMAN)*

on a chair next to my leg. Eventually they let us go and we went back to SST. I never found out what happened to the guy with the coke. A few weeks later, I was in a burger place up the street from SST. One of the pigs that busted the party came in and spotted me. He stood over me and hit the seat with his stick like the other guy did at the party. He stood there until I left. I didn't get to finish my meal.

19 VALENCIA CA & W. COVINA CA: This was a great day. We were asked to play in a classroom at Cal Arts. I don't remember what the class was about, but there we were, playing with a seated class in front of us. I climbed on the teacher's chair and screamed all this shit at her while we're playing. I remember the spit hitting her glasses and her looking very nervous. She seemed to understand that it was all part of the "artistic experience" that we were trying to bring to them. After that, we stood in front of all of them and answered questions. The teacher didn't say anything. We packed up and played this party in a back yard of some kid's house in W. Covina. Typical thing where the nervous kid needs us to run his party for him and take all the heat when the pigs come in by climbing over his fence. We got a few songs off anyway.

21 PALM SPRINGS CA: Did the show with strep throat. It hurt. I was running a fever and it was a trip. Pulled it off though.

HENRY, DINAH CANCER AND KEITH MORRIS, CLUB LINGERIE, LOS ANGELES, CA / 1982 *(EDWARD RASEN)*

GREG GINN / **12.10.82** (*GLEN E. FRIEDMAN*)

DECEMBER

02 PHOENIX AZ: At this time, we were playing new material and it was making some people at the shows a bit hostile. We did that a lot. We would do entire tours with new music in the set, sometimes only doing a few older songs. People were not always that open-minded about this and would yell that we had sold out. I can't think of a band that was accused of selling out more than Black Flag. We got shit for releasing an album because real bands didn't release albums. We sold out because we didn't cut our hair or because we had a song that was slow or longer than three minutes. Sold out because we had instrumental music in the set. We did *all* the "wrong" things. All the time, we were working our asses off and we were dirt poor. We would read the sellout bullshit and laugh. It might not have been bad if we had been able to get three meals a day out of our big sellout moves. Imagine having to take shit from these minuscule fakes like Maximum Rock n' Roll and Flipside. Anyway, we're playing away and people in the crowd are screaming for the old songs and we're doing what we want. They're getting mad. I took off my clothes and jumped off the PA on top of them. They hated that. I stood up on some partition and started dancing around. A security guy shined his flashlight on me to get me to stop, but I just started yelling "Fuck you, pig" or something. I eventually got back onstage and we finished the show. It was one of those nights. It became very hard to have a good attitude about "fans" with the shit that people gave us all the time.

UKRAINIAN HALL, LOS ANGELES, CA / 12.10.82—D. BOON BEHIND GREG'S RIG. *(NAOMI PETERSEN)*

10 LOS ANGELES CA: The Ukrainian Hall show — one of our most ambitious flyer campaigns ever. We put them up all over the place. We made them into stickers and put them in every phone booth we could. We went and put them up around the police station in San Pedro just to say hello. I remember Dukowski kept yelling out songs to play well after the set was over. It was a long set. I was doubling over from cramps afterwards. I had torn my stomach up with the mic as well. It was a good night.

CHUCK DUKOWSKI, SAN FRANCISCO, CA / 1.8.83 (GLEN E. FRIEDMAN)

MUGGER, REDONDO BEACH, CA, 1982 *(GLEN E. FRIEDMAN)*

1.25.83 ARIZONA: Left SST in the van. Went through the desert. It's great out here — cruel and honest. I want to die out here.

1.26.83 TEXAS: Getting colder. Sundown.

1.27.83 SOMEWHERE: Drive, night watch, riding shotgun with Davo. The mountains are beautiful — snow and trees and a full moon. Makes me think of werewolves. We're going to drive all night. Everyone is in the back of the van asleep, except for us.

1.28.83 FALLS CHURCH VA: Got here at 7:30 a.m. Got a little sleep and then went out. Went to the record store and checked that out. Went to my old work place and talked to Vincent and Andy. Strange being in there walking behind the counter and looking out the window onto Wisconsin Avenue and remembering how many times I wanted to get out of there.

    Visited some friends. I wish I could take all my memories and put them in a book, and then put the book on a shelf and take it down when I damn well please. It's hard to take. Harder to get away from. I haven't been away from here for very long, but still, it's hard to talk to these people. So much has happened since I left. I notice that I speak differently now. I can't help it. I hang out with different people and it happens.

1.29.83 LONG ISLAND NY: I sucked tonight. Soundcheck was bad on my part. The gig was cool enough. The people were alright. I gave it my best shot. I sucked though. People should have had their money refunded. I got kicked in the head a few times. I forgot where I was. Got my lips busted by one guy who shoved the mic into my mouth. That counts for something doesn't it? No, it doesn't. None of it means shit. I wish somebody had killed me.

1.30.83 BOSTON MA: At the Channel. I thought we played good. I bashed up my left elbow and can't move it very well now. I don't care as long as I played better than last night. When I play bad, it's all I think about until the next show. Playing is all that matters. Playing well and trying to keep up with Greg and Chuck.

1.31.83 BOSTON MA: We have a day off. I am sitting in someone's house. I forget the name of the person to whom the place belongs to. We always end up on someone's floor.

I was walking on the streets in DC the other day and it seemed that I hadn't even left. I still knew my way around. All the buildings were still there, but I looked just to make sure. I don't know what the hell I was looking for.

Later: Now in New Jersey at Dez's brother's house. I hope I get bashed up soon. I need the pain to play. I need to have to play for my life otherwise it's not worth it. Nothing's worth it. I don't talk to anyone right now. I find it a waste of time. Nobody understands anybody. What's on my mind is not important to anyone except me. I have to keep that in my head and I'll be okay. It's too easy to talk too much and make a fool out of yourself.

I talked to this girl I go out with on the phone tonight. She doesn't like being alone. She should go out with someone that's home all the time. Looks like I'll be out all the time now.

GOOFING OFF AT PRACTICE PLACE — LONG BEACH, CA / JANUARY 1983 *(GLEN E. FRIEDMAN)*

2.1.83 NEW YORK NY: Doing van watch while the guys go to the music store to get gear. We're trying to book practice time so we can work on stuff. Chuck has been trying to get in touch with Mi Casa, the place where I auditioned for the band. That would be strange to go back inside that place.

Later: At a practice place, not Mi Casa though. Tomorrow we play in New Haven, CT.

2.2.83 NEW HAVEN CT: Played okay. Nothing special. Packed up and left for DC.

2.3.83 WASHINGTON DC: Tonight was two sets at 9:30 Club. Played as hard as I could. The lights were cooking me during the first set. Between sets I had to lie down. While I was down, I got interviewed by a man from the Washington Post. I could barely think straight. I was tired and thinking about the next set made it hard to concentrate.

It doesn't matter how hard you play. No one likes us here. You sweat. You spill your guts out. People just laugh at you and try to find ways to make you look stupid. It works. I feel like a jerk for playing this town. As if anyone in that fucking crowd could pull this off night after night. I would like to see them try. Laughing at me is like laughing at thin air. It makes me want to move to a place where no one lives. Tonight hurt a lot. Sometimes I'm almost afraid to play because it hurts so much.

TORRANCE, CA / 1.14.83 *(NAOMI PETERSEN)*

2.4.83 BALTIMORE MD: At the Marble Bar. Fucking cold. If I ever get an apartment or a real place to live, it will not be as cold as this place. The inside of the club is colder than the outside. How the hell did they pull that off?

I remember seeing some shows in this place a few years ago. I saw DOA tear this place up. They were so good. Jello got up and sang with them, that was great. I got in a fight next to the stage. I was so pissed off after the show that I took a piece of wood I found on the floor and ripped my right arm apart with it. Felt good at the time.

2.5.83 PHILADELPHIA PA: Picked up the Minutemen. Ten people in this van now. We are packed in like sardines. The drives are going to be hell, but that's okay because get to play. Now at the Eastside Club. What a dump. All these guys running around like they're in the Mafia. Give me a break.

BILL STEVENSON, SANTA BARBARA, CA / 1.7.83 (GLEN E. FRIEDMAN)

I cut myself up with a piece of broken glass to get myself ready to play tonight. I don't know if anyone would understand that.

Tomorrow we leave with the Minutemen for England. I hope the plane doesn't crash into the sea. To be free you have to speak a different language. You have to think in another frame of mind. There's no hope in life. You get temporary breathers and that's it. Sometimes I need a dark room and stupidity to dull the pain. There's no such thing as friendship. You just get what you need when you need it as fast as you can. The only reason that people give is so they can take later on.

I went walking. Ended up in front of a 7-11. I saw an old woman huddled in front. That will be a tough one to deal with. A place to sleep without freezing to Death. This is a cold place. No one lives here, they just die. People are disgusting. So tough, so mean, so scared. I can speak some of their language, but I can't translate it to save my life. I walked along this street and looked into the windows of all these bars. All the people inside staring off into space. What a lost place we are stuck in.

2.7.83 LONDON UK: Landed okay. Now at some lady's house. Don't know who she is. I guess she's a friend of the promoter or something. Oh shit, some of the guys from the Anti-Nowhere League just came in. What a drag! Trapped in a cold, fucked up house with no money, no food and these punk rock shitheads.

I don't like touring with other bands, but I guess it's cool that the Minutemen are with us. Everybody should get a chance to see them. Their new record is finished, but it's not out yet. It's great. Tomorrow is practice and running. Thursday we hit it. We have to destroy them. If you want to destroy, you have to prepare. You have to practice. You have to learn your pain.

The fact that there's a lot of people and almost no room on this tour is going to make it hard. The Minutemen have hardly been out the door let alone on a Black Flag tour. We'll see how they hold up.

You're not an American until you leave America. The people at this house aren't letting us forget where we're from for a second. I would rather be a human being than an American. Whatever, it's all over when we hit stage. Like Dukowski says, "What the fuck. Fuck shit up."

2.8.83 LONDON UK: Listened to Electric Ladyland with Dez today. The bitch of the house didn't like it, but hey, it was in her record collection. Practice was okay. We are going through rented equipment so Greg is having a hard time of it. I think Dukowski never sounded better. The practice place is a cold, fucked up room with bad lights. It took us a long time to get here because we didn't know which side of the river the place was on and ended up crossing bridges for over an hour. I hate England. I knew this was coming. We are out of food and money.

2.9.83 LONDON UK: It's 9 a.m. and everyone is asleep. I'm in the kitchen. Today will be a bad day. Long practice and little or no food. I am used to it, it's the Black Flag thing. The only thing I want besides the chance to play, is a meal and the chance to get some sleep.

I think that deep inside we are all running from something. Thinking about the time I was in DC recently makes me see that. The lady from Melody Maker asked me why I am so heavy. I'm heavy? I tried to explain the way I see things. I don't think it worked. I could tell by the way she looked at me. I walk through life with a heavy heart I guess. It makes me go. A heavy stone. I would rather try to write it out

TORRANCE, CA / 1.14.83 *(NAOMI PETERSEN)*

than talk to anyone about it. There's nothing to say to anyone anyway. Maybe some girl I could talk to.

My brain moves from meal to meal. That may seem pretty funny, but that's the way it is right now. I can't wait to be able to think of other things and not have to be preoccupied with thoughts of where the next meal is coming from. It makes me mean. The bottom line is that we get to play.

2.10.83 LONDON UK: Sitting here at the 100 Club. This place is heated. Ate okay. We loaded the PA in as well as our equipment. It's snowing outside. We are leaving for Amsterdam tomorrow. Can't wait to get the hell out of the UK. Skinheads will not be allowed in tonight.

The stage in this place is so small. The last time I played here sucked real bad. It was in 1981. I got punched out by a skinhead. I had my back turned and he hit me in the back of the head and I went down. I got up and didn't know where I was. That shithead really rang my bells. The roadie from the UK Subs got me out of there. He told me later that the skinhead was mad at me because his skinhead girlfriend kissed me on the cheek and he got jealous again. Ha ha. The next inhospitable town to be played is Amsterdam, Holland. I have never been there before. Wonder what that will be like. I'll find out if these people don't kill me first.

2.11.83 CROYDEN UK: The show last night was cool, people showed up and everything. Did another interview in a pub near the 100. It was with NME. Now I'm in a room with a stereo. I am playing Hendrix. Soon we leave for the boat. Tomorrow night we stay in a real hotel.

Later: Now on the boat. This boat is huge — saunas, disco, a movie theater. I am sitting far away from the others. Mugger is running around screaming, "Blow jobs!" I don't want to be involved. He and the

AMSTERDAM, HOLLAND / 2.13.83 (*PATRICIA STEUR*)

drummer are running around trying to meet girls by yelling at them. Somehow I don't see it working all that well for those guys. This is a strange trip. One night I'm in some grimy club and the next night I'm in a boat that looks like the lobby of a hotel. I'm tired, but there's really no place to sleep except the floor which is no big deal. I don't want to get my stuff ripped off as I sleep. So if you steal this, send it back when you're done with it.

Flash!! Piercing screams from the upper deck, followed by rowdy American low-rent rock stars yelling to stay because "There's a party up here!" Four young things come tearing down the stairs and run past me. People on my deck gasp in disbelief. We have yet to leave the dock.

2.12.83 AMSTERDAM HOLLAND: Didn't get much sleep because of Mugger and Co. It's 7 a.m., we are docked in Holland. It's dark outside. Mike Watt sure talks a lot of shit. Sure would be good to get some sleep before the show.

Later: the hotel in Amsterdam. I have to stay away from everyone until I get a grip on all of this. It's strange to see Greg unsure of what's going on. I don't blame him. We're in Holland for the first time and we're doing it on our own. I have to get it together.

2.13.83 GERMAN/DUTCH BORDER: About last night. The Nig Heist got through one song before skinheads jumped onstage and started attacking them. One asshole was swinging a mic stand at Mugger's head. The Minutemen were freaking out before they went on. They thought that they were going to be killed. It just made me mad. I wanted to kill those fuckers.

When we played, one skin got onstage and was looking offstage to show off to his friends. I kicked him off and he fell a long way to the floor. He didn't dig that too much. 850 people showed up, but I bet that there will be a lot less people next time. D. Boon had the best move of the night. During their last song "Fanatics", D. jumped offstage with his guitar on and ran through the crowd screaming, "FANATICS!!!" People didn't know what to do. He knocked those skinheads over like bowling pins.

The countryside is beautiful. I've never seen anything like it. Thatched roofs on the houses. Snow everywhere, the sky is so blue. I'm 22 years old today.

2.14.83 HAMBURG GERMANY: Played last night in Hanover. Real good show. The place was small and packed. The air was mostly smoke so it was hard to breathe. Played a 24 song set. We kept going off and Dukowski kept saying to play more. Fine with me. It was hard though. Bill and I kept grinning at each other because we knew how the other was hating the heat. Pulled it off though.

The gig here was at a place called the Markthalle. A lot of people. A lot of really fucked skinheads. Watt got mugged at the bar when they heard his American accent. When we played, the skins were all up front telling us to go home and pushing people around. They kept swinging at my head when I got too close to the edge of the stage. Finally I asked the crowd how many of them thought that the skins were assholes. The place cheered. The skins shrank back and just stared.

I played hard. I poured myself out. I feel like a dry sponge. You can play until you drop and no one cares. There's a lot they'll never know. I don't want the things they tell me to want. I'm losing all hope for people. I don't feel like writing anymore. I hate everything and I'm lonely and I think there's no way out. Destroyed by the eyes of the world.

2.15.83 HAMBURG GERMANY: On a day off in Hamburg. Didn't do much. Some guy came to talk to us. The guy, Dukowski and I went out and walked around. We got on this train and the guy told us that you didn't need a ticket unless you were asked to show yours. You could risk getting shit, but if you went for it you could ride for free. We went for it and it was fine. On the way back, we ran to catch the train and we all got on except for the Duke who had to pry the doors apart. This little boy comes running up to him and starts trying to push him out the door. The little fucker is yelling loudly and causing all the people to look over at us. Right then, a pig came over and took us out at the next stop and proceeded to give us a lot of shit when

we couldn't show our tickets. We tried to play it like we were stupid American tourists, but it didn't work. He knew we were sleazy. He kicked us out. Other than that, I ate a lot of oranges and slept a lot. I needed it.

Greg went off on the guys who were running the food store below the hotel. They were trying to rip us off and I didn't think much of it because I expected these guys to be sleazy. But Greg was so pissed. He and

THE MINUTEMEN, MUNICH, GERMANY / 2.19.83

Dukowski started eating food out of the refrigerator and yelling at the guys. The guys behind the counter knew they were busted and had no choice but to let them do it. They looked at the rest of us and realized we would have beat the shit out of them. There's something about your eyes when you haven't eaten for a while and you've been fucked with by skinheads that just says don't fuck with me.

2.17.83 KÖLN GERMANY: Didn't write yesterday. Last night, I met Volker and Eric Hysteric from the Vomit Visions. They gave me some of their records that I had never seen before. It was so cool to meet those guys.

It was a wild show. The guys at the door pulled a few knives and a gun from people coming in. When we were playing, I saw a guy about to club another guy with a piece of lead pipe. I grabbed it out of his hand as it was coming down toward his head. That was crazy.

The press people and the hangers on were treating me like I was some kind of star. Interviews are ego rollercoaster rides. They are self-indulgent wastes of time unless they are informational. Some people feed on the star treatment.

Later: Now at the club in Osnabruck. Cold in this place. Skinheads are in here for some reason. It's not even soundcheck and they're here. They make me nervous. I don't like the pressure of playing under the stare of some stupid army faction. Power is a dangerous thing. Organizations are evil. Unity is evil. Only a cowardly idiot would align himself with a unified faction. This

MUNICH, GERMANY, 2.19.83

shit can be hazardous to your health. The outsider presents a threat to the power of the uniform. If you can't convert the outsider, you must destroy the outsider. Maybe that's why the skinheads hate our guts.

Soundcheck is over, went okay. The skinheads make me nervous. It's hard enough to play these gigs let alone have to deal with these shitheads. There's always too many of them. I never see them alone. Tomorrow we leave to go to Berlin at 7:30 in the morning. Mike Watt never stops talking. It's not like there's any place I can go hang out in here. The room is small and we're all stuck in here and I think I'm going to

MUNICH, GERMANY, 2.19.83

punch Watt's fucking lights out before all this is over. Fuck it. Maybe I should go get a job in a library, live in a cave. I don't know.

2.18.83 BERLIN GERMANY: Hello, here at the SO36 club. Inside is cold. The heating is broken and it is painfully cold. Do you know the meaning of cold? If you haven't been to a cold place, then come on down to the cheery SO36 club here in Berlin, just 5 minutes from the Berlin Wall.

We crossed into Berlin no problem. The place we played last night, Hyde Park, that was something. One song in, someone cut the snake and we had to play the rest of the gig with no PA except for the monitors. We turned them toward the crowd so they could hear the vocals. It was alright, sounded like one of our practices. No one seemed to give a fuck. Shit, my pen is blotting because of the cold. Mugger is keeping Greg's hands warm by putting a lighter underneath them.

2.19.83 MUNICH GERMANY: Been driving since 8 a.m. It's now evening. Last night was pretty wild. The Minutemen were great as usual. 3 songs into our set, I got hit square on the forehead with an unopened can of beer. Good shot. I grabbed a mic stand and begged the guy to come and get killed. He ran out of the place. The rest of the gig was a lot of sweat and smoke. These people seem to smoke as much as they breathe.
At the end of the set, the PA got turned off and we did "TV Party" without it. The crowd joined in *(see back cover photo).* After that, we got some food and slept in some freezing rooms. We had to double up in the beds. There was no hot water.

2.20.83 AUSTRIA: Just crossed into Austria. The gig last night was good — about 1100 people came. We played the Lowenbrau Keller, a huge beer hall. Before we went on, I was checking out the size of the beer mugs these people were drinking out of. They must have weighed a few pounds on their own, no lie. All I could think of was one crushing my skull. I wrote a postcard to someone and told 'em that this might be the last gig. You can't sing too well with a head full of glass. No one threw a thing at us. They did wreck the barricades and scare the living shit out of the security. Before we went on, people were telling us about how Hitler had spoken on the same stage here many years ago.

2.21.83 SOMEWHERE: Last night in Vienna was real bad for me. A guy took the microphone from me, called me a pig and bashed me in the mouth with it. People spat at me, hit me in the face. One guy burned me a few times with a cigar. I got these big burns on my leg. Some big guy got onstage and the bouncers were trying to hit him. I got between them to try to save the guy and for my trouble, the guy hauled off and punched me in the jaw. After that, it got wild. The police came and the crowd beat the shit out of them, the police dog too. Some punks were wearing the pig's hats. During the Minutemen's set, someone hit D. Boon with a trash can. It bounced off.

Felt bad afterwards. Real lonely and I felt like fucking myself up real bad. I don't know whether that's bad or good. All I know is I felt it. We ate some fake food in this frozen kitchen area with some of the people that run the place. Ugly junkie types with green hair, white skin and too much makeup.

Later: In some gas station. Cold outside. The sun is going down. Music like you hear at an ice skating rink is on the radio. What am I doing in all these places? We are on our way to Italy. It will be a long drive.

2.22.83 MILAN ITALY: The drive was long. We went through the Alps. The night came and we climbed and climbed. Our van has no snow tires and we were going through heavy snow. A few times I thought Dukowski was going to

MILAN, ITALY, 2.22.83 *(M. COPPINI)*

dump us off the side and down into hell. Mike Watt of course would not shut up. He's a one-man freakout. At one point, I thought Duke was going to pull over and punch him out. All the while, we had the live King Crimson album going. The weather is warmer here.

The poster for the show tonight is so great. It's a Pettibon drawing blown up real huge with our name underneath it. Maybe the crowd won't be so hostile tonight and we can get some playing done for a change. We have no shows for the next 3 days. I don't know where we are going to sleep and how we are going to eat. This is going to be a hard one I think.

2.23.83 ITALIAN/SWISS BORDER: The Italian border is on strike. They don't want to let the equipment van through. They threatened to beat up Davo. Last night was real cool. When we got to the club, there were all these kids there. We pulled up to the front door and they started rocking the van and pounding on the windows. I thought they wanted to kill us. I was getting ready to get out of there as best I could without getting hurt too bad. When we got out of the van, they all started hugging and kissing us and giving us presents. A lot of them had Black Flag logos painted on their jackets. They thought that the Minutemen were Hüsker Dü.

After that, a lot of people started coming to the place and wanted to get in for free. The owner

MILAN, ITALY, 2.22.83 *(M. COPPINI)*

went outside and told them no way. The kids started throwing rocks at the club's windows and started fucking the place up. In the main office, they had a video camera set up and we watched the whole thing from inside. The police came and started kicking ass on the kids. A couple of hours later we got to play. It was wild, to say the least.

So tonight, if we get out of Italy, we play Geneva. After tonight, we have a three day spaceout. The drive here was amazing. I have never seen castles like these before. I've seen some in England years ago, but they weren't like these. The Alps blow my mind. Everywhere you look, looks like a postcard. Tonight's crowd will be the basic German type I bet. We were spoiled in Italy, all those people being so nice to us and all. Now I guess it's back to the hostile shit.

I wonder what we're going to do for the next three days. We have no money to stay anywhere. By now I'm used to this. But in Switzerland? What will this be like? The next three days are going to suck. Davo has to drive back to the border to get some paperwork filled out that they wouldn't do the other day. What a waste of time. You should have seen these assholes — fat pigs. One of them tried to buy Dukowski's watch.

Denmark is a two day trip from here. That's the next show. Food will be hard to find. Tonight's crowd is coming in, not many of them either. They look like the basic punker type.

Later: At the hotel. We played real tight. The toughest skinheads were total chickenshit. A guy threw a cup of piss on Dukowski as he left the stage. Duke went berserk man, it was wild. He started wrecking the dressing room. I have never seen him like that before. I have never had a cup of piss thrown on me either. I gave it all I had, but it's hard to dig all the way in with a bunch of gluehead punks casually spitting on you. Some dick spilled his beer all over my bag tonight. All my stuff is wet. I wanted to kill the guy, but he was a friend of the promoter. Dukowski and I packed up all the food that was left in the dressing room. I made myself a sandwich for later. Who knows when the next meal is coming around this place.

2.24.83 GENEVA SWITZERLAND: Still in Switzerland. Hanging out in some punker squat. Tonight we will stay here and then we will go on to Denmark. The people in this shithole are gross. All they do is rip shit off, get drunk and listen to shitty punk rock.

Dez had some fun with one of the punkers. He put in a ZZ Top tape into the community blaster. All the punkers started yelling at him. Dez told them that the tape was the new Exploited album. The punkers were stupid — they all believed him. One guy started crying, no shit.

These days off are bad for us. We lose our momentum. The last few days have not been all that great. I liked Berlin the best so far. I like the desperate shows the best. I don't play good unless I'm pushed. I know that sounds stupid, but it's true. The more bashed up I get, the better I play. One of these days someone is going to get me good and that will be it.

2.25.83 OSNABRÜCK GERMANY: Back at the Hyde Park place. Connie, the lady who owns the place said that we could stay anytime we wanted. We drove out here to see if she meant it. She put us all up in the rooms upstairs. I have my own room. We're getting fed good too. We have been in the van since last night. It's great to be out of the van and in someplace warm.

Found out that the Birthday Party are playing the Lyceum the night that we leave the UK for America. What a drag. That would be such a great show. My hand is shaking from too much coffee.

2.27.83 OSNABRÜCK GERMANY: Richard Hell played here tonight and let us and the Minutemen open up.

We went off. I got all cut up. I bit a skinhead in the mouth and he started to bleed real bad. His blood was all over my face. While we were playing, D. Boon was in the crowd and gave me a glass of beer. I broke the glass over my head. I am all cut up. Hell went on and told the crowd that Black Flag kills. No shit. I took a bath and had to wash myself three times to get all the dirt and glass out of my skin. We leave for Denmark in an hour.

2.28.83 COPENHAGEN DENMARK: Now in Denmark. I don't know who I am. We left Hyde Park at three in the morning. We have been traveling since then. We just got here. It's time for soundcheck.

We have found a way to get Watt so pissed off that he might have a cardiac arrest. It's simple. We start telling him that his girlfriend is with some punker with a mohawk now that he's away from home. He always goes for it and gets mad and calls us all a bunch of motherfuckers. Another thing to do to pass the time is to get Watt and D. Boon in one of their epic arguments. It's easy — set up any topic. Chances are that they already disagree. When one guy says something, anything, just say to the other, "Are you going to let him say that kind of shit to you? Don't take that shit from him unless you're just scared of him. Well, I guess I see who REALLY runs this band." After that you just get out of the way. Boon and Watt will go at it like Siamese fighting fish.

We have been listening to Mike's tapes because he gets so freaked out about who gets to play what and he starts talking about fascism when someone puts something in the deck. He has been put in charge of playing all the music just to shut him up. He has turned me on to some cool stuff — James Blood Ulmer, Albert Ayler, this really cool live Curtis Mayfield album — all kinds of shit. It's worth putting up with Watt because he's such a great bass player and the Minutemen are so amazing.

It would be nice to be touched by hands that didn't want to kill or congratulate me. Sometimes the hands that want to kill me are mine.

3.1.83 AARHUS DENMARK: Hard show last night. People took snow from outside and made snowballs and threw them at us. One guy was fucking with me so I went out and bit him. I crawled up to him from the floor, and pulled myself up his legs and bit the fuck out of him. People were throwing money, the coins with the holes. I don't know what we did to get that. The gig looked cool when we got here. I was so excited to be here for the first time and then they take it all away by being assholes.

Later: In the hotel. The show went great. There was this kid that came on a train all the way from Finland. He was so wasted on glue that he passed out on the side of the stage and was out for all three bands. Mugger put all this echo on us and it sounded strange. Came off okay though. People didn't know what to make of the Heist boys. They played and people didn't get the jokes. There were a lot of fucked up people. Next we go back to the UK.

3.3.83 CROYDEN UK: Didn't write shit yesterday. Spent the whole day getting here. Dez, Davo and I are here at Boswell's house listening to Black Sabbath. We play tomorrow night and we leave on Sunday.

That's three days away. Can't believe that we have been through all these countries. This house is depressing. There's nowhere we can go and everything's cold so we just sleep, drink tea and hang out.

3.5.83 CROYDEN UK: Last night was pretty rocky. People were throwing plastic mugs at us. It was hard to sink into the music while dodging the projectiles. A man with a mohawk started to fuck with Greg, and I beat him up. His mohawk made a good handle to hold on to when I beat his face into the floor. The bouncers were afraid to break it up. They stood nearby and asked me to please let the guy go. Punk rock

(GLEN E. FRIEDMAN)

shithead. It would be so cool if we could just kill these posers. Next time a guy fucks with Greg, I should let him punch Greg's lights out. Sure would be better than having Greg call me a macho asshole. If that guy slugged Greg, instead of me getting him away from his face, he might have seen it a bit differently. That's not the part he sees. He just sees me hitting some guy. He doesn't see the part where it would have been him getting his fucking lights punched out. I don't bother talking to him about it because you can't talk to Greg. You just take it and keep playing. Whatever.

I don't enjoy playing unless I see blood or get hurt. I bet that people would think that's crazy. Maybe Nick Cave understands this. The world is cold and no one understands you anyway. Fuck it.

I just called the girl I go out with long distance. She told me that she doesn't want to go out with me anymore and then she hung up. Fucking hung up on me long distance. I guess when I get back home, I will be alone again.

3.10.83 BROOKLYN NY: In a club called the Brooklyn Zoo. Last few days, I spent in DC. I had a good time. Hung out with Ian, went to a few record stores. Took the train up here on my own. I feel older than when I left DC. I know I'm older in years, but I have seen a lot of shit since I have been in the band. I deal with people differently. It took me a while to get used to how differently they treat you. People that you thought

were your friends give you shit about working hard. All I know is that we play hard and a lot of this shit is not fun. Playing is great, but the way we live is not the life of a rock star. When people tell me that I'm a rock star, I tell them they can go get fucked. Like I said before, the world is cold and no one understands you. I never knew how alone you could get. Now I know a little more.

3.12.83 CLEVELAND OH: In a diner. Last night in Baltimore was cool. We played good. There were some girls up front grabbing me. I never had that happen before. The other guys gave me a ton of shit about it.

Later: Have been in front of the club now for a few hours. They aren't open yet. I am in a hole in the back of the van between the door and the cabinets. There's enough room for me to kind of lie down and sit. I have managed to sleep here as we wait for the place to open. I hope they open soon because it's getting cold out here.

SAN PEDRO, CA / 1983 *(KEVIN SALK)*

3.13.83 NEW YORK NY: At this club called Great Gildersleeves. We will be playing two nights here. This place is another shithole. Two nights here will be plenty. It's a real hole.

Last night was Cleveland and it was pretty cool. I was crawling all over the floor and rubbing myself on people and grinding my face into the floor. By the end of the gig, I was covered with dirt. I washed off in the sink in the men's room and got back in the frozen van and we made the drive here.

3.17.83 CHICAGO IL: Have not written in a few days. Fuck it. There's nothing to write about. The other night in New York, Allen Ginsberg, the poet guy came to see us. I don't know what that guy's trip was. I have seen some of his books at my mom's house. I remember seeing a picture of him when I was very young. He said I moved like a kabuki dancer, the way I "writhe and undulate," whatever the hell that means. Played Detroit last night — played good.

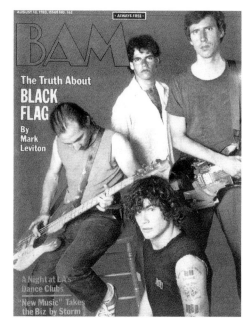

3.19.83 MINNEAPOLIS MN: Played here last night — real good time. Will be back in LA soon. Ten more shows to go on this one. I am pretty tired. I like playing though. That part of the night always seems to go well no matter how I'm feeling before. I can always play. The last trip to Europe was hard and some of it was scary. It's hard to be in this band sometimes. It comes with the territory. I can handle it.

I had a bad one in Chicago the other night. We were in the second set, and I was pulled off the stage and thrown to the floor by the audience. Most of my pants were torn off and people started kicking me. I remember feeling the glass that was on the floor going into my back. Dukowski pulled me back onstage and then I kind of freaked out during the next song. Duke carried me offstage and that was the end of the show. I sat on the stairs and shook for about 20 minutes. No one said shit about the fact that we left off a few songs from the set. It was weird. Maybe I'm too worn out right now. All I remember was I lost control of myself.

HENRY AND IAN, LOS ANGELES, CA / 1983 *(NAOMI PETERSEN)*

3.20.83 DENVER CO: Sitting in the lobby of the Rainbow. A lady that does shows here looked at the infected cigar burns in my leg and asked if I was on heroin. It was a hell of a drive to get here. It's cold and my throat is swollen. I am more exhausted than I have ever been. I feel pretty freaked out. I am still thinking about the night in Chicago. That was scary. Tonight is the last show of this tour. I don't know what we'll do when we get back. If we're not on tour, life just slows down. When we are out, it's hard. Whenever we get back, all I think about is how great it was being out there and when we get to leave again.

SOMEWHERE / 1983 *(NAOMI PETERSEN)*

That's all of the journal from 1983. Here are some things that I remembered about the rest of 1983.

SPOT ON CLARINET — MIKE MUIR'S GARAGE, SANTA MONICA, CA / 4.30.83 (GLEN E. FRIEDMAN)

A P R I L

30 SANTA MONICA CA: We played a party in Mike Muir's garage. It was a good setup with plenty of room. I bit some girl. I don't remember why. She bit me back. It was cool. Spot was playing clarinet. I don't know if he could be heard over the music. It ended up being the last show with Dez on guitar.

MIKE MUIR'S GARAGE, SANTA MONICA, CA / 4.30.83 (GLEN E. FRIEDMAN)

DEZ'S LAST SHOW WITH BLACK FLAG—MIKE MUIR'S GARAGE, SANTA MONICA, CA, 4.30.83 (GLEN E. FRIEDMAN)

J U N E

11 SANTA MONICA CA: We played with the Misfits at the Santa Monica Civic. It was a pretty cool show. We had Dez and Chavo, the two old singers in the band, play short sets before I went on. It was kind of like the history of the band live. It was a drag that Keith Morris didn't make it to the show. I don't remember why he wasn't there. Perhaps he didn't get along with some of others.

SANTA MONICA CIVIC, SANTA MONICA, CA / 6.11.83 *(GLEN E. FRIEDMAN)*

L-R: Danzig, Rick Spellman, Doyle (seated), Henry, Robo, Mark Rude, Jerry Only. Santa Monica, CA / 6.11.83 *(Naomi Petersen)*

A U G U S T

05 PORTLAND OR / 06 EUGENE OR / 07 SEATTLE WA / 08 VANCOUVER CANADA: This four show outing with the Meat Puppets was some of Davo at his finest. He drove and drove and hardly slept. He kept himself powered on large Cokes from gas stations. He referred to them as "99 Ouncers." Pretty much the only music played in the van was the first Dio solo album and *Heaven and Hell* by Black Sabbath. On the way to one of the dates, we stopped into a college radio station and took calls. We got this strange call from this hick sounding guy who said something like, "We're kicking back on the porch having a few beers and twisting up a few doobies and we're listening to your music on the radio and hearing what you have to say. We wanted to know if you have any Dio in your music?" Pretty strange question considering that all we've heard on the way up was the relentless playing of Dio. Greg fell for it hook, line and sinker. I went out to the hallway and saw the Meat Puppets gathered around the payphone talking to Greg on the air.

20 / 21 LOS ANGELES CA: We played two nights at a club called The Vex. The club was located in a bad part of town. When we got to the gig, there were local guys hired as security. They were carrying guns around the parking lot and people were getting pretty freaked out. When people walked in the front door, they were searched. The girls got searched extra carefully — the security guys getting a good feel in when

THE VEX, LOS ANGELES, CA / 8.20.83

they could. One guy had his chopper parked inside the lobby and warned people not to touch it or he would beat the shit out of them.

After the opening bands played, we got ready to play. I looked at the stage and saw that the huge guy that had the chopper in front was standing onstage looking out at the crowd. I went to another security guy and asked him to tell the one onstage that we would be fine and we didn't need him there because he was scaring the audience, and also the stage was so small, he took up about a third of it. The guy made a big deal out of getting this man off the stage. He kept asking me, "Are you sure you want him to get off?" I didn't see what the big problem was. I figured the guy would be happy to kick back and not be bothered with a bunch of sweaty people. I was thinking that it would be safer to have him as far away from us as possible, considering the size of the knife he had strapped to his leg. Eventually he was told that his services would not be needed and he left the stage.

We played and everything was fine. Later, everyone had left and I was hanging around waiting to leave. The bouncer that left the stage came up to me and asked, "Do you want to get paid?" I told him that stuff was handled by our manager. He said, "You better go to the office if you want to get paid." I didn't know what he was talking about, but I figured I would go up front and talk to the promoter and say hello anyway. I walked past the guy and headed toward the front. When I got there, something hit the side of my head. All of a sudden, I was on the ground trying to get up. The bouncer had hit me in the side of the head when my back was turned. I got to my feet not knowing where I was. He kicked me in the balls and I went

JUST WHEN YOU THOUGHT IT WAS SAFE TO DROP YOUR PANTIES...

"THE NIG-HEIST

— THE BAND THAT CUMS IN YOUR MOUTH NOT IN YOUR HANDS —

"SLURP INTO THE 80's"

IN A BENEFIT FOR MUGGER'S AIDS:

SATURDAY JULY 2

AT **VEX**
2580 N. SOTO
E.L.A.

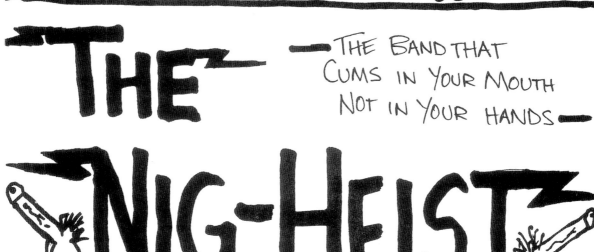

THE NIG HEIST IS:

MUGGER: VOCALS, LEAD COCK
BILLY: GUITAR, LEAD EGO
DAVE-O: BASS, LEAD POSE
MERRILL: GUITAR, FAGGOT
SPOT: DRUMS, NEGRO RYTHYMS
B. BOON: BOUNCER, ANAL ROADIE

WITH: THE DESCENDENTS AND SUICIDAL TENDANCIES AND SOME STUPID PUNKER BAND.

GIRLS: GET THERE EARLY TO FLOW BLOW-JOBS TO THE BAND TO EN-SURE A ROCK 'N' ROLL SHOW NOT TO BE FOR-GOTTEN! (NO SLEAZY PUNKER BROADS)

CALL 372-1848 TO BE AN OFFICIAL NIG-HEIST GROUPIE.

down again. I was trying to get up and I saw that he had his knife out and was coming toward me. He was

screaming, "I'll kill you, you fucking punker!" I got up and put my hands in front of me. It occurred to me that I was going to get stabbed. His friends tackled him and wrestled the knife away, just like some movie. The promoter came out of the office and told the guy to leave. He took his bike and staggered out. Apparently he was dusted. The rest of the security guys laughed at me. My face started to swell up pretty bad. Hell, that was only the first night. We had to come back and play this fucking dump again the next night. Luckily, the guy with the knife didn't show up again. Thank goodness for small miracles.

SST / SUMMER 1983. L-R: GREG, BILL STEVENSON, CHUCK, HENRY. *(NAOMI PETERSEN)*

D E C E M B E R

29 TORRANCE CA (PARTY): This was Kira's first gig. What stands out to me about this one is that we played all three songs from side two of *My War* in a row. Three slow songs all timing out at about eight minutes each. It was the only time that we ever did that and it was great. Too bad we didn't do it more often. Later on, we were to find out how much these songs infuriated some audiences.

NGELES, CA / 7.4.83 *(GLEN E. FRIEDMAN)*

LOS ANGELES, CA / 7.4.83 (GLEN E. FRIEDMAN)

INTERMISSION

There's a noticeable gap in the journal here. It's due to the fact that for a long period of time the band was involved in a legal battle with a label distributed by MCA. It's a long and boring story. Basically, it kept Bill, Chuck and Greg up to their eyeballs in legal work. We practiced and kept writing songs that would eventually comprise the *My War* and *Slip It In* albums.

We were strapped financially and it was hard to keep spirits up. I spent a lot of time running and working out at the beach. I helped the Ginns build a house. D. Boon and I were the two employees. We had a great time working together.

We were living like dogs at the time. At one point, we had all the band members living on the floor of SST. D. Boon was living there for a while too. At night, it was snoring bodies, dirty socks and bugs. In the morning, it was a record company. It was hard to take when someone said that we had sold out.

I remember the day John Belushi died. Dukowski and I walked up the road toward the beach. We stopped in a market. For some strange reason he had some money. He bought some raw beef and we stood in the line eating it as it was. People must have thought we were crazy.

A good eating stunt was to go to a local Mexican restaurant and wait for a group to get up from a meal and sit right down at their table while they were still putting their coats on and start eating from their plates. Food became our obsession. We were constantly talking about food. One time I had a cheese sandwich hidden in my desk. I got in the door to see D. Boon about to eat it. I told him to get the fuck away from my food. He drew a protest picture of a man holding a gun in front of him. The caption quoted my "get away from my cheese sandwich" line. It was a hell of a time.

During the summer, I visited Washington DC. I saw Minor Threat blow the Damned off the stage so badly that it was tragic. After the MT set was over, I saw Rat Scabies and asked him if he saw that and he just winced. They were that good.

In November, I did my first spoken performance. A local producer named Harvey Kubernik was organizing shows where he was getting people in bands, actors, performance artists and poets together and having them kick it live onstage. These shows came off really well. A typical night with Harvey would be Wanda Coleman, a fierce and talented, Black woman poet along with actor Harry Northrup and then some legendary LA musician. He really mixed it up well. Harvey was also involved with making spoken word records. He asked Dukowski to be on one and I went to the session and met him. Months later, Harvey asked me if I wanted to be on one of these bills. He said I could do whatever I wanted — read something I wrote, tell a story, whatever. He said that he had two gigs booked and I could have my pick. I asked to be on both. I figured what the hell.

On November 25, I went to this place called the Lhasa Club on Hudson and Santa Monica. There were a lot of poets on the bill. I listened to them and it didn't do anything to me. When it was my turn, I went up and told a story about growing up in Washington DC, watching the riots as a little kid. It was strange to be onstage without the band, but it was cool. People seemed to like what I did. They were asking me how many years I had been doing "spoken performances" and I told them about twenty minutes, which at the time was the case. I started doing more shows of this kind and it continued to be a good thing.

Later in 1983, Kira Roessler became our bass player and we started to practice every night. Kira learned things so fast I thought we were good to go after a week. Greg said that we weren't and said we were going to practice for months until it was perfect. So we did. We cranked through the *My War* set two times a night. The room was small and the heat got going. Some nights felt like gigs. Black Flag practices were as heavy as the gigs a lot of the time. Some nights, Joe Cole would come down and watch. I didn't know him then — he was a friend of Greg's. He would just sit in the corner and watch without saying a word.

After many practices, we were ready and a tour was booked. 1984 was a great year. We played all over and all the time. We had the fiercest attitude on earth. We had been in the practice place for months. Our first record in a couple years, the *My War* album was out and we wanted to kill everyone. The shows were great. Kill Everyone Now was the agenda. KEN mode all the time. It was good to be out on the road again with an album out and an excuse to live.

AT THE PRACTICE PLACE / 1984. L-R: KIRA ROESSLER, BILL, GREG, HENRY. *(GLEN E. FRIEDMAN)*

SANTA MONICA, CA / 7.22.84 (NAOMI PETERSEN)

L – R: Greg, Bill, Henry, Kira, Los Angeles, CA / 7.22.84 *(Glen E. Friedman)*

3.25.84 Tucson AZ: Maybe Phoenix has changed. Last night was cool. Didn't used to be that way. I met Mo Tucker a few minutes ago. She sat in on a jam with Dukowski and Troccoli. She was great. She put her beer down by her feet, put her head down and went for it. It was cool. She has that thing she does with the snare that sounds totally primitive. It was so cool to watch. I bet no one in the place knew what they were seeing.

3.28.84 New Mexico: A long and gross story. Cold and frustration. The problem: everything. We left from Tucson yesterday afternoon and drove east. Woke up this morning — snow everywhere. One of those Black Flag stories of misery that there are so many of now. It is freezing. Forget that other shit. Rollins mode now in motion. There's nothing besides this.

3.29.84 Over Air: Going down to San Antonio. Tom and Chuck are with the van. Last night we played in Norman, Oklahoma. A good show for the amount of time we have been out.

3.30.84 Austin TX: If I could wash my hands of it all... but my hands aren't dirty so that one's out. Born into the grave. The earth is a massive grave. You get dragged into the back room, slapped around for a while and then it's over. You're all done up.

Last night's show was plagued by equipment failures and bad mics. They cut us short because of "bar time". That pissed Greg off big time. Me too. These clubs aren't into the music. They want to sell their beer and when that's over they want everyone out. You get no respect if you're in one of the bands on the bill. It's as if you're the biggest pain in their ass.

3.31.84 DALLAS TX: My throat is tender today. Makes life more difficult. We have been told that tonight has nearly sold out in advance. We'll deliver. Last night was real good. I sang hard. I am starting to get my wind. Body giving me trouble. Takes me all day to get loose enough for soundcheck. Need to get some real sleep.

Later: Now en route to Houston. The Mofomobile's electricity system burned up and it's stranded on the highway. We are now all in Chuck's van. Last night we played well. I think that next time we play there it will be even better.

Later: Now at the Lawndale Art Annex in Houston. Tomorrow we hook up with the Meat Puppets. That should be interesting.

4.2.84 NEW ORLEANS LA: At Dave Slut's house. The Meat Puppets are a great band but they are children. They think that everyone owes them something. It's funny to see them deal with things as the rich kids that they are.

Strength from within. Underneath my flesh. I don't hide behind art. Behind my eyes, I wait in ambush for you. Not caught up in their little world. I escaped from their trip. The pettiness, the bullshit, the lightweight world. It's swampland down here.

4.3.84 BIRMINGHAM AL: Will be in DC in 3 days. The journal is a good way to keep things to yourself. It's good to help me cut down on talking. The last thing I want to do is talk too much. I always hate myself when I do that. When you work within your confines you are going to have more impact with what you are trying to do.

HENRY AND IAN IN IAN'S ROOM, WASHINGTON, DC / APRIL 1984 (*NAOMI PETERSEN*)

4.4.84 EN ROUTE TO ATLANTA: Played to about 80 people last night. Not the best gig I remember us doing, but I'll take it. I'll take touring over anything or anyone. The places we've been playing are a little too clean for my liking. I like the ones that are fucked up. Gives me something to work against.

On this tour, there's no girlfriend to think about. When I would leave someone to go on tour, it gave me someone to think about and to focus on. But it was also distracting to have to deal with missing her. Having no girlfriend is better. Now it's just the music. That's where the real destruction starts.

4.5.84 ATLANTA GA: At the 688 Club. This time around is the rematch gig. Last time we played here in '82 with Biscuits on drums, we sucked. This time I know that we have to destroy the place to make up for our shortcomings last time. It's all I'm thinking about. I felt so bad the last time we played here. I wanted to kill Biscuits for being such a fuckup.

　　Later: We tore the place up. Great gig. I feel redeemed. Some guys were throwing squashed beer cans at the Meat Puppets. I grabbed this one guy and nailed him pretty good. It would be great to just be able to shoot these people on sight.

RICHMOND, VA / 4.9.84 *(NAOMI PETERSEN)*

4.12.84 PITTSBURGH PA: Last few days have been good. We're back at the Electric Banana again for the whatever time. Whenever we're here, I can't wait to leave and get on to the next show. It's a pretty depressing place to be stuck in all day. The shows in DC were real good. I have never been happy with the shows we've played there and this time it was good to stick it to them really hard.

　　That's all there is on this mission. You play and play and don't think about it too much. I have found that you can deplete yourself every night and still be able to get up and do it again. You have to keep rising. You can't have too much hanging off of you. The less you have, the less there is to separate you from the music. If you have too much on your mind with this way of living, it will be ripped away from you.

4.15.84 BOSTON MA: We played three shows in three states in 24 hours. We pulled it off. It was great. We played at the Reggae Lounge in NYC first — it was an early evening show. The Meat Puppets went on first. After they finished, they took off to Connecticut to start the show up there. We did our set and ran the gear right through the crowd into the van. Mugger was mowing people down getting the shit out of there. It was funny to listen to him yelling at people. We got in the van and hauled ass up north. We got some coffee and went into the hall. Loaded in the gear and set it up in front of the crowd and played our asses off. It was a good set. After that, we drove up to Boston for a noon load-in at The Channel. 1150 people there to see us. As usual, the Boston crowd was great. After the set, we were pretty wiped out. Nothing like the Dukowski booking method to get you in a lot of places in very little time. Sometimes I wonder if he looks at a map when he books the band. If I saw the gig list that said Miami to Seattle to New York to London, I wouldn't be surprised.

4.17.84 SYRACUSE NY: Did an in-store. What a piece of shit that was. These people rip the insulation right off me. I hate people when they idolize and flatter. I also hate it when they come up with their little words of weak contempt. Hardcore... They don't know the meaning of hard. Some guy wanted me to sign a copy of his Barry Manilow record. He thought he was being cute. I put a big swastika on it. He bummed out. Fuck these little pigs. Like they could ever pull this off. They can say what they want, but I know the real thing and I know what we do would wear them out in a few days.

4.18.84 SYRACUSE NY: Still in Syracuse. No show in Montreal tonight. In a hotel. Tomorrow will be busy — border crossing and a long drive. The weekend show will be in Detroit.

The initial inception must be pure. All energy must be put to use. The end must never leave your sight. Complete destruction must be had. You must maintain drive that goes beyond obsession, beyond purpose, beyond reason. Every movement must be in the forward direction. When in the woods, seek the clearing. The path shines so bright it's almost blinding. When you work within your confines, when you realize your limitations, that's when you can break through them. You have to know what you're made of. If you don't take that step, you'll never know what the fuck you're after. While they flail about, you will remain calm in the knowledge that you possess strength from within. With every breath, you destroy them. The straight line. It borders on insanity. People tell you that you're crazy or brainwashed to be doing what you're doing and to be doing it like this. You can't listen. If you listen to them one bit then they pull you down. Even if they're telling you that you're great, you can't listen. The more they tell you that you're good, the more you have to let it go. They will fuck you up and take your eyes off the trail.

4.21.84 MILWAUKEE WI: The shows have been okay. I didn't like Detroit at all. People onstage all the time. Knocking into me, making me forget the words and shit. I know one thing — I hate interviews. They make me feel like I have been fistfucked.

4.22.84 MINNEAPOLIS MN (two sets): Played good in Milwaukee last night. For our trouble, the front tires on the Ryder truck were slashed. The Ryder people couldn't come until 5 a.m. to bring some new ones. We got on the road at 6:00. Been driving ever since. Just got here. We have two sets to play. Fuck people. I want to kill them.

4.25.84 DENVER CO: Apparently the show has sold over 800 advance tickets. I'm looking at the press. It's fairly raving. I think there are ten shows left on this tour.

There's not much that's given to you — like really put in front of you. There are a few things that are mine. I see this now. Like today, sitting in this diner. This time is mine. These thoughts are mine. Memories are mine. I don't own much. It's nice to know that there are some things that no one will be able to take from me. These days, besides meals and the music, there's not a great deal that's mine. It's good to get some time to think things over.

4.26.84 SOMEWHERE: Fuck, where am I? Somewhere in Wyoming I think. Thirty degrees outside, snow everywhere. The van just broke down at a gas station. Sometimes you get lucky. Sometimes your van breaks down in the middle of a snowstorm. I'm sitting in a Burger King and it doesn't look good for the show in Salt Lake tonight. Last night in Denver was pretty wild. Sure was a lot of people. Mugger and Tom were arrested for being naked onstage when they were playing their set as the Nig Heist. The promoter came onstage after they went on and assured the crowd that they would never have to see such a disgusting thing ever again. We got them out of jail at 3:30 this morning. Barry Fey was the promoter — a real scumbag. He's horrible and will probably be around for many years to come. The shitty ones always are. These classic ripoff artists never really get what they need... like a baseball bat to the head.

We have a few days off in LA and then we take off to the UK to start a tour in Europe. I am lonely. If a woman touched me right now, I would melt.

I have a hard time with all the adulation that I get these days. I don't like getting complimented on what I do. I just want to play. The opinion of others really doesn't matter to what we are trying to do. Sometimes hearing what they think is very distracting. It's hard enough as it is.

PORTLAND, OR / 4.28.84 *(SEAN COX)*

4.27.84 SEATTLE WA: The Village Voice reviewed our show in New York. Damn man, that guy Tim Sommer hates my guts. I don't know what I did to deserve that. He really went out of his way to nail my ass to the wall. Seems to me he could have just talked about the music, but it seems that he really has a problem with me personally. It's hard to read that kind of shit and not be able to do anything about it. I was giving it all I had and the guy cuts me down. Maybe I will meet up with him someday and then it will be different. He wouldn't like to deal with me the way I would deal with him. I know that's for sure.

I read *Black Spring* by Henry Miller for a few hours today. This is the coolest book I have ever read. I don't understand what these people want from us. They are abusive as shit. That's okay by me. I can take it. Makes me play harder. But for the life of me, I can't understand what the trip is. Critics and girls hate me. At the start of a set, there will be a lot of girls up front. As the set goes on, they shrink back. By the end of the set, they're laughing. I must look funny to them, all sweaty and bent out of shape. I wonder what a woman would see in me anyway. At the end of the day, all of these people can go get fucked. We're not here to entertain.

4.29.84 EN ROUTE TO VICTORIA BC: Last night we played in Portland, OR. Playing about a mile away was a band called the Dinosaurs — ex-members of Jefferson Airplane and Big Brother. We got some guest passes and went to see it. I thought it was a load of shit. Robert Hunter made a special appearance and the place went apeshit. The audience were hippies and bikers. The music was awful retread rock and roll. At one point, they had the crowd chanting "San Francisco" over and over. How much are you supposed to be able to take before you just napalm the whole place. Fat, fucked up hippies with their butt faced women. The bikers were some of the ugliest people I have ever seen. Made me feel like a million bucks.

5.1.84 SEATTLE WA: Day off today. Played last night in Vancouver, Canada. Not bad for once. I usually hate that place. Some of the shittiest people known to man. Vancouver types are hilarious. All dressed up in their limey punker gear and all they do is drink, shoot dope and pass out. They get pissed off when you laugh at them for being the fat, fucked up pieces of shit they truly are. But last night it was not as bad as it has been before. Maybe the shitheads have been off heroin for a half hour and have seen the light.

I woke up this morning in the truck. I like sleeping out there, it's quiet and dark and I get left the fuck alone. The rain was falling on the roof and it was good. I heard the sound of tires screeching, followed by a loud crash. I looked outside. There was a head-on collision. The song "Dead Joe" by the Birthday Party came immediately to mind. There was a little kid sprawled on the sidewalk in the rain. The mother was in hysterics. Whenever the kid would scream, the mother would scream and stomp the ground.

I know a girl whose brother was killed on his way to school by a drunk driver as he was crossing a busy intersection. After that, the city put a big set of crosswalk stripes at the intersection. She calls it her brother's "memorial crosswalk." It has a wheelchair ramp and everything. What are they going to do for you when you fall off the planet?

The following written using Curt Kirkwood's guitar as a desk: Talked to Chuck today. There will be no Italian shows on the tour. The schedule sounds rough. Oops, there I go again. I will live through the next tour as I have lived through all the others. I have read back some of this book. I must be sick.

5.2.84 EUGENE OR: Spring has sprung. It's beautiful here. The streets remind me of Washington DC. Tomorrow we'll be in California. You knew it had to end sometime.

5.4.84 SAN FRANCISCO CA: At the On Broadway. No, we didn't play in Arcata last night. We pulled up to the club and they had no knowledge of us playing. It was great. We were loading in the equipment, telling people to get out of the way. There was a band onstage soundchecking. We figured that they were the opening band and we told them to get off so we could start getting soundcheck together. We looked like flaming assholes when we found out that they were the headlining band for the night. Bill and I hauled out the gear double time.

We drove to Berkeley and stayed with some friends. It's real strange to me that you can get out of the truck and be in New York, and get out of the same truck and set your foot down in California. I can look at the truck and see crud that has been there for over a month and remember the place where we picked it up. I know that no one thinks of stupid shit like this besides me. 43 days, 40 shows. If we didn't have those 2 cancellations, it would have been 42 in 43. I want to do the Black Flag Hot 100. One hundred shows in the USA in one tour.

Had to do interviews on the phone today. Don't even know who I was talking to. I hate those things. This is Black Flag not Tiger Beat. Will be

PASADENA, CA / 5.5.84 *(DAVID HERMON)*

glad to be out of California. I did all the normal things I do when I play this club. Coffee in the same place, tofu from the same place. It's cool, but at the end of the day, it's all the same bunch of assholes who don't care about you anyway.

When they compliment me, I always put myself down. I have to. If I acknowledge any of that shit then I'm finished. Looking forward to getting back to the shed. Have to get ready for the next mission.

PASADENA, CA / 5.5.84 (ROBBIE ROBINSON)

5.8.84 SHED: Did a talking show tonight at Bebop Records out in the Valley. I think it went okay. I am new at these things. It was the first time I ever headlined a show. Not a lot of people. These things take time, experience and a lot of work. Went to Deirdre's house and did the *SNAP* show with her. Interview with Creem tomorrow. Leaving a few hours after that.

5.13.84 LONDON UK: Been here a few days practicing. Playing our first show in a few days. The good news is that I saw Nick Cave's new band. They were billed as the Cavemen. They were great. Blixa wasn't with them. Barry Adamson played bass and keyboards. They played "I Put a Spell on You" by Screamin' Jay Hawkins. Hung out with Nick after the show. He insisted that they were awful. He was wrong — they were great. They don't even have any records out yet. I took the bus back to London with Jim Foetus. I played his new record on my headphones.

5.14.84 LONDON UK: Played the Marquee tonight. Bill and I are on fuck everybody mode. We came here two times before and got fucked with by these assholes and now they can go get fucked. Before we went on, we made the DJ play ZZ Top's *Eliminator* album all the way through. He apologized to the audience because he hated them. Figures the piece of shit has bad taste in music. It saved us from having to listen to some weak punk bullshit.

So Bill and I are backstage stretching and Gene October comes in. He's the guy from Chelsea that kicked me in the side and talked the shit about the band in Leeds in 1981. He wants to use the bathroom.

Bill looks at him and asks me if this is the guy I'm going to kill. I say yes. Bill looks at me and says, "Kill him now. Kill him now." Totally deadpan. Gene baby freaks out and starts blubbering a bunch of shit about how he always liked the band. We started laughing and told him to get lost. What a piece of shit. So many people should just get killed.

It was hot as hell in there. I passed out in the middle of one song and climbed up Greg's leg and kept going. We played well. People seemed to dig it. Doesn't matter if they did or not. During the breaks in the beginning of "Slip It In", Bill was standing up and screaming, "Fuck you! You limey pieces of shit!" It was great and it made me play even harder. Fuck these people.

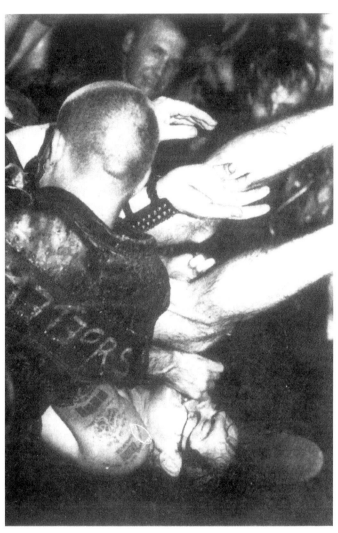

LONDON, 5.14.84 *(KERSTIN RODGERS)*

5.16.84 2:00 A.M. LONDON UK: Hung out with Nick Cave tonight. He gave me a copy of the new Bad Seeds album. It's called "From Her to Eternity". It looks great. Too bad I don't have a way to tape it. He's on his way to Holland. I hung out with him in this strange hotel where he and Hugo are in. The woman who owns it has pretty much given the two of them the run of the entire place. This old drunk man came in. He has been living there for years. He sits down in front of us and demands tea right now. Nick gets up and puts a towel over his arm like a maitre d' and crawls across all these tables to get to the stove to make him the tea. Fucking hilarious. After that, I watched Nick pack to go out on tour. His suitcase was a trash bag full of clothes and pieces of paper. Nick told me that Scotland is a rough place to play. That's where we are headed next. Some French lady from a magazine was trying to scam on him. He took me aside and asked me if I could get her out of the hotel so he wouldn't have to deal with her. I managed to get her out and into a cab. She gave me a tearful story about how she had come all the way from France to meet him. Then she hit on me. Bye big lady. I'm going to Scotland.

5.17.84 GLASGOW SCOTLAND: Last night we played in Birmingham, England. It sucked. The punkers laid on the floor and flipped us off or fell out because of all the glue they were on. I wasn't into it at all. I asked the one punker closest to the stage if he thought things were better in '77. He said yes and then lay down on the ground and flipped us off for the rest of the show. To think that the mighty Black Sabbath came from this town. I bet they don't live here anymore.

Later: Back at the hotel. What a nightmare that was. I walk onstage and before I get to the mic, I get hit with two pints of piss by a guy on the balcony. Before we had played more than a few songs, we were covered with spit. One guy had a lot of blood in his spit and so it looked like I was bleeding. Somehow I got through the set. They hated our guts. The best was yet to come. We were in the dressing room and I was stinking up the place. I saw the shower and I was thinking relief is on the way. Of course, it didn't work. At this moment, we hit an incredible low. We are hated. We are covered with spit and piss. Life sucks. At this moment, the band that was playing across the street at the Apollo comes over to say hello — Ultravox. They came into our dressing room with their slippers, puffy pants and flared sleeve shirts. They looked at us like we were a bunch of idiots. You could see the stench register on their faces. They told us that they had seen a bit of the set and thought it was "dross" and then they split. We felt pretty stupid after that. I knew that we were chumps right then and there. To have to take that kind of shit from punkers and then get fucked with by some guys who looked like they just got out of dance class. Perfect for us.

5.19.84 LEEDS UK: We are headlining a punker festival. How the hell did we get ourselves into this shit? Leeds is full of punkers from all over Europe to see this thing. It would be great if we could be the first band on and get the hell out of here.

Later: What a nightmare. We played. It's over with. It was a series of ordeals with people who should be dead. First, it was the punker that got into our corner and told us how we shouldn't even be here because Reagan is such a bastard. I fell for it. I actually tried to reason with this jerk. I tried to tell him that we were just there to play and it didn't matter where we were from. I gave up as soon as I came to my senses. Next was the writer shithead, Steven Welles. He wanted to know what I was going to do about all those coal miners. I listened for as long as I could and then I had to split. He gave me some record that he did. He'll never know how close he came to getting his ass kicked. We played well. These punkers are such a joke. Too drunk to do anything. Pathetic. I don't see why we even bothered coming to this shitty country again. We should be on the continent where people are real and they get into the music. The punkers here are just into their fashion show. Shitty bands as well.

5.26.84 ROTTERDAM HOLLAND: Played here last night. I know these different countries have different customs. I will not believe that the guy who tried to light my leg on fire was just some random asshole trying to torch me. Maybe this is some Dutch thing that I don't know about — Torch the Yank. It was funny to see the guy with the Black Flag tattoo on his neck, walk over and punch out the guy with the lighter. Nice shot. When the Nig Heist went on, there were a lot of skinheads up front — big ones. I figured we should make friends with them as quickly as possible. I took all the beer that we had backstage and gave it to them. By the time we hit stage, they were all toasting us. All these girls were yelling, "Go home, you Yankee shit!" We kept playing. We didn't go home. We went right up their asses. Tell me to go home — I should move in and ruin your fucking fat Dutch neighborhood. After the show, a lot of them were backstage trying to hit on us. Fuck these people. I want to get into some fights like right now. It will be enjoyable kicking the punk dog shit out of some of these people.

The shows in England sucked. We played well when we could. Skinheads were at all the shows and they were a pain in the ass. At one of the shows, they were spitting mouthfuls of dark beer at me. One threw a folding chair onstage. I looked at all the other members of the band and looked into the crowd and said that if another folding chair hit the stage, we would leave. We all braced ourselves for the chair that we knew was coming our way. It hit the stage and we happily walked. Thanks for the free money, shithead. I don't think we'll come back here again. If I ever come back again, they'll have to pay me plenty.

5.27.84 VENLO HOLLAND: Last night was good. They were into it. The skinheads had to be kept out of the show. Bill and Kira are hard to take. It's none of my business. They are the way they are.

5.29.84 GRONINGEN HOLLAND: Last night's show in Nijmegan was at least interesting. The Heist got shit-canned because of their "texts". They were bottled off the stage and then these intense lesbians came up to the back room and gave Mugger a ton of shit which Greg got on tape. Came out sounding funny as hell. When we got on to play, people were drunk and just standing around. That was until there was a huge fight that cleared the hall. Some skinheads from the next town over had rented a bus and came over to get in a fight with the skins from Nijmegan. It was pretty wild. We were told to get off the stage. I went onto the floor to watch the shitheads beat each other up. They were going for it too. These drunks were really pounding each other. The promoter was trying to break up some of the fighting and was punched out in the process. Finally the police came and the show was over. Some night. I didn't want it to stop! It was great seeing all these shitheads beat the fuck out of each other. I wanted to thank them and pay them to keep it up.

JAKI EL DORADO, OUR GERMAN TOUR MANAGER, GERMANY / 1984

Tonight is the last show for us in Holland. Some people in this group are complaining. People should shut their mouths talking about how this is hard. We have seen a lot harder. Some people should have been around the last time we came to Europe.

5.30.84 GERMANY: On a ferry about to leave for Sweden. Never been there. Last night was alright. We took all the beer that we had backstage and sold it to the punkers out front. Made some dough off of it. The *My War* album has been released in Sweden. When we play new songs that no one knows, the audience gets mad as shit. They always scream, "Gimmie, Gimmie, Gimmie! Six Pack! TV Party! You hippie bastards!" I am sick of those songs. They are good ones, but I think that we have played them enough.

No quiet place on this boat. Moms with their kids. Nowhere to sleep. If I had a kid, I would want it to be male. Maybe it would come back and kill me. Isn't that what's supposed to happen?

Good to be away from the others for a while. We are so cramped all the time. Being in front of a lot of people all the time makes me hate people. When they want to talk to me with their booze breath, it makes me sick. Those Dutch kids were spoiled brats — drunk and in your face.

I hate booze. It turns people into assholes. It really fucks with the Dutch punkers when you don't take their shit and give it right back to their drunk asses.

After this tour is over, we'll be home for four weeks and then out again. I should try to get in some readings at the local radio stations. I want to do things outside of Black Flag. I would like to do more talking shows. Just got hit for autographs by a bunch of kids. Here on a fucking boat in the middle of nowhere. What next?

Discipline is money in the bank. A real friend — true strength.

5.31.84 STOCKHOLM SWEDEN: Now in Sweden. We are playing at a house and staying there as well. It's full of hippies and punks, but they seem cool. We got here in the morning and been hanging out all day. I fell asleep in the truck and just got up.

6.1.84 KARLSHAMN SWEDEN: This place reminds me of DC. It's moist out and the bugs are biting. The gig was fun to play but not very involving. We set up in the living room and went for it. Between songs, the bugs would get us. Everybody was flying and falling all over us. Mugger was pushing them around, calling them all Sid and Johnny.

5:31 p.m.: Now at the club. Looks pretty stylish. Looks like a scaled down version of the place we played in Switzerland. Slept in the van last night to try and avoid the attack of the killer bloodbeasts. We had to do nine hours to get to this place. I don't even know what the name of the town is. We were driving through town and we heard some Black Flag music coming out of a window somewhere with all these people singing along to it. It was pretty cool sounding. I guess they're getting ready for us.

The sun sets and it gets dark for a few hours and then the sun starts to come up again. We have ten shows left on this one. Something about this club gives off a bad vibe. I like it though.

Later: The opening band was a trip. When they play they have two skinheads onstage wrapped in Swedish flags. They were standing at attention. One of the band members came into our dressing room and gave Kira shit because she had on red socks. He started calling her a Communist. These people should go get killed. It's a drag to have to put up with these people who should just be hit by cars.

6.2.84 GÖTEBORG SWEDEN: At a real cool looking club. It's in an old building. This place has a shower. We must be moving up in the world. We'll be home soon. I don't want to go back to America. I like it better out here right now.

2 a.m.: I played hard tonight, but people just laughed in my face all night. I have to concentrate on the

music so nothing will distract me. Some of these people are so stupid. You'll be playing a song as hard as you can and someone is tapping you on the shoulder yelling a song title in your ear over and over.

6.4.84 3:10 A.M. JÖNKÖPING SWEDEN: Back at the hotel after playing a festival. Played hard. It was satisfying to be able to pull off a gig at one of these shindigs and be able to feel like we gave them the real thing.

6.5.84 2:55 A.M. MALMÖ SWEDEN: We were supposed to do a two night stand in this place, but the crowd was so small that they canceled the second show. We have a day off tomorrow. Amazing.

Davo and I went walking around town. Must have covered three miles. We saw where they were going to build a 7-11. There was a 7-11 staff car parked in front of the site.

The gig was fun. People were cool and we played good. This journal is becoming my best friend. It's the only one I talk to.

After the day off, we leave for Germany. Touring does a strange thing to my sense of time. I like it out here though. People are hard to understand. They are rude as hell at the shows. The women are beautiful and won't give you the time of day and it's easy to get lost.

6.6.84 12:52 A.M. MALMÖ SWEDEN: Did a lot of stuff today. Took a hydrofoil over to Denmark and hit a great record store.

It's raining tonight. The smell of the streets reminds me of Washington DC. Like walking home from work to my apartment. Going over to my friend's house. Going to the store and getting ginger beer. Those were some good times. They were uncomplicated.

I used to believe in destiny and fate. Now I think it's a bunch of bullshit. I want more than the normal human life, but now I see that I have to create it for myself. There will be no miraculous happening in my life. It's just a lot of getting in the van and going to the show.

I want to reach a higher level of concentration and intensity. I know I can hit it harder than I have.

The smell of summer rain pulls the puppet strings on my brain. I'm thinking about my last walk up my old street. The pet shop I worked at was turned into an Italian restaurant. They put in bulletproof glass inside Pearson's liquor store. Nicky's Pub uses frozen pizzas. The MacArthur Theater is now the MacArthur 1-2-3. I'm 23 and I sound like I'm 55. I'm feeling sorry for myself which isn't so good. But when it's all you've got, it's at least a feeling that lets you know you're alive.

I get sick of the fact that there's never enough room anywhere we go. We're always living on top of each other. Life is a movie these days. I can't speak the language here and it makes me eat less because I feel strange pointing and asking.

I must work on my discipline. I see now that it will be my ace in the hole when I need to go places in the future. It's all in your head. You have to be able to maintain at all times, no matter what's happening. There's no way to relate to anyone but yourself. When I get sad, I write it out. The less I talk, the better. I'm better than last year but still not good enough.

I'm glad we'll only be home for a short time after this tour is over. I don't like being in LA in the summer. I must burn from the inside. Strength from within. I must try to understand this idea better.

Wasted energy. Excess exposure to humans — social bullshit. It always wears me down and wastes my time. If I flap my mouth like the wing of a bird, all I'll ever be is one of them. One is the perfect number.

IF IT WEREN'T
FOR PUNK ROCK...

DAVO DRAWING

The more things I do alone, the better. In Miller's *Black Spring*, he talks about the joy of being able to enjoy one's own company. I think there's nothing better than being a loner. I think it's the best way to be. There are no mysteries to life. All the doors are open. People don't always want to go through.

The guy who is promoting all the shows here just got out of jail. He has this distance with people that chills them fast. I don't know how to describe it. It's as if he looks at them and deals with them from a few feet away. There's something really cold about him. You can tell it works on people too. They bum out on him. He's like a shark. I like him. He's cool to us. Society is a lab experiment. The only reason to exist is to tour and destroy.

I know some people who will never get out of the town they live in. They'll call me and tell me that they're going to get married and they'll invite me, and I'll tell them that I can't make it because I'm a running man. My hometown tries to pull me back. I see others trying to get out. Home lets out the leash a little then pulls it back and then gives it a sharp tug. I watch them fall and choke. They gain weight and fall apart. They tell me that I'm a rock star because I play all the time. I think that they can all kiss my ass.

6.8.84 BREMEN GERMANY: The hall we're in tonight is one of those industrial strength punker anarchy pit places. Reminds me of Stollwerck in Koln. We're eating in the restaurant. All these punkers are outside watching us. When I look up, they pick their nose and stick their tongues out like Sid. Whatever. Someone should just shoot these people. We're trying to eat.

6.9.84 HANOVER GERMANY: Last night was belligerent as shit. The front row was all skinheads and all they did was fuck with us. They had a good scam. They had this little shithead up front and he would spit on me endlessly. I knew if I hit him, all of them would jump us. I had to take it. They knew that we knew and they loved it. One took a swing at Greg's head and I blocked it. No one else in the crowd seemed to care. They all sat or stood far away from us and the skins.

After the show, this one skin was all fucked up and came backstage to hang out with us like we were old buddies. He was taking a piss down a stairway that went down into who knows where. I helped him by kicking him in the back and sending him down there. I guess he passed out down there because he didn't come up.

Right after that, a girl came up to me and asked if she could fuck me and I said sure. Since we all were piled up in the hotel rooms, she and I had to go into the van. Gee... sex in the van. How strange. Never did that before. Anyway, she was a nice girl and the sex was forgettable at best. She left afterwards. The train station was conveniently located across the street.

6.10.84 1:43 A.M. HANOVER GERMANY: In the hotel. Good gig tonight. Lots of people and they were cool. Davo and I saw this awesome blonde woman. She was the Deutsch dream — tight black leather pants, boots, leather jacket. We dubbed her "Heroin Mamma". We played this place before. It's a small room that stinks and is damp. And when the punkers come in, it gets real hot and you can't breathe because they all smoke so much. It was a good gig though. I think I smoked a few cigarettes from just being in the same room with all that smoke.

5:48 p.m. Berlin, Germany: This place looks a lot better than the last hall we played here. This place is called the Latin Quarter. The place in '83 was called the SO36.

Davo and I walked around and found this great store that only sold guns, knives, beer mugs and tobacco. It's all you need for the beginning of a good party. We found this great place for coffee right near the gig. The lady serving them up was another beautiful frau. We dubbed her "Cappuccino Mamma" and she will live forever in our hearts.

Sometimes certain members of our group get into some bullshit. It hits like a wave. It goes through all of us. I don't let it knock me over. I duck and it washes over me. Some people are funny when the joints are passed around. You would think that pot had some kind of power. I mean come on, it's a plant, not a reason for living. One smokes out, the other gets mad about it and stomps off. I could give a fuck. Controlled by a plant. How hilarious. A plant. A fucking plant.

6.12.84 4:28 P.M. BERLIN GERMANY: In the hotel. Gig was cool except for the guy that punched me out. This big guy was up front and just hauled off and whacked me one. It didn't hurt really. He put me on the floor, but I got up and kept on playing. But now, I'm a little fucked up. Robert Hilburn from the LA Times was there. He liked it. He's doing some article on European bands or something.

When we were loading out, some guy took off with one of Greg's guitars. The fucker just grabbed it and ran up the street. We were told he was probably a junkie. I barely saw the guy, it happened so fast.

I don't talk to them much anymore. I'm in my own world. There are six of us in one room. We are on top of each other. I spend as much time as possible away from them.

I had to do photos with the Times photographers. We did shots at the Wall and Check Point Charlie.

We're playing here again tonight, some small club. I hope that the guys from Die Haut come to the show — one of my favorite bands. They live here. I have a black eye from last night. Fuck it. Three more shows on this one and then most of them fly back to LA. Greg and I stay to do press.

I did something funny today. I picked up on a girl and didn't know it. I came into the lobby and saw this gross American guy talking up the pretty girl behind the desk. He went away and when I went up to get my key, I asked if it was fucked to have to be nice to people like that when you really want to smack the shit out of them. We started talking and I told her we were playing at this club tonight and she asked if she could go. I figured that anyone could go and told her of course. I told her that we would put her on the guest list. I thought nothing of it. It's not as if we know anyone here. She shows up to the gig all done up and excited to see me. At the end of the show, she's trying to get me to come home with her. Whoa.

I think that Black Flag has reached it's high point. Each record sells less and less and we can't outdraw shitty bands in LA. I think that the new songs bum people out.

6.13.84 1:21 A.M. HAMBURG GERMANY: Show was okay. About 600 people showed up. Three girls got their tops torn off. It was like a feeding frenzy. One girl lost her shirt and then all of a sudden the shirts were flying. Guys were tearing their own shirts off. I gave my shirt to a girl. She put it on and it was torn off in seconds. So much for my good deed.

They had those barriers up tonight. I hate those things. It's not good for me to play with those things up front. They make me weak. If you're not up against it every night, then you lose something and then the fuckers will be able to push you around. You can't back away. You'll only fuck yourself up. Sometimes I want to fuck these fat Germans up so bad. They come rolling in, giving us shit about this and that, telling us what songs we're going to play. It's funny when I tell them to fuck themselves.

6:14 p.m. Bochum, Germany: This place looks real cool. This is the last show on the tour. Last night, I had an idea. The sound, the records, the money you pay to get in — it's all filthy. Don't touch the PA, it's dirty. Don't look at the band, they don't matter. It's just the music. That's all you need to know about. The rest is filth and bullshit. If you need to touch something, touch yourself. The rest is dirty — the tickets, the t-shirts. It's all filthy except for the music.

LOCATION UNKNOWN / 1984 *(DEBRA LOCKROW)*

X was here. Billy Zoom autographs every backstage room he plays it seems. Sixty-five shows so far. Feeling pretty good.

6.14.84 SOMEWHERE IN BELGIUM: You have to keep your perspective. I keep thinking that we work hard, but it's nothing like what a construction worker does. The best thing to do is not talk and just do. I hate doing these interviews. I feel like a damn idiot talking about this shit. A man that welds steel doesn't get asked for his autograph, but I do. I can't see it as anything other than bullshit. If you find yourself caught up in it in any capacity, it's dangerous. Nothing good comes out of it. I feel like an asshole who should get shot when I get asked to sign some fucking piece of paper.

6.15.84 2:25 P.M. LONDON UK: It's wild that Hendrix played the Marquee. I wonder what that must have been like to have been able to walk into a place and see Hendrix play. I can't imagine it.

Word from back home says that we have been kicked out of the office on Phelan Avenue. I hope Carducci has found us a new place to live. Otherwise, we'll have to go for what Davo calls "body storage".

At least I can go for a walk around here and nothing will happen to me. I'm scared to walk in my neighborhood in LA. I'm afraid of getting picked up by the pigs. I've had enough fucked up experiences at night with them. I'm afraid of getting picked up and getting the shit beaten out of me by the swine. This hotel room is getting to me. We will be here a few more days before we leave. It will just be me and Greg staying here and doing press. It's a drag. I'd like to leave this country. Nothing to do here.

I hope no one asks me about how the tour was when we get back. I would think that I would be all into telling stories of what happened, but now I think differently. I don't want to talk about it. I don't know why either. Maybe it's because a lot of what happens escapes words. If you weren't there then you'll never know.

6.20.84 12:08 A.M. LONDON UK: Just got back in. Walked all over the place with Chris Haskett. We walked by all these clubs and shit. It was cool to see the Hope & Anchor. We went to the Marquee. Phil Lynott from Thin Lizzy had some kind of jam night there, and by the time we got there it was over, but Lynott was drinking at the bar. We stared at each other for a second and Phil raised his eyebrows and nodded slightly and then I turned to Chris and said, "Look it's the Thin Lizzy guy," and then we split. It was good to get out of the house and go somewhere. I have been doing these interviews and photo sessions with Greg. It's funny how we used to get so much shit from the limeys. Now they kiss our ass. I can't trust them, but it's funny to watch them fall over themselves when they deal with us. It's funny, but at the same time, it makes me sick that someone would lower themselves to something like that.

6.22.84 2:44 A.M. LONDON UK: Just got back from seeing Hanoi Rocks at the Electric Ballroom. I never seen that many good looking girls at one show in my life. It was painful. Hanoi was a cool band. The singer has all these different poses. He goes for some Iggy, some Bowie and some Jagger. They rocked hard as shit.

A big ball of scars, blood and the sound of screaming. There's something in there, but I don't know what it is. I wonder why I do this shit sometimes. I'm here to prove something I think. The upward climb to subhumanity? I don't know. I watch these bands like Hanoi and I see it as so safe. Good band and all, but very safe. It never gets any farther than the drugs they're on the night of the show. I can live through just about anything and I will continue to do so. I will not burn out. Maybe that's the thing. Maybe the whole thing is one great endurance test to see how long you can last out here with all of these fuckers.

On plane going to USA: Finally out of the UK. I hope we get real big or real small. Something has to happen to stir things up. I don't care about money. I want action. I want life to be a life and Death experience.

Looking forward to getting off the plane and getting back to my shed and sleeping on the floor with my roommates, the snails and the ants. I wonder if they've missed me. ·

It's a joke you know. When I get out of this plane and get into the real world then it's back to the same shit of not having enough money to make ends meet. We'll be poor and tense until the next tour starts and then we'll get to live again. That is — we get to play and eat again. We get all these pictures taken of us. People want our autographs. We get to ride the plane home. If they saw how we live, who knows what they would think of us. I'll have to be strong to deal with this upcoming time off the road. It won't be long, but it will be hard. When we're home, everybody gets a chance to get an attitude going and it fucks all of us up. When we're out on the road, there's no time for that shit and we all drop it.

6.23.84 LONG BEACH CA: One great scene after another. I go to the Tropicana Hotel to find Nick Cave. Marcy has called and said she's at the end of her rope looking after the Bad Seeds and would I do it for a while during the day.

So I show up at the room and it looks like a tornado has been through there — clothes, a few girls are passed out on the bed. And then there's Nick and Blixa. They look like they haven't slept yet. Blixa must live

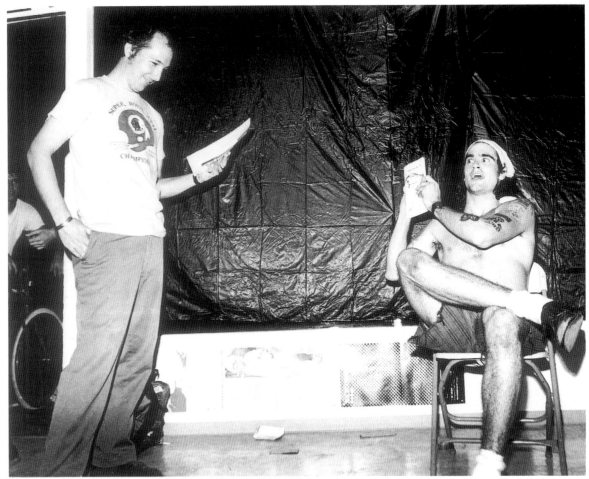

CHUCK AND HENRY, SANTA MONICA, CA / SUMMER 1984 *(NAOMI PETERSEN)*

in those leather clothes because they sure smell ripe.

So now we're at Zed Records where the boys are doing an in-store appearance. People are making assholes out of themselves trying to get to the them. It's kind of sickening to see these gothic types losing it over these guys. I mean Nick Cave is the greatest and so is Blixa, but I thought the goths prided themselves in being so removed from life. Whatever. They sure are making a fuss over them.

Black Flag doesn't get girls coming up to them like these guys are right now. I guess we're not that kind of band. I can't see why they would be into it. Looking the way we do and the fact that we don't give a fuck about anyone.

6.24.84 AT MARCY'S: Yesterday was really interesting. The in-store finishes and I'm in charge of getting the two boys into this girl's car and getting them back to the hotel. I see Nick in the back of a carload of scummy people. He looks at me through the window and waves weakly. Someone tells me that he went with those people because they have drugs or something. So okay, I've still got Blixa who is now drunk. We get into the car and we are going fast, back to LA. The girl is looking bad and driving poorly. I ask her what the matter is. She's on heroin. Great. Blixa sees an oil pump and touches the window and says, "Umm nice." Then he says he has to take a piss right now, pull over. The girl says that she will when it looks good to do so. Blixa says that he is a human organism and he must urinate now and calls her a bitch. He grabs the steering wheel and shoves it hard. The car lurches over two lanes. Cars beep and hit their brakes all around us. I ask him what his fucking problem is. Blixa says, "What is the matter? It is not you that would have been killed!" He says that he is going to take the piss now and opens the door to get out. Whoops. The car is going about 60 mph. I grab him and pin him to the seat until we pull into a gas station. He says nothing all the rest of the way.

We take some of the Bad Seeds to the Music Machine to see the Gun Club play. They stank. Mostly because Jeffrey was so shitfaced he couldn't play. It sucks because their new album *The Las Vegas Story* is so cool. It would have been a great show. They did play a good version of "Walking With The Beast". Blixa is falling down at this point and I am holding him up. He starts waltzing with me. It was great. I haven't slow danced since 8th grade. I ran into John Doe and Chris D.

6.28.84 HERMOSA BEACH CA: The show went well. Saw a movie with Mr. Ginn — *Spinal Tap*. Kind of depressing. I mean it was depressing in that it was true about a lot of shit.

I'm fucking tired of being poor. It never ends. It's good to be able to go into the shed and cool out. I have that tape player in there now and it's cool. This is a strange way to live. I sleep on the floor of a cold, damp shed. I own next to nothing. I am grateful just to eat. I tell the truth and I get shit for it. I get lonely in the shed. Hits me like a brick.

6.29.84 HERMOSA BEACH CA: Big Friday night. Pettibon is listening to jazz and watching the baseball game. Anything could hap-

SUMMER 1984 *(NAOMI PETERSEN)*

pen. Anything? Well, it's really a big fat zilch. Nothing ever happens around here. Kind of cool in a way. You get time to yourself in this house. No one ever calls. No one comes over. Pettibon never stops working. He rarely talks. He just draws and reads and he never stops. It's incredible. At the end of the day, there is a pile of drawings on the floor. All great too. I don't know how he does it.

7.1.84 10:25 A.M. HERMOSA BEACH CA: Played a party in Lawndale. That was a lot of fun. A bunch of stoners were hanging out while we jammed. We had a great time. I like those kind of gigs. Everybody's cool and there's none of the bullshit that usually comes along when we play. That party crew are actually cooler than any of the people that come to the real shows. They don't yell at us to play this or that and they get off on the music and they don't have time for bullshit attitudes. If we could have people like them at all the shows, we would have a lot more fun playing. So many of those punkers have nothing to do with music. It's all just a pose. They give us shit about the music we play, but they're more into their makeup than any music. I can't take any of them seriously.

7.3.84 7:02 P.M. GLOBAL: Dukowski, Greg Cameron of SWA and Ted Falconi from Flipper are jamming downstairs. Sounds amazing. Violent shit. Ted is one damaging guitar player.

My hang-ups make me see that I'm all hung up. Sometimes I want to throw myself away like trash. I know it's all bullshit, but it gets real enough for me that I get caught up in it — stuck to it.

People hurt. Things hurt. It just hurts. Alone doesn't always work. Rotting in your apartment. Together doesn't always work well either. We rot in your apartment. We are leeches leeching off each other. We are addicted to each other but we cannot digest each other's blood. We are each other's heroin. We want to kick so bad but we can't do it. We exist only to suck each other's blood and make each other weak and mean. We know nothing else.

SAN DIEGO, CA / 7.7.84 (*KLIK ABSTRACT*)

7.7.84 7:19 P.M. SAN DIEGO CA: Now at the Adams Hall. Last night went real well. I did a show in the Valley by myself and then did a show with Black Flag in Hollywood. The show last night at Lingerie was cool. I always hated that place so when I play there I always have an attitude. In the middle of the show, I took a knife off a guy and started swinging it at people in the front row. I put my other hand in front of my eyes so they could see that I couldn't see. I hope it bummed them out. Next, a guy handed me a syringe that looked full. He said that there was coke in it. I took it and threw it into Greg's cabinet screen. It stuck like a dart. After the show, some fucked up guy was trying to crawl into the van with us. I pulled out Dukowski's .45 and put the barrel on the man's forehead and told him to get the fuck away.

7.8.84 NEAR PHOENIX AZ: In some restaurant. Last night's show in SD went well. Some girl scratched the shit out of me. DC-3 and St. Vitus were great as usual. We drove all night and we still have some more to go.

8:51 p.m.: At the hall. Looks like we got some metal meisters in the crowd. Some surfers, some hot looking women. Last time we played here was real good. I don't want to do everything. I want to do anything.

7.11.84 VENICE CA: At Radio Tokyo Studios. Greg is mixing an 8-track tape of our show at Perkins Palace. I saw the sleeves for *Slip It In* and *Family Man*. They look great.

7.13.84 HOLLYWOOD CA: At this house that Nick is living in right now. Not much going on, just hanging out. We had some fun today though. Since Nick and the film crew for his video are all Australian, they called and asked the Australian Consulate to see if we could

HENRY AND NICK CAVE, SANTA MONICA, CA / 1984 *(NAOMI PETERSEN)*

come over and check out this party celebrating Australian filmmakers. They said we could attend so we went right over. The place was intense. Security all over the place. All these people dressed up... and then there was us. Nick had his bright green skintight Elvis outfit on. Looked like he hadn't slept for a few days. The rest of us just kind of stepped in behind him and went with it. We were in this back yard and Nick had a big glass of whiskey. I was eating all this free food. People were coming up to us asking what film we were in and we gave them so much bullshit. They were so stuck up and polite that they had to take it. Nick went up to one woman and put his index fingers and thumbs together so they looked like a triangle. He looked through them at her and told her that he was looking to set up a shot and could she please stand still. He told her that the reason that he had his fingers like this was because he was the only director in the world to use triangular film. She asked where he was from. He replied, "Nazi Germany." She just stared and walked away to a group of people and pointed at us from afar. We talk to others and give them a bunch of shit. Meanwhile, we stuff our faces on all the free food. Nick is drinking and eating grapes by the handful. I talk to some old man who knows me. A few minutes later, I look over and Nick is on his hands and knees crawling around on the grass. He crawls up to a large woman and bites her on the ankle. She bails. It looks like it's time to go. Nick takes a large handful of bleu cheese that was in a large mound and stuffs it into his mouth. He takes a napkin and wraps it around a big hunk of cheddar. Grabs it and some grapes and we are out of there, escorted by men with wires coming out of their ears. They walked us all the way to our car. On the way back to the house, Nick whipped out the piece of cheese and said, "This is a symbol of my discontent." I grabbed it from him and bit it in half. He threw it out the window at the car in the next lane. I leave at 5 a.m. to go play in Berkeley.

4:16 a.m.: Saw the Gun Club play Lingerie tonight. They were good. I hate sleep because I know I need it. Like tonight, I have to stay up so I can catch the ride up north for the show. We will all be packed in the van and no one will really get any sleep. It's hard to sleep knowing that whoever is driving is as tired as you and might fall asleep at the wheel and kill you. Fuck it. I just get used to staying up in the van at night. Sleep is the enemy and the friend. I wish there was a way to not have to ever close my eyes.

1:40 p.m.: At some truck stop en route to Berk. Got a few hours sleep after daybreak. I feel good enough to play. Tonight we play Ruthie's. What a shithole. I hate playing there. The people are always the same. Always fucked up and they think they can tell you what to play.

7.15.84 MONTEREY CA: Last night was the typical Berkeley bullshit. Some guy got onstage and cracked me one in the face. Knocked me out cold. I came to at Greg's feet wondering what the hell was going on. People yelling at me, telling me, "Get up you faggot! You're not hurt! Get the fuck up!"

I wonder if the Monterey people are as fucked and should be exterminated like the ones in Berkeley. We are near Santa Cruz — a town full of hippies, assholes and police.

I am an alien man. I don't understand anyone's anything. Nothing they say makes any sense to me. Their problems aren't mine.

GEARING UP FOR GLOBAL DESTRUCTION AT DUNKIN' DONUTS *(NAOMI PETERSEN)*

The opening band is soundchecking. They are really something. The guitar player has Greg's guitar. The drummer has the same setup for his drums, same dimensions as Bill. Every song they play sounds like "Thirsty and Miserable". They are called Blast. The rest of the Flag are watching them and laughing when they aren't looking.

The streets lie. The sidewalks lie. Everything lies. You can try and read it, but you're gonna get it wrong — all wrong. The summer evenings burn and melt and the nights glitter. But you're going to get it wrong and it's going to sink its teeth into your flesh and pull you to the bottom. Home is like that. Underneath the homes and the streets, there is a river. It moves with crippling power — a crushing muscle. It strangulates and lures, chokes and attracts. It says, "Come here and stay with me." And it lies.

7.17.84 10:45 P.M. SHED: Here in the shed. The Monterey show was the typical Northern Cal trip. I just went for belligerence. I got shocked so hard by the mic during "Slip It In" that it threw me through the air. It sucked. Played well anyway. The opening clone band was a real sight. They seem like cool people. They should play their own music though.

After the show, I was making out with a girl in the hallway and I reached into her pants and came back with my hand all bloody. Moments later, I was in the van stuck with all this blood on my hand for the ride back to LA.

That shot to the head fucked me up. I feel like I'm underwater. We leave for tour in a few days and it's a good thing too. It seems to be the only thing that makes sense.

7.24.84 COLORADO: I died... Not much going on. We're driving the gear out to Chicago for the first show. The van is a drain. It's packed with gear and bodies. I don't know how it all fits. We have the Sac Trust boys in there as well as people from the other band. The Chicago show will be good. It's great to be out of California.

TOM TROCCOLI / 1984

The other night I did a talking show and a Flag show in Santa Monica. Deirdre cooked me and Nick Cave dinner. It was cool to hang out. The shows were good as well.

7.25.84 CHICAGO IL: At the Metro. I love this place. I have been thinking about putting out my own book. It's not as if any publisher would want to do it. It might be a cool idea. I will get a ton of shit for it and they won't sell, but I should do it anyway so I can say that I did.

7.26.84 CHICAGO IL: At a Denny's. Played hard last night. Had a good time. Place was packed out. I scammed on this girl and was making out with her okay and then I went out to play. When I finished, she was gone. Doesn't matter if she was around. Where would I be able to go with her? Forget it and move on.

Last night, I slept on the hump of the wheel well in the van. I stared at the plywood of the upper level of the shelf. A guy on either side of me. A guy in Sac Trust blowing his beer breath on me all night. No room, no sleep and eighteen more shows to go. Twelve people in one van. It's okay though. You have to learn to make space in a small space. You learn to get out of the van fast and get all the time you can to yourself. There are ways to hide from interviewers and shit like that. Ways to melt into the crowd and not get recognized.

7.27.84 ST. LOUIS MO: Finished the show. Now we're at some rich kid's house. His parents are out of town and the place is full of people. Sometimes you sleep in a pile of shit, sometimes you sleep in a pile of roses.

Crowd really gets pissed off when you don't play every song they want to hear. They make all the demands instead of just getting into the music. I think there's a big difference between playing the music and listening to it. I know who's having the better time.

There's some hurt that won't leave you alone. Seems that one should be able to do something with it. I must concentrate on that. I feel crazy all the time. I should put all of it into the music. It makes me mad that I can't talk to girls. I would like to, but I'm too fucked up. When they talk, I don't know what to say. I usually have nothing to say to them and making shit up is making shit up. Fuck it. There's only one thing to do. Destroy every night and then sleep. There's some shit you can't scrape off your shoes.

Later: Talked to this girl for a while. I found out later that she fucked Tom in the shower. 16 years old. What a life.

7.28.84 Denny's: Yup, at a Denny's again. Where else? Tom ordered a Grand Slam breakfast in honor of the four girls he had sex with the other night. Gig last night was a trip. Belligerent people — so I got belligerent and smacked some guy.

Last night we slept at a caretaker's place — a fucking funeral home. I slept in a room with all these show coffins. It was trippy to look inside them and think that they went to all that trouble to handle some dead person. I mean it's pretty stupid if you think about it. I always thought the pine box was the cool way to go out if you have to go in a box. The insides were all done up in velvet. Davo and I wanted to get in one, but the guy said that wouldn't be cool. Tonight we play Columbus, OH.

Some people like to be served. I'll be fucked before I'll work for a boss again. That's bullshit. No way to live. I don't understand the autograph thing to save my life. It makes me uncomfortable doing that shit. I'm just like them. That's all that occurs to me.

Later: Two set night. The second set ripped up. Some of the people in the Midwest are kind of complacent. They stand and drink beer. They are like cows in the field.

Had fun watching a girl who took her shirt off during the set. She would get onstage and throw herself on the audience. People were trying to get away from her.

7.29.84 Columbus OH: Slept in the truck. The others went in this house and slept on the floor. Too noisy in there. I like it better alone with the sound of cars passing outside. I tried to get happening with this girl, but she wasn't having any of it. I gave it my best shot. It's all I can do being a guy from out of town and all.

7.30.84: In some diner. Long one today. Border crossing into Canada. Long drive. It's hot out and the van is packed full of people. That's the way it is, but sometimes it's hard to take.

Toronto: Canada is a funny place. They tell you how fucked up your country is and that all you want to do is be like them. And then you see their cheesy imitation bands and all you can do is laugh and get into it.

8.3.84 Marlboro NJ: At some huge roller rink. I don't know how we'll sound in here. The Canada dates went okay. The last one had some great fights. These cheeseheads beating the shit out of each other.

The show is being promoted as a "punk rock festival". The promoter is real clammy. What a depressing place this is. Makes me think of something David Lee Roth once said about his ability to endure anything. I bet he got that strength by playing a lot of nights in places like this.

It hurts to want. Whenever I find myself wanting, I find myself in a bad place. It's not a good place to be when you're living like we are. I am afraid of liking a girl too much. I know that it's not good to want. It will only kill your ass out here. The less you take with you out here is the less they can take away from you.

You come out here with a lot of anything, be it clothes, thoughts, emotional bullshit — whatever — you're only going to get it ripped off your body and you will feel the pain.

The man who runs the PA is a typical piece of shit. He wants to run the PA real low because he's afraid of something. I guess he's afraid of using his equipment. This is a show for the books I'll say. All you can do in a situation like this is focus on the music and make your way to the stage.

8.5.84 TRENTON NJ: Last night was Southgate, NJ. Never been there before and hopefully will never go there again. Our set got cut short by the biker/bouncers that didn't like what our audience was doing. One of the shitheads went up to Davo and grabbed him by the back of the neck and told him to "Turn it off." I'm surprised Davo has a neck left after that shit.

Greg's song "Can't Decide" is one right on song. It's how I feel right now. If you fuck a lot, you think about fucking a lot. If you don't fuck much, you don't think about it as much. You might for a while, but then it goes away. If you don't talk a lot, you lose some of your ability to do so. When the time comes to speak, you find yourself at a loss for words. They don't work well for you and you end up saying a bunch of shit that you don't mean or don't understand. What a fucked up position to be in. To talk and not understand yourself as you hear the words come out of your mouth. I think that's the definition of being full of shit. I feel like a damn fool when I open my mouth.

8.9.84 NEW YORK NY: At the Ritz. Second time here in a short period. Of all the bands in the world... the Sisters of Mercy will be opening for us tonight. Smoke machines, all kinds of lights were brought in for them. What a crock of weak-assed shit they are.

We drive to Florida after the show tonight. A long sweaty night after the long sweaty set. No real sleep for a good long time. Oh fuck, the Sisters are soundchecking with "Purple Haze". I just did something funny. I yelled at them, "Leave Hendrix's ass alone, you limey fags!" They stopped playing and looked at me. That was the funniest thing I've seen in a while.

8.11.84 MIAMI FL: The show at the Ritz was one of the best ones we've ever played. The best part was seeing the poor Sisters trying to maintain their pose with the front row trying to beat the shit out of the singer, swinging at his head and shit. What great crowds we get. After the show, this kid told us we could shower at his place and that it was on the way. We drove all over the fucking place until daybreak and found out that it was out of the way and his mother wouldn't let us take a step inside. We drove about 30

MIAMI, FL, 8.11.84 *(CHRIS BARROWS)*

hours to Tampa and played this outdoor place and it was okay. Crowd was kind of fucked but whatever. Now we're in a dive in Miami. I have some days off coming. I'm going up to DC.

Later: A girl shoved four one dollar bills down my shorts during our set. That's cool. I dried them off and bought myself dinner.

HENRY AND IAN, WASHINGTON, DC / SUMMER 1984 *(NAOMI PETERSEN)*

I am drowning, but it's my own hands that are pulling my feet to the bottom. I seem unable to stop myself from killing myself. It's a continuous drowning process.

8.15.84 SOMEWHERE IN UPSTATE NY: Doing this film with Lydia Lunch and Richard Kern. I think they're going to call it *Right Side of My Brain*. It's pretty fucking stupid, but I'm having a good time anyway.

I was in DC the other day. I walked up Wisconsin Avenue to Ian's parents house. I walked by all the old places I used to work at and hang out in. They sure have changed the place since I lived here. The Calvert Wine and Cheese Shop has been leveled. The Leonard Hair Salon is gone. Adriana's Mecca of Middle Eastern Dance is no more. Used to have some great times back there skating and getting chased out.

8.18.84 NYC: Did a reading at the Pyramid. It was a waste of time I think. A bunch of people talking through the thing. Luckily for me, I wasn't onstage for very long. I don't know what it is about shows here. They tell you not to go for very long. I think people just want to see you so they can say they did and then bail.

Yesterday, Kern and I were coming out of a restaurant and suddenly I was surrounded by all these skinheads. One had a chain in my face. They were pissed off that I told them to leave our show at the Ritz the other night. We played there on that New Music Seminar thing and they were in there fucking with people. I went to their leader and told him to take it out. Now they were all pissed off with me. One of them asked me why I didn't like them. I told them that I didn't like them because of all the fucked up shit that they did. It really took them back a step that I answered them so plainly. One skin told the guy with the chain to get it out of my face and then they all shook my hand and left. Strange.

8.22.84 TORONTO CANADA: Did two sets of reading at this club. Both sets were an hour each. It's the most I've ever done. Felt good though. Between sets, I went to a radio station and read there. After it was all over, I was tired as hell. But it was a good night.

DAVO DRAWING

8.25.84 6:48 P.M. SACRAMENTO CA: Flew in and had time to go to practice from the airport, and then we drove up here. Nine hour drive. Now we're in this shitty club in a shopping mall. What a drag this place is. Something about the people at the shows here in Northern Cal. They're so dead. Their eyes are dead stones.

8.28.84 10:05 P.M. SHED: After Sacto, we played San Francisco. We taped for a live video and album. I don't know how we played. It's a lot of pressure to be taped for video and audio. I know that Bill was choking big time. He hates all that kind of shit. He always plays too fast and too conservative when we record this kind of thing.

I talked to Cave today. He's in good spirits. I'm working on putting together a small fold and staple book of my writing so I can sell it at shows. I want to save money to do a real book someday. I know that it's probably never going to happen, but I've got to try.

9.2.84 2:09 P.M. SHED: Yesterday we played a party with the Alley Cats and October Faction. It was fun.

HENRY AND NICK, LOS ANGELES, CA / 8.31.84 (*NAOMI PETERSEN*)

OCTOBER FACTION, 1984. CLOCKWISE FROM CENTER: GREG CAMERON, JOE BAIZA, TOM TROCCOLI, GREG GINN, CHUCK DUKOWSKI. *(NAOMI PETERSEN)*

Last few days have been cool. Hung out with Nick a lot. We did a talking show together at the Lhasa Club. It sold out. Quite a few people left after Nick went on. He was good, but a bit nervous. I don't think he's used to that kind of thing.

6:29 p.m.: Went to the used record store this afternoon. Walking around in Redondo Beach can be a depressing and alienating experience. Especially if you're a cynical bastard like myself. A woman walking around in an "LA '84" shirt, overweight in bell-bottomed pants. Walking with some disgusting guy both in search of the ever elusive Coors. Beach burnouts are a trip. White trash and the smell of sea salt are enough to send a lesser mortal over the edge. I can see why they drink. All you have to do is look at the smokestacks in the sunset and realize that you'll probably never get out of this town. Sprawling scattered ghetto. Okay, this is a gross overexaggeration of the truth. But it sure is fun to write all of this while the sun goes down on another day of loneliness.

9.8.84 9:07 P.M. SHED: My book is at the printer. I called it *20* since there's 20 things in it. I didn't know what else to call it. Now I'll have to sell them. I hope I can handle that well.

9.14.84 11:53 A.M. SHED: We leave for Mexico soon. Tried to get my workout in yesterday, but I was hampered by the fact that I whacked my head on a cymbal at band practice. Hard to work out with the head pain. I did the best I could but still fell short. I wish I had more access to weights so I could work out like I used to.

Later: In Mexico. We seem sleazier than these guys. What the fuck. Ha… We win.

9.17.84 11:39 P.M. SANTA MONICA CA: Mexico was a trip. Some Mexican punk band opened. They were intense. They were into a real political thing. I was getting followed into the bathrooms and hit for autographs and pictures. A lot of kids didn't have money to get in so they hung out in the parking lot outside and listened. There were a few hundred out there, all dressed up in their cool duds. A lot of them had cameras. Me and Greg took pictures with them. It was cool.

9.22.84 9:44 A.M. GUERNVILLE CA: At some coffee place. We drove all through the night. I got a good sleeping spot so I'm doing good. Next to Brewer again. I always end up sleeping next to him. I'm listening to men talking up girls at the counter. They sound like they're talking to children. How gross. People suck.

Later: This time out, we're bringing our own PA, Rat Sound. It's a lot of stuff to load-in every day. We had to load in the PA up this flight of stairs today. This will be a shitload of work every day. I feel sorry for us. It sure is good to be back on tour again. Life is back to normal.

Later: Gig went well. A lot of people showed up. I found a small room to hang out in before the show. I found a piece of broken glass and started slamming it into my chest. Blood started flying all over the place. It felt good to feel pure pain. Helped me get perspective. The owner of the club came in and saw me and bailed fast. He must have thought I was crazy. Like I give a fuck about what he thinks. I went into the shower and turned the water on hard. The water made the cuts in my chest burn. I like the feeling. It's pure, direct and not muddled up by personal, mental or other trips. I wish everything was as pure, direct and simple to understand. Just finished soundcheck. I am having serious throat problems. This is really frustrating. I cannot figure out what it is. It puts me in a really bad mood. I hate throat problems worse than anything. I'm gonna have big problems if I can't get It together. I sound hoarse like I did two years ago.

9.26.84 SEATTLE WA: Played last night in Seattle. Show went good. Throat feeling better.

9.27.84 SALT LAKE CITY UT: At the Indian Center again. Pulled in a while ago. All loaded in, now just hanging around. I feel kind of detached — floating. My writing slacks off in this environment. I have thought of things to say and do and write, but a lot of the time they never make it to paper. We are hitting colder weather as we drive east.

There are two vehicles on this tour: a van and a large Ryder truck. The van carries people and the Ryder carries all the equipment. I live in the Ryder with Davo, Ratman and Tom. I like it in there. We take turns being up front. Being in back is a strange way to travel. You are detached from the drive. I live in total darkness most of the time. I can

THIS USED TO HANG OVER THE COFFEE MACHINE AT **SST** *(Davo)*

lie down on a blanket spread over the speakers. The truck makes a lot of noise and it throws you around a lot. You don't know what's happening out there except for maybe rain on the roof or something. I spend a lot of time in the dark, staring at the ceiling of the truck. I think about a lot of things. I think about this girl. I think about running my hands over her body. I think about her hips. I think about her eyes. I think about her smile. In my mind, I come up to her and put my arms out. She pushes me away firmly with determination. She shakes her head slowly "no." Her eyes are fixed to the ground. "No." I turn around without saying a word. I walk away and away and away. I walk forever through darkness. I look straight ahead. I can see clearly. There's nothing to see. In darkness, I can do no wrong. There is a lurching halt. The truck comes to a stop. The door pulls up. Bright Utah sunlight comes streaming in. The darkness vaporizes from my eyes

D. BOON, ALBUQUERQUE, NM / 1984 *(D.D.W.)*

and from my mind. I emerge from the truck. I went into the men's room. I can remember staring at my reflection in the toilet bowl. I can't remember feeling uglier in all my life.

9.28.84 WYOMING: At a diner. Just read the Denver Post's thing on Black Flag. Seems like they like us okay. Morrison thing again. I am getting tired of that shit I tell you. Come on guys. How about some new comparisons like... to Cyndi Lauper.

Pretty nice being back at the Rainbow. I wonder how it will go. I'm looking forward to playing. There is some tension in the ranks. No tension with me, I'm okay. It's snowing here in Denver. I don't like snow much. I always figure we'll crash the truck or something. It sure was cold in the truck today. Being in the back is like being in a tomb or something. Lying prone, wrapped up and waiting for release.

More on Salt Lake City, Utah: We played at the Indian Center which is run by Indians. I don't think they were much into us paleface motherfuckers. I walked up to the main office where about six of them were seated and asked if there was a backstage area for the band. One said no. Another one said, "No. Why don't you go change on the street?" There were Indians posted on both sides of the stage and in order to get through, you had to show your hand stamp. No matter how many times I went by the same guy, he would stop me, grab my hand, scrutinize my hand stamp very carefully and reluctantly let me pass. In the men's room there was a lot of anti-white graffiti on the walls. After the show, an Indian man was sweeping the floor. He walked past me and said, "I should be on that stage — not you." I just sat there and watched him sweep the floor.

Now at Denny's in Denver. Show over with. About half the amount of people as last time. This is the second time in six months we've been here and Rank & File were playing down the street.

Played okay. That's the way I always feel about playing on that stage — the show is just okay.

Now we go for an overnight drive to Lawrence, Kansas. I feel lonely. The weather and the thought of getting into the truck and freezing does not make me feel all that great. It snowed today. 29 degrees.

9.30.84 OMAHA NE: Just your average hall. I wrote a letter to Nick Cave just now. I don't really feel much like writing. I usually don't like to near show time. Slept in a room full of junk and trash last night. There was a mattress in the middle of it all. Got some more sleep in the Rolling Tomb. I was reading Henry Miller's *Tropic of Cancer* today while sitting on the ground in Lawrence, Kansas. Miller talked about how good everything looks when the sun's out — even the look in people's eyes. When I was sitting there in Lawrence, the sun was out and everything looked good. All of a sudden, it was the most beautiful place I had ever seen. I couldn't remember what any other place in the world looked like. I felt like I had been there for a long time. I felt a need to articulate. I couldn't do it with a photograph. It would have to be with words.

Now hours later, I can only remember the feeling. I can't even remember what Lawrence looks like. Being here really reminds me of being back in DC. The people look the same and the streets, houses and buildings look like Washington. The weather is a contributing factor to this home feeling. I spent a week in Washington in late October '82. Tomorrow is October '84 and now I can remember that week very well. I think the temperature and landscape egg this on. I like to be moving forward so fast that I don't really have a chance to look backwards. It always seems to leave me feeling a bit empty. It's a Sunday night. I'm sitting here in this Bingo Hall in Omaha, Nebraska. It's cold in here. There's no stage. Lots of long skinny tables and chairs. The air reeks of the popcorn machine in the front lobby. Lots of florescent lights all around. Florescent light makes me feel lonely — crummy. My fingers are cold. Soundcheck is going down. Greg is playing his guitar. Two or three people who were watching just walked out with their hands over their ears.

Later: Place filling up. I'm sitting at a table. Lots of people staring at me, pointing and shit. Makes me feel funny. There's no backstage here or I would surely be there. I find more and more that I have less and less to say to people. I just can't get into answering the same questions all the time. This is no fault of theirs.

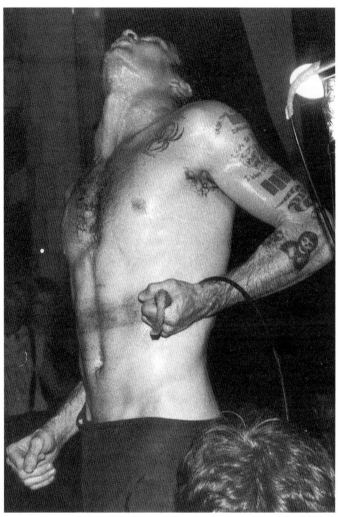

(CHRIS MAGERI)

Twenty minutes later: I just signed about 25-35 autographs. All these people just lined up and started handing me stuff to sign. It makes me feel stupid.

10.1.84 COLUMBIA MO: Pretty easy drive getting here from last night's show. Last night in Omaha was good. I thought we played well. I have nothing to say to any of these girls who come up and start talking to me. Most of them get offended when I don't talk to them. I do not like to make idle conversation with people. I feel ugly around girls. I always have. I feel like a leper. In darkness, I'm not ugly. I'm not anything at all. I like that. I have been with a few girls over the years. I'm surprised that I ever got laid in the first place.

This girl from San Francisco told people that I raped her and beat her up. I sure didn't do that. When I walk on the street and I see that I'm behind a girl, I always drop way back. I don't want the girl to think that I'm going to attack her. I've had girls run into stores and wait until I pass before they come out. I just keep my eyes to the ground and try to be low-key. I like the dark. I sit with the lights off if I can. The truck is dark — pitch black. Devoid of light, devoid of me. If I can't see my body, then it can't be bad.

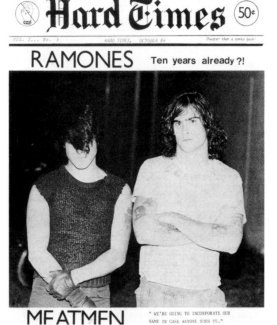

Today is the first day of October. I like October. Good things happen in October. The leaves turn and all that cool stuff. Last October, I was in LA. That was a drag. That's no place to be if you ask me. I'd rather be somewhere else, like Missouri. I hope I don't have to do all that autograph stuff again. Last night was too much. I don't like signing pieces of paper. It makes me feel crummy. I like gigs with dark corners where I can sit and no one even looks in my general direction. If you don't feel like talking, which is pretty much all the time for me, then you have a hard time when someone sits down while you're reading or thinking and starts talking at you. I don't know what to do. If you say something like, "I was reading" or "I'd like to be left alone," it really comes off sounding nasty. The person probably feels embarrassed, stupid and thinks you're conceited when the real deal is that you've been driving all day listening to a lot of talk, loading in equipment, feeling shitty from little sleep, etc. But fuck that! This is no excuse. I guess I'm what they say I am. Fine. Turn off the lights and there will be nothing to worry about. In darkness, there is nothing but darkness. The sound of my breathing and the absence of light. The eyes. If you can see nothing, then you can see nothing wrong — bad or ugly. I see women when I turn the lights off. They can't see me.

10.2.84 NEBRASKA: Drove all night. After tonight's show, we drive to Minneapolis for two sets. I slept okay last night. I like to sit alone when I eat. I noticed that this seems to offend certain members of the crew. There's just no way that I'm going to sit and listen to all that conversation when I don't have to. Last night's show was okay. I couldn't hear myself too well so I pushed my voice too hard. Some guy spat on me and I took his shirt and wiped it off. Last night, there were these people giving me all these compliments. I don't know what to do. I say thank you and try to smile but it comes out funny. I think it's really cool that people dig Black Flag. I don't know how to handle the compliments. I try to be polite because they're being cool but I don't take praise well. I remember when I met Nick Cave at Club Lingerie a couple of years ago. I just held my breath, walked up and introduced myself. He was real cool. I told him he was my favorite singer. That guy looked like he wanted to crawl underneath the table. One time I walked up to Tex Jones from Tex and the Horseheads and told her that I really liked her singing. She smiled like she was really surprised and pleased. When people say they like my singing or something, I think that they have brain damage.

10.3.84 MINNEAPOLIS MN: Pulled into Minneapolis about two hours ago. I have slept about one hour. I feel like I'm dead. I took a walk down the street to find coffee. I found a record store and a McDonald's. I went into the record store to look around. I saw our new album *Family Man* on the shelf. I went into the used record section. I overheard this couple talking as they went through the records. Man: "This place is great! I found the first Black Flag album for three bucks here last week!" Woman: "Three bucks? I'll give you mine for free!" I left the record store and headed into McDonald's. Inside: 4 lines in front of the counter, mostly male. They looked like they were in line to use the urinal. I was standing behind a woman with a big ass. There was a draft and I caught a breath of what smelled like fresh shit. I thought to myself, "Has this lady shit her pants? Couldn't she have waited until she got to the counter first?" Through the shit stench and urinal queue, was a woman walking in and out of the lines surveying the customers, asking the kind of questions that those kind of people ask. She looked like a medic during wartime or a stewardess on an airplane. I expected oxygen bags to fall out of the ceiling at any time. I checked out her legs. No shit stains. Got my coffee and crawled through the smoke and the bodies to a foxhole in the front. The phone rang. Comfort Woman picked it up. "Hello!... Welcome to McDonald's!... Yes!... Pretty darn good!... Thank you!... Have a nice day!... Good bye!" I made a run for the door. I looked behind me, the McDonald's Courtesy Woman was standing on the counter. She was bleeding from the head. She was yelling into a bullhorn, "Maxine, we need some more straws! More Quarter Pounders, large fries, splints! Where's that goddamn plasma! Hit it! Thank you! Pretty darn good! Have a nice day!" I wandered the streets for a time and made it to soundcheck with minor injuries.

10.4.84 OSHKOSH WI: Good buddy, pulled in about 90 minutes ago. Live in Oshkosh. Here's how it went down. Pulled into the place, a video-activity-recreation center. PA loaded, I hit the streets in search of coffee. I walked down N. Main a few blocks. I saw a beauty parlor. Inside, women sitting in chairs with huge black cones over their heads. They looked like suburban automatons. What was going on in there? Some kind of Midwestern brainwashing operation? Modernized psychotherapy? Plastic surgery while-u-wait? The attack of the brain suckers? I didn't stick around long enough to find out. Up ahead in the distance, I could see a beacon shining against the evening sky... *Burger King*. Sure, I had the money — strong American currency. But would it work here? I ventured in. The man at the counter was so nice it made me cringe. I sat down with my coffee. A man and his son went up to the counter and ordered food. The guy behind the counter smiled at the little boy and said, "Hey-y-y! I've got something for you. Do you like candy? Here!" The man handed the kid a red lollipop. I felt like jumping on the counter, pulling out my cock, waving it and screaming, "Don't take candy from strangers, you little shit!" Busted out of there and walked back down Main and back to Videoland.

10.6.84 MILWAUKEE WI: In this house that was supposed be quiet. It's just a bunch of noise. I don't understand how you can sit around and talk about mundane shit all night long. I'm in this basement. I can hear all these people walking around upstairs, making a lot of noise. Last night in Oshkosh was real good. No dressing rooms so I couldn't hide out. This is nowhere. Tonight's show was good. I think we played well. I would like to play a little longer. It seems to go so fast.

10.7.84 MADISON WI: Sitting at a coffee shop. Man, this is some righteous coffee. We're loaded in. I walked here, not very far from the hall. I kind of know my way around here from previous tours. A man across from me tells the woman he is sitting with that his friend has AIDS and it keeps him from sleeping. My father came from this area. I think I can see what happened to him. This is a college town. That's easy to see. I usually don't like college towns much, but this place seems to be okay. I guess that we'll be here tomorrow since there's no Chicago show. There's probably not much here. I slept in a basement last night.

    Back at the hall. That coffee shop was a trip. There was this guy behind the counter. He was totally wired on coffee. I sat and watched him handle customers. It was great. I thought that he was going to fly through the ceiling. One customer wanted to know the difference between Nordic Blend, Viennese Roast and Espresso Roast. The request sent this young man into fits. He started breaking down the coffees like wines. He was great. The store was great. The entire establishment totally devoted to coffee.

IN A SLUMP WITH A BROKEN KNUCKLE. GOT IN A FIGHT AT THAT NIGHT'S PERFORMANCE—ST. LOUIS, MO / 10.8.84 *(HILLARY D.)*

10.8.84 ST. LOUIS MO: Sitting at this guy's house. The black van isn't here yet. The Ryder came out first. Don't feel all that tired. I'm sitting in a stylish basement. There are Black Flag posters everywhere in the room. I have nothing on my mind so I'll stop right here. At this kid's house talking to the cleaning lady. Decaf on the pot. I drank a cup by mistake. What is this bullshit? 97% caffeine free is 97% not my kind of thing.

10.9.84 ST. LOUIS MO: At Denny's. The same Denny's I was at the last time I was in St. Louis. In fact, I'm even sitting in the same seat. Last night's show was good. This guy gave me shit so I beat him up. I broke his nose bad. I think I might have done some damage to his cheekbone as well. I gave him a lot of chances to back off, but he wouldn't so I dealt on him — simple. After the show, I had to go way out into the middle of nowhere to do a radio interview which was taped for later use. Went okay. Didn't get back until real late. Long drive today. I don't even know where we're playing.

I am ready for whatever's coming. I expect nothing but to be let down or to be turned away. I am alone. Goddamn. The shit hurts sometimes, but I realize what I am, what I have become. The alien man waved his arms up and down and noticed that he couldn't wave in the right language so he stopped.

In the club. Just got here about 45 minutes ago. Loaded in real fast. Hand all swollen from punching that guy out. I think I broke another knuckle. Walked down to the liquor store to get a soda. Passed a bunch of taxi drivers. They didn't like me much, judging from the looks on their faces. Walked into the liquor store. The guy in there says, "Good golly gracious. Great balls of far!" Yes, "far" like "My paints are on far!" Bought a Coke. Walked back to the club. A bunch of guys pass me. "Alright Henry!" I open the door and walk into the dimly lit hallway. It reeks of sweat and rotting beer. The hunchback owner man-thing sits slumped over a stool with a cigarette in his hand. Inside: Ugly woman putting quarters into the jukebox inciting the vomit of John Cougar and Loverboy. It's a Tuesday night. We were here six weeks ago. In goes another quarter, out comes some shit. I don't know who. Pinball game noise. The place stinks of the men's room. Places like this make me sink so low that I think I'm going to melt into the seat I'm in. Loneliness. I am on a lonesome trail.

10.10.84 FLINT MI: Played well yesterday. Tonight, a small hall and our huge PA. Man, we're going to ruin them tonight. I watch a lot of people go by. They never look around. There's so much to feel, so much to look for. I can feel myself on fire. I'm burning all the time. If I'm crazy, then you're boring. All it takes is one good scare for them to run home, sit down and shut up. Premature Death. I want to die over and over. If I'm a coward, then I'm nobody's hero and nobody's fool. My closet is cluttered. I want to

FLINT, MI / 10.12.84 *(MURRAY KAPPEL)*

throw open the doors and let all the junk fall out for all to see. Like going through life with your pants off. Like the way we all start out.

I don't want to drink from their coffee pot. I don't want to catch their slowdown disease. We're being buried alive. I don't think anyone sees it. I see it.

Soundcheck is over. Man, is this system loud. Writing interrupted by four girls coming up and saying, "Ohmigodyourethesinger! Weworshipyouguys!"

The youth here are drinking Stroh's Lite. What is this *lite* shit? To purchase lite beer you should have to be over 30 and have ID to prove it. These kids should be dropping shooters of straight grain.

10.11.84 FLINT MI: Last night's show was pretty good. I played hard and spent most of the set slipping on my own sweat. The front row was girls trying to kiss me. This one guy in the front kept grabbing me. I grabbed him back hard. He bummed. I thought he was going to cry.

Slept in someone's house. Baby in the next room cried a lot but I still got enough sleep. Now in Kalamazoo. Last time I was here was about two years ago. Dukowski had to be taken to the hospital because he passed out. He and the drummer Emil were so sick, they could barely speak. They had some kind of walking pneumonia. In a span of three days, we did six sets. That was a pretty tough stretch.

At Denny's today, there were a great bunch of women sitting near us. They were talking about K-Mart. I picked up two names, Esther and Priscilla. One of them said that there was a great selection of Rubbermaid stuff there. The rest of them said a bunch of "Oh my!" and "Oh my, yes!" type statements. I thought of how great it would be to have these ladies around on the tour. I don't know what they would do. They would just be there hanging out. The possibilities would be endless. The woman at the cash register asked if we were campers. I told her that in a way we were indeed campers. I told her that we were avant-garde terrorists roaming the midwest wiping out stupidity with the use of flamethrowers. I told her that we were on our way to Kalamazoo and many would die. The woman froze for a second and then looked at Brewer and asked if I was kidding.

10.14.84 3:38 A.M. KENT OH: Played two sets tonight. Had to load the PA down a flight of stairs. Not the easiest thing I've done in a while. After the sets, we loaded out into the cold night and the only thing open was this biker bar next door. We were loading and having to be careful not to knock over the shitheads'

TRENTON, NJ / 10.19.84

bikes. They were watching us like drunken hawks. Some fight started and they fought right through load-out and we just kept putting the equipment in the back of the truck.

9:14 p.m. Columbus OH: Tonight is a night off so we're here watching the Meat Puppets. During soundcheck, they played this new song called "Away". I think it's the best thing I've ever heard them do.

The people at the show are tripping out looking at us. I guess they didn't expect us Black Flag types to show up.

10.16.84 2:27 P.M. HOBOKEN NJ: Have not written for a few days due to the drives being long and little time to stop. Oh yeah, one last thing about Kent. Two bikers were fighting in the street outside. One of them was begging the other to hit him. "Please hit me! Come on man!" They walked back into the bar with their arms around each other. Buddies for life.

10.17.84 6:12 P.M. STORRS CT: I think I was born on Mars. I don't fit in with people in the real world. I think I've written about this idea before. We live in a different world than they do. All we see are people that come to our shows. We rarely talk to straight people at all. I don't know how long I'd last out there in their world. I never remember them until I'm right in the middle of them and that's when I start to freak out. We speak a different language. We say things that make them hate us. For us it's nothing. We hate their fucked up world and they hate ours.

The day after tomorrow will mark the fourth week of this tour. I don't remember the first week very well. I feel fine physically, but my mind is slipping around a little. Happens to me on tour.

My trail will never end. It's lonely because I'm the only one on it. I'm in a band with musicians. I'm not one. Don't know how to play an instrument. Don't want to know. I don't see why all these people like me. I really don't. I wouldn't like me.

Looks like our show at the Palladium will be with the Ramones.

10.22.84 6:11 P.M. WORCESTER MA: Haven't written in a few days. Hung out with Ian when I was in DC. He was great as always.

We played in DC and after the show, the old bass player in SOA came up to me and gave me this whole rap about how I should have stayed in DC and all this other bullshit. That's so typical. All he can do is get drunk and give me shit for doing what I'm doing. I don't want to talk to people from there anymore if they're going to be like that. What is it with them? I don't see them doing anything. All I know is that they couldn't handle the way we conduct business.

We did two sets in Trenton the next day. Danzig showed up. Hadn't seen him in a while. We drove all night to Providence. Played two sets there too. I slept under the truck in the parking lot when we got there. Cool people — played hard.

10.23.84 4:10 P.M. BOSTON MA: Last night we played in Worcester. Some real shitheads were there. These redneck guys were trying to beat up the entire club. Like they're going to show all these punk-ass motherfuckers how it's really done, that kind of thing.

The Boston show was good. Hard on me. Two sets for the two days before and then an afternoon show in Boston. Kicked my ass, but we destroyed them.

There's nowhere I can go. We're all cooped up at some guy's house. Tom has taken control of the tape deck and all he plays are live tapes of his band. It's not like we don't hear him enough — like every night. It's cold and raining out. No food near here. Nothing to do. Here we are. So many nights like this where you just end up in a place and nothing happens except hanging around trying to stay warm and fed. That's why I spend so much time in this book. Where the hell else am I going to go?

It's funny to watch the others argue amongst themselves and vie for control. What's the point?

Days off are depressing. I'd rather be playing. I think that's the same for all the rest too. None of us know what to do with time off after the laundry has been done.

10.27.84 3:19 A.M. CHARLOTTE NC: Sitting with this drunk guy because there's nowhere else to go. The show was at the Milestone. One fuckup after another. Have to find some place to get some sleep.

1:14 p.m.: At a diner in Charlotte. The show was stopped halfway last night. There are several stories as to why. All pretty bogus if you ask me. Mostly, the owner of the place is a total fuckup. Stayed at this kid's house last night. Mom gone — just the kid, his brother and his father. There was a burlap and yarn plaque over the toilet — *We love you Dad*. Beer cans and bottles all over the floor in every room. Dead roaches in the bathtub.

The last few days have been pretty gross. On the way to Philadelphia, the front tire of the Ryder sprang a leak and the rear lights of the van caught on fire. Great so far. We pull into the rear of the Eastside Club at 10 p.m. The people who work there are gross, junior Mafia cokeheads who don't want to know you. We play the show and go to get some sleep at a guy's house in town. He's in a pretty fucked neighborhood. We go to the van the next morning and find the van's window smashed out and all this stuff missing —

Tom's tape deck, all the t-shirt money, all these tapes and shirts. There's blood all over where the guy must have cut himself making his getaway. We follow the blood all the way up the front steps of a house. We knock on the door and an old woman comes to the door and tells us that no one lives there except her. We look up and some guy is watching us from the window. What a bunch of shitheads. We should have just taken her outside and shot her in the head, waved at the guy and driven off.

So that was the last few days. I just talked to Chuck. From what he says, it looks like we'll never come home. We finish this tour in LA with the Ramones at the Palladium on November 17 and then leave almost immediately again for another 6 weeks. That will make this one a 14 week tour. Oh well, fine with me as long as my throat holds out. I'll be doing some shows on my own for a couple of weeks after that.

10.28.84 1:01 A.M. COLUMBIA SC: Tonight's set was good. We have two sets tomorrow. We leave in a few hours for Raleigh. I don't feel tired. I'm starting to hear voices when I try to sleep. It's fucked up. I can hear voices talking in half-sentences. It wakes me up.

Tonight, people were coming backstage asking me to autograph copies of their *Family Man* albums. I have nothing to say to these people. They're cool, but still I don't know what to say. I feel so far away from them. To know us is to ride in the van and do the whole thing. Otherwise, you're on the outside.

I would like to go hang out in the desert for a while. I really took to that place when I first went out there. The desert knows about the *alonity*. Yes, the alonity. That's my word. It's being alive and living with yourself. Sometimes the alonity hurts because it's real. It hurts, scars and strengthens. I spend lots of time in the alonity. Most people busy themselves with meaningless rituals and assorted bullshit. They fear the alonity. I don't. I feel at home with it — in it. They get caught up in how they think their hair should be cut. If they could see inside themselves, they would freak out. It's a crime against time, to waste it on such bullshit. I don't beg for understanding. I live on earth. I just wonder if I got the wrong address.

Later: Finished the first set here in Raleigh, went okay. No room onstage, real hot, no air to breathe. A typical night.

10.30.84 2:22 P.M. TALLAHASSEE FL: I'm sitting at the bar listening to the bartender telling a story to his friend. He has this regular customer that got real plastered the other night. He asks for a ride home and some other guy says he'll do it. The guy who drives the regular home is a stranger to everyone. The guy gets to the regular's house and reaches over and stabs him in the stomach and throat. The regular somehow survived. The bartender said that the regular is going to stop drinking altogether now. "It kind of devastated him you know?"

10.31.84 3:25 A.M. TALLAHASSEE FL: Back in Kentucky, I was talking about that guy who sat in the rancid hallway smoking cigarettes and not talking to anyone. It seems that the man did a long stretch in prison for a multiple homicide. Some guy was telling us it was 45 years. Who knows?

11.2.84 4:03 P.M. ATLANTA GA: At the 688 Club. Played in Tampa last night at that Cuban Club place. We drove all night to get here. Two sets today. Show in Miami was pretty cool — Halloween and all. I had some fun with the crowd. I passed a cup to them and told them to fill it with money and I'd do something really gross and stupid. They did. I took a large cup and wrung out my socks and shorts into it and filled it to the top with my sweat. I toasted the crowd and drank it. Made enough money to buy myself a meal at Denny's afterwards.

11.3.84 7:10 P.M. NEW ORLEANS LA: Got my ninety dollar weekly paycheck and lost forty of it somewhere. I don't know where it went. I'm not too happy about it.

Played really hard in the second set last night. We played this long encore and I'm walking offstage and people are yelling shit like, "Play more Henry, you faggot!" I saw one of the guys who was talking the shit and dumped the rest of the water in my bottle on his head. I should have just broken it over his head. What the fuck. That's why I'm always going to tell you, "Fuck you." I'm a walking "fuck you". I'd like to get a baseball bat and club the shit out of some of you. That would feel so good. See you spit on me and then crack your stupid head open. Burning me with cigarettes. Grabbing my balls and giving them a twist. Punching me in the face. Fuck you. I should just start smacking people at random. Fuck them. All of them. I used to like audiences. Now I see what the fuck the deal is. They can go get fucked. They are going to get hurt if they fuck with this animal.

I walked around the French Quarter today. All these people and their little comments. Nice shoes, nice hair — that kind of thing. My stock replies were "Fuck you" and "Give me some money." That shut them up fast. Fuck these people. It would be great to carry a gun and shoot people all the time.

I have to be cool because of my broken knuckle. Losing that money really burns me. I don't know what I'll do for food next week. Fuck it.

11.6.84 8:43 P.M. LAFAYETTE LA: The show in New Orleans was cool. Right before we went on, Davo was playing a tape and a pig came over and told him to turn it down. Davo turned it down. Then the pig said, "I said turn it down!" And with that he pulled all of the faders on the board down, ruining Davo's settings for the mix. These fucking pigs should just be killed. We were good anyway. Like you're really going to stop us.

11.8.84 2:43 P.M. AUSTIN TX: The gig the other night in Lafayette was great. It was a gay bar. The tripped out part happened when all the transvestite regulars came to see the band and mixed in with all the Flag types. Awesome. Punkers standing next to big men in dresses. Ratman was outside lighting off bottle rockets. A sheriff's car pulls up and Rat figures he's busted. The pig is drunk and just wants to know if the owner's inside. Great one-liner from the pig: "Is Martin inside? Tell him I'm horny as hell and I want my black boy."

Davo drew all these stupid tattoos on me. I had Devo men on my knee caps, a Quiet Riot one going up my thigh, "Cyndi Lauper" across my chest. I went to the bar part of the club and would get next to women and try to pick them up by showing them these horrible tattoos. Of course they thought I was an idiot. I went up to this big blonde girl and did my shtick and she said a few "oh my's" and then said in a very deep voice, "You better take it somewhere else, fella." Yeah, it was a big man in a wig. Later, he pulled off his dress and paraded around the club in his wig and underwear. It was great.

The next night was San Antonio. The pigs came and busted the show halfway through. We've played there three times in the last three years and never once have we completed a set.

Austin was a piece of shit. We played that outdoor place Liberty Lunch. We played good, but the audience was a bunch of fuckups. There was a single black guy in the crowd and he got the shit kicked out of him. The pigs came in and busted the show three songs from the end. I dodged a few bottles that barely missed my head. One of the bottles hit me in the balls. I went through the crowd looking for the guy who did it, but no one would tell me.

Today is a day off so we're doing the laundry. Today makes it seven weeks out. Whatever. I would like to do something else for a week or so.

Sometimes being in Black Flag is a thankless job. I reckon we'll be poor and dirty forever. I'm not looking for the house on the hill, but sometimes this is a hard deal. A year from now we'll be flea-bitten and behind on sleep, but we'll be free at least.

All I know is that when I've pulled into the place, loaded in the PA, played so hard I can't even think straight and then loaded the PA back into the truck, I don't have time to listen to anyone telling me that I'm a rock star. I can't listen to little yapping dogs like Tim Yohannon telling me that I'm something or other. They have no idea. None of the people that talk the shit could ever tow the line that we do. It's good to know that.

Hell, I figure all of my problems are solved. I have nothing except to play this music and die. There's nothing in my way. My knuckle is swollen from hitting that guy. My balls are still hurting from that bottle, but fuck it. At least I have some clean socks on.

LOS ANGELES, CA, 11.17.84. L-R: JOHN DOE, HENRY, JOHNNY RAMONE.

11.12.84 EL PASO TX: Last night was Houston. The night before was Dallas. The shows went okay. I broke my finger on a guy in Dallas. Some guy told us he had a place for us to stay and then at the last minute he couldn't get it together so we had to get a hotel that we couldn't really afford. At least we all got showers. Went to sleep at 5:30. Got up at 9:00 to drive to Houston.

In Houston, there was a guy who wouldn't leave me alone. He kept trying to take the mic away from me by pulling on the cord. I bashed him in the face with it and he went away. Soon enough, he was back again and pulling the same shit so I had to help him out. I smacked him in the eye with the mic and that seemed to get him in line. He came back later with all this blood coming from his eye, waving an insurance card at me. I just laughed in his face. I hope it kills him. I hope it kills all of you. Fuck you.

11.15.84 PHOENIX AZ: Tonight we play with the Ramones. We have to leave right after we play because we have to drive to San Francisco for a show tomorrow night. After that, we have to rip down to LA and do the show at the Palladium. Should be a fucked few days with no sleep. I'm burnt to the point to where I have to be told about the shows we're doing a few at a time because I can't remember too much.

11.22.84 2:57 A.M. LAS VEGAS NV: In Las Vegas at a Denny's. A lot has happened in the last few days. I have been either too busy or too tired to write about it. I think I'm getting sick. Both sides of my neck are hot and swollen. I can't afford to get sick.

Last night was the show here. These people are a bunch of shitheads. We had the Meat Puppets play with us. People threw stuff at them and they lasted a total of fifteen minutes. Fuck these people. Never playing here again. Seal off the crowd and gas the fuckers. Kill them. I have to get some sleep. I think I'm going out of my head.

11.23.84 5:34 P.M. BAKERSFIELD CA: This is some place. Never have I been in such a hovel. I don't like Bakersfield. Home of the brain-damaged youth. Still feeling like shit. 23 years now! I could barely move this morning. If I was a good man, I would take all of my meager earnings and devote them to a good cause like the total destruction of Bakersfield by firestorm. Gas, napalm, whatever it takes. I'm going in. If you don't hear from me in eight hours, *you* call in the airstrike. There's nothing like the Californian redneck. He does all the usual things that you would expect a redneck piece of shit to do — drink, drive, fight and fuck. The Californian will do all of this, but still wear an Oingo Boingo shirt. He will tease fags and listen to KROQ. You will see him fly past you in his Bronco with Billy Idol blasting out of the system.

11.24.84 10:18 P.M. SHED: I know I should be in Reno. But I'm sick enough to cancel a few shows so here I am. I'm glad I don't have to play. I wouldn't be any good. I'm sicker than shit.

It's good to be off the road for a few days. It's good not to be seen by people for a while. I don't like being that thing that can be recognized all the time. It strips the insulation off me.

12.2.84 TUCSON AZ: Feeling better thanks to some penicillin I took. Real strange. Fell asleep in the van, woke up in the desert. Good deal if you ask me. Great to be out of California.

I hope my throat makes the next four weeks. It's never been this bad. It's swollen every day. I can see it from the outside. I know that's not right. I just play and try to sleep. I don't know what day it is or where we're playing next. I just go and I don't question it. It's better that way.

12.3.84 2:37 A.M. TUCSON AZ: At a Waffle House. It's beautiful out here tonight. Tonight's show was real good. I like playing out here. Tonight we drive to Albuquerque.

LOS ANGELES, CA, 11.17.84 *(DAVID HERMON)*

12.4.84 ALBUQUERQUE NM: Played here last night. Playing again tonight. It's cool not to have to move the equipment. It's cold as shit outside and the place has all these holes in the wall so it's cold until the people show up. You know the second show in this place will be empty. I have no idea why we're playing two nights here. Enough of this mundane crap. Let's talk about something interesting like the shit written on the walls of the men's room — "Scorpions #1", "Break Dance" — this is great stuff. The drive to Santa Fe is only fifty miles so it looks like we'll get some sleep.

12.5.84 SANTA FE NM: Last night's show was pretty cool. The time being sick really knocked my stamina back. The place we're in tonight is cold too. I hate the cold. It's hard to get the muscles loose. At least we get to see Saint Vitus every night. They're great guys.

I'll be doing a talking show in Albuquerque in a while. I spoke to the guy that I will be doing the show with. He kept talking about "us poets". That shit made me sick. I'm no poet. You can save that shit.

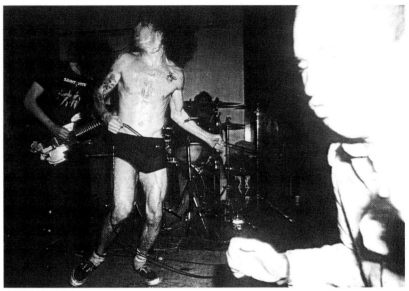

ALBUQUERQUE, NM, 12.3.84 *(D.D.W.)*

There's a single wood-burning stove that heats the entire club. It's all the way at one end. I think if we're here any longer, Jack London will show up with White Fang. The promoter told me that I should just keep filling the stove with wood. I told him if I run out of wood, I'll just stuff his little kid in there. He didn't think I was funny.

Last night a girl came up from behind me and grabbed me. Without thinking, I threw her into a wall. I didn't know it was a girl. I don't like people coming up behind me. I hate drunk assholes that think that they have the right to come up and talk their stupid shit in my face for as long as they want. They seem to think that if they bought a ticket then they own a part of you. Man, it's cold in here and there's hours to go before we play.

12.6.84 OKLAHOMA CITY OK: I have no voice whatsoever. I have no idea how I'm going to pull off the next set.

These two set nights kill me sometimes. It's strange though, I don't remember one night where the second set wasn't a killer show. I rode up front in the truck last night and didn't get much sleep in there. I got more sleep in the club this afternoon. Apparently this place used to be a gay disco. The owner was telling me that they were cleaning the place out and found all these pictures of these guys fucking each other and all this other shit like dildos, etc. A great one-liner from the guy: "Yeah, pictures of guys fucking dogs and shit. Want a beer?"

Well hell, at least I'm not in Santa Fe anymore. The people were real cool, but there was nothing happening there, except for a lot of people looking at dirt.

"Hey, what are you gonna do?"

"I'm gonna look at some dirt."

"Then what are you gonna do?"

"Put some water on it, mush it up with a popsicle stick, look at it some more."

"Cool, can I come over?"

See what I mean? Nice folks, but not my idea of a good time or a bad time or any kind of time at all. Tomorrow's show is in Tulsa, Oklahoma. We played there about two and a half years ago. I don't remember it. No wait, I do. That was the show where two, count them, two people came. It was cool, they sat way in the back. We couldn't even see them so we were playing to nobody. That's just like playing to a crowd in England. The only difference is that you can see them, but you're still playing to yourself. There are a lot of cynical people in the world and I'm one of them. Maybe I'm two or three of them.

I remember Dukowski taught me something that night I will never forget. We were hanging out in the parking lot right before we were going on and I was complaining about the lack of people there. He totally laid into me. He said that there might only be a couple of people there, but they came to see you and it's not their fault that no one else came. And that you should play your guts out anytime anywhere and it doesn't matter how many people come. I played my ass off that night.

I've noticed that my writing in this journal has taken on a cynical edge in recent weeks. I think this is due to exhaustion. I'm sure that other people might have a better word. It's the people, drunks in my face, interviewers, people who want autographs, etc. The shit makes me sick. I'm happy that I get to play, but I don't get into this personality parade bullshit.

Sleep has been hard lately. I finish the show, load out, then I sit up until about 5:30 a.m. I hardly remember what city I'm in. I feel almost unprepared for tour even though it's pretty much all I've done for the last ten months. It can be a bad insulation trip. I went into a drugstore to get some pens and Listerine. People stared at me. Made me feel like wrecking the place. On tour all you see are stages, fans and truck stops. You get used to that mode and it can be weird.

I was listening to the radio the other day in California and one of our songs came on and I jumped because I couldn't find my microphone. Now that's damage.

When I was in 10th grade chemistry class, I had a teacher named General Price. One day in class, he was showing us how alkali metals react in water. He dropped a little hunk of sodium in a beaker of water and it went pop. Not much happened. We weren't impressed. He cut off a big old hunk of sodium and dropped it into the beaker. This time it went POW! General Price yelled, "HIT IT!" and dove to the floor behind the lab table. It was great. War damage. He came up a few seconds later and mumbled that he was sorry. During fire drills, the sound of the buzzer did something to his head, made him freak out. He would run up and down the hall yelling, "EVACUATE! EVACUATE! GOD DAMN IT!" He once told me, "Henry, you don't get to be a general by being namby-pamby." What a strange word. He's my favorite General.

12.7.84 OKLAHOMA CITY OK: Did the two sets last night. Played good. Slept at some guy's house. Now sitting in the Ryder waiting to leave. I think we play two sets tonight. I think my throat will be okay — held out okay yesterday. During the second set, the crowd was that curious college type. They have what I call "R.E.M. Sensibilities" and Black Flag has a tendency to make them react in strange ways. There was this one girl who looked like Madonna Jr. She massaged my feet and stared at me without smiling. Guess I didn't fuck with her R.E.M. Sensibilities.

Now in Tulsa at the club. It's sunny outside and raining inside. No, really. There's holes in the ceiling and the water is pouring in. Buckets all over the place. A few minutes ago, an entire ceiling panel fell down followed immediately by a shitload of water.

12.9.84 KNOXVILLE TN: At the club. Played in Memphis last night. Real good show. All the bands played good. I slept in the truck last night. It wasn't very cold outside. I went to Vanderbilt University to do an interview for the radio station there. Another typical trip.

Later: One thing that saves me — the ability to live by myself. I have learned over the years that I need to exist on my own. The last two days I've had all these people treat me like a fucking celebrity. I understand that none of it's real. What they say, what they think. If I can keep that fact in my mind, I'll be able to keep up what I'm doing.

I did this college interview today. I couldn't relate to the people asking the questions. Their conversations seemed ridiculous. I hear all

ALBUQUERQUE, NM, 12.4.84 *(D.D.W.)*

these people talking and I can't believe that they're serious. Okay, I'll just assume that I'm the one who is full of it and I'll just keep to myself. I feel confused and resolved at the same time. My thoughts and dreams plague me and keep me from sleeping. I feel at ease with alienation. I have allies — DISCIPLINE and INSANITY. With these by my side, everything is everything.

12.10.84 NASHVILLE TN: In the truck with a flashlight. Played okay tonight. Voice giving me trouble. I have a lump in my throat — literally. It's gross. Every time I swallow I can feel it. Makes me feel cancerous. Lots of drunks tonight acting stupid. I hate drunks. One guy from Jason & the Nashville Scorchers came up to me after the show and said I reminded him of Charles Manson. Girls trying to scam on me. One girl told me she loved me. Give me a break.

12.15.84 AMHERST MA: There hasn't been much time to write. We had three cool shows in Tennessee. We were driving out of Knoxville toward DC. Two hours into the eleven hour trip, the Rat Van broke down. We spent our day off sitting around Bristol, VA waiting to get the van fixed.

By 4:30 p.m., we found out that the van couldn't be fixed there. Highlights of our stay in Bristol include the following incidents. Davo and I went to a Wendy's to get some salad. We looked real sleazy, dirty and unshaven. Neither one of us had slept the night before. We ordered our food. The lady gave us everything "to go" even though we had said that we wanted it for here. It was clear that we were not wanted inside Wendy's. Of course, Davo and I sat down and proceeded to eat slowly. I started to notice that everyone in Wendy's was staring at us. Fine. The best ones were these two well-to-do ladies sitting behind Davo. They were staring at us real hard. One lady on the left took one bite of her burger, looked at me and said, "I can't eat this." The counter lady came over to the woman. She pointed at her food and then at us. Our appearance and conversation bummed this gal into nausea. Triumph!

Davo hooked the bumper of the Ryder on a phone pole and pulled the bumper out so it looked like a battering ram. We hitched the van to the Ryder and took off to DC. I'm the only one who went in the van while it was being towed. I liked it, looking up and seeing no one at the wheel.

We arrived in DC at about 2:30 a.m. We left the next morning for NYC for our show at the Ritz. Ratman stayed behind with the van to get it repaired.

12.16.84 SYRACUSE NY: At the club. I got the shit shocked out of me the last time I played this place. The Ritz show was real cool. Played hard and a lot of people came. People wouldn't leave me alone. I went down to the men's room. I'm in the stall and some guy starts knocking on the door. "Hey Henry! Hey, come out. Fuckin' Henry, alright!" This waitress cornered me and started working on me. She managed to tell me her name, her age and the fact that she was sexually viable, all in one sentence. Incredible. I spent most of the night sitting in the dressing room waiting to play. The crowd was cool, they sure didn't used to be. NYC used to be a fucked up gig for us. It's strange how places change.

We took off to Adams, MA after the show. Mitch Bury of Adams, Mass scheduled me for an appointment with a throat doctor. The doctor took a look at my throat, made me hold all these notes and stuff. He told me that my vocal chords were swollen about three times their normal size and that they were infected. He told me that I should stop singing for at least ten days. I can't do that. It makes me mad sometimes. I like playing, but now it hurts so much that I wince at soundcheck. We can't afford to cancel shows. I don't want to sing. I am tearing up what little voice I have. I shouldn't be playing, but there's no choice. I ripped my shoulder up somehow, can't lift my arm above my head. Makes carrying the equipment difficult.

Playing in Adams: Went well until the security guys came for their pay. They were just off-duty cops. The pigs were yelling at Mitch, calling him a "prick". The pigs wanted to be paid in cash. Mitch wanted a receipt for his income tax. The pigs made it clear that if Mitch wanted a receipt, he was going to have "trouble" in the future. What can you do? That's why I'm overjoyed when pigs get cut down.

Later: Just did three interviews — two regular ones and a video one for the local public station. Relatively painless I guess.

We played at the University of Massachusetts at Amherst last night. I was sleeping on the floor next to the stage. I was awakened when something smacked me in the face. I got up and there was this guy standing there. He said, "Get up, Henry." I picked up this metal trash can and bashed the guy with it. No problem. Otherwise it was a good night. The penicillin is helping my voice.

The show was videotaped for the University. They were filming people in the crowd. This one girl was interviewed. She was telling me about it. She told me how the camera people "amused" her. She pulled up her sleeve and showed me about 9-12 cigarette burns along with three safety pins skewered in her flesh. The "amusement" went more than one way I bet.

So now I'm sitting in the cold, damp club waiting to play. Today's drive was bleak, cloudy, gray and cold. Houses out in the middle of nowhere, not much more than rundown shacks. Sometimes I feel like one of those houses — cold, dark and vacant. I need to have some time to myself. Maybe in January when I get back from tour.

Life has no instruction manual. Parts and labor can be impossible to find. Many go down the road with parts that are in great need of service. A breakdown is eventual.

12.17.84 SYRACUSE NY: At a Denny's a few blocks down from the show. Played hard. Lots of creeps. People telling me what to do. Lots of people talking to me, saying nothing. After the show, I hid in the DJ booth so people wouldn't do their autograph trip. Shoulder feeling better. Not getting left alone enough. I have become this celeb type. Crowds make lots of noise when I hit the stage. It's always Henry this, Henry that. It's cool I guess. Most of the people are real great and mean well, but it can be a drag. When I hear my name yelled, spoken or mentioned, I wince. I'm sitting in a dark corner, writing and someone will sit down and start talking. Some guy says, "Are you busy?" Come on! I'm sitting there with my head down, writing away and this guy asks me if I'm busy. I say, "Yeah, I am." The guy leaves mad. Well shit, what can you do?

Later: Quebec, Canada. I feel like I've been in Europe all day. Everything reminds me of it — the restaurants, the signs, the people — everything. It was cold and raining today. I have slept about 2-3 hours. The border guards had us tied up for a long time. They searched the van and the Vitusmobile, shaking out socks, pulling out window liners, the works. They jerked us around for two and a half hours. Been driving since last night. My throat aches. Awww, isn't life a drag? I haven't been to Quebec since the 1982 summer tour. The people in the crowd didn't speak English. They were polite and reserved, but real cool. Shoulder feeling better. I need some sleep. The weather is a lot warmer than we expected. The promoter told us that the Canadian post office opened up the promo stuff we sent and confiscated it. They were crass enough to send a letter telling the promoter. The Post Service said that we were immoral. That's cool. I'm waiting for the PA to be hooked up. All around me, I hear people speaking in French.

THE SOOKEY BROS.

12.18.84 QUEBEC CANADA: Show over. About 30-40 people. The gig really wasn't all that bad. It wasn't easy playing tonight. I fell asleep on the floor after soundcheck and woke up feeling like a popsicle. That's life. We're getting ready to load out the equipment. I don't look forward to this, considering I can barely keep my eyes open. The old throat has had it. I've got no volume at all.

Load-out finished except for a couple of things. I can't load anymore tonight. I'm beat. I'll be glad when the tour is over. I'm into the playing, but I'm not into tearing my throat up and I don't like to play when I can't give it my all. I need a break from being in front of people. It's a welcome relief to be able to walk around without people talking to you or pointing and whispering.

Later: Got some sleep. Feel okay. At the same house when Black Flag played here in '82. It's snowing hard outside. We have 180 miles to go. Travel will be slow. Throat is feeling good. The pain and swelling are down. Shoulder is pounding. It's time to bail for Montreal.

Now in Montreal. Sitting in a Dunkin' Donuts located 4 or 5 doors away from the club. Load-in was okay. Up some steep stairs but I'm still here. The doors open in about 90 minutes. Nazareth are playing a few doors up the street tonight. Remember them? This old queen is staring at me. Everyone speaks French. They seem to get offended when I speak English. My right knee is aching. Makes carrying stuff hard. I guess it's the cold that causes this.

A couple of years ago, we played in Montreal and my right knee just fell apart. That ended the tour. I eventually had the knee operated on and had some cartilage removed. I'm looking out on a busy, well lit street. Lots of flashing neon, colorful window displays. People hurrying home, hurrying in and out of stores. A vagrant man just walked in — ate half of a donut that was on a table. People looked at him with disgust. I'm a foreigner. I like this feeling. It's a change. It humbles me. This is always good. Nazareth's semi totally eclipses the street. I watch the people pass against a clean white background. They look like they're on display. The vagrant comes up to me and shows me two books he has written. They have his picture on them. I don't speak French, he doesn't speak English. He goes away. No, I'm not a writer, but I bet I look like a bum! I walk around here and I forget that I am playing. I don't remember what I'm here for at all. The people on the street appear to be happy, but they barely show it. Maybe they are protecting their little happiness, keeping it warm under their coats. They walk quickly, briefly glance at me, look at my limp and move past me. It's getting close to soundcheck.

I hate the inside of dingy clubs. They're so dark and depressing. I wonder if that's to get you in the mood to drink yourself into a stupor. Why do they call it Happy Hour? Because the rest of the time these places are lonely pits of carpeted limbo.

Now in the club. This place is a hole. Out of one hole and into the next. I will be in places like this for the rest of my life. Maybe at some point when my throat has been surgically removed, I can get a job working construction. I spend a lot of time with my brain on idle. Touring burns me out. Drive... Load... Play... Load... Drive or sleep depending on what's happening. I must look pretty ragged. People look at me with disgust, distaste or fear a lot of times. Who do they look up to? Cops? Someone they saw on TV? What do they think of themselves? Fuck this.

12.21.84 CHICAGO IL: At my usual hangout, McDonald's. Drinking coffee and getting some time to myself. The Montreal show was okay. Fell asleep on a couch upstairs and woke up with all these skinhead guys around me. They asked me all these questions. I wished for a place to hide. I'm starting to crack a little. I can feel it. I wanted to jump out of my skin rather than talk to those people. I hid after the show so that I wouldn't have to deal. The next night was London, Ontario. We played this dismal bar-hotel place. When we loaded in, all these drunk half-dead people just watched us work. It was real depressing to be in there. I played real hard last night. I barely remember the set. During one song, my right side started to shake uncontrollably. I split for Chicago. In a situation like this, I usually have a lot to write down. I feel burned out, exhausted. Last night I was riding in the back of the Ryder. I heard a voice. The voice said, "Check it out... Henry." I said, "What? Check out what?" Nothing answered back. Fell asleep. Woke up and when the Ryder door opened, some border guard said, "Rise and shine. Time to meet Immigration." Emma? Emma Gration? Never heard of her. Got back in the truck after doing the dance with these jerks. A few of our guys pissed in the parking lot just to show them. I woke up a few times and ended up here in this McDonald's. I feel real sore. I can hardly move my neck and shoulders. I need to pull out for a little while. I know I have to. I am starting to flake, burn out and burn up. An ambulance came to the McDonald's. Two attendants led this smiling black lady out. As she passed me, I noticed the shit stains on her pants. The ambulance took her away. I feel like a zombie. This has been a long train. The discipline and the insanity are much stronger than I am. They're taking their toll on my body. I looked in the mirror last night. I look like I have miniature black eyes. What a drag. The other bummer is that I have started to lose weight again. That's okay. I'll finish these shows and then I'll get some rest. The weight will come back. It sure is strange to travel so much. The only thing that remains a constant is the Ryder, the set and the load-in. There's a man sitting across from me who has been writing steadily since I came in here over an hour ago. I wonder what his trip is. I wonder what mine is. These shows leave me feeling broken up and shallow. I hope I never have a night like Montreal again. Seclusion is the key to keeping it together for the next few weeks. I have no idea how I will handle.

Now sitting in the Metro. Feeling a bit more awake. Went back to McDonald's, got some more coffee. Load-in starts pretty soon. The rain has stopped. The sun is coming out. It's pretty warm outside. I walked past these mirrors. Man, did I look old! Ha! Old Man Rollins. Where's my wisdom? Nowhere in sight. Time to load in.

Load-in done. I fatigue a lot faster now. Just tired I guess.

12.22.84 CANADIAN BORDER: At the border office trying to get into Canada again. Apparently our papers are not together. The promoter from Winnipeg is being called now. The temperature is 20 below zero. I was freezing cold from running ten yards from the truck to the customs building. Now people have decided that this is the time to lose ID's and equipment lists.

The Chicago show was one to remember. Some people were not too happy with the ticket price the promoter slapped on. They took out their grievances on the security and the band. The shit bums me out. I hate having to listen to the bullshit. Trying to get left alone in the dressing room and these people come in, sit down and make themselves at home. The head security comes in to talk to me about all the shit that went down. I need this? No. Fuck you. It's nights like this that make me act the way I do. It makes me want to run away and hide. I'm sick of people. Drunks yelling my name, spitting on me. I don't need it. Some guy jumped onstage, kicked me in the side as he jumped off. Just another night. I hope we get out of the cold tonight. It will kill us if we don't. It's funny. I'm watching myself come to the end of my rope. It looks pretty ridiculous. I think I'm losing my crackers. A lot of things that are important to me aren't anymore. I wish I had something in my head, but I don't. This has been the usual for a couple of weeks.

12.23.84 WINNIPEG CANADA: 35 degrees below out. I'm sleeping in a closet. Got some soup in me, feel okay. Going to try to sleep. I talk too much. Believe it. Slept okay. Pretty warm. If you live in Miami or in the desert or some shit, here are a few descriptions of a place that is radically different than the place you live in. Breathing outside: Inhale and the hairs on the inside of your nose freeze. Exhale and they melt. Fine. You walk ten yards outside and everything in you says, "Fuck it, I'm bailing."

Now here's an update. None of the vehicles will start. The tow trucks have come and gone. It looks like we will be getting a new Ryder — a Canadian Ryder equipped for cold. Ratman says that if the PA can't thaw enough, the speaker cones will shatter. The cables have been brought inside so they can thaw. If they are unwound, they will snap. It's now 5:00 p.m. We were supposed to be at the hall about four hours ago. It's supposed to hit 45 below tonight. I don't know why we're here. Thanks, Chuck... I just went outside, the snow makes a queer crunching sound underneath my feet. Why did I go outside? To get my stash of granola from the Ryder. That was a pretty long trip, about 1-1/2 minutes. Froze my ass off. I guess at some point, we will be loading in tonight. How? Somehow! The weather report says that we are in "the frostbite region," temperature-wise. I'm just sitting here inside my closet, passing time. Feeling mighty low right now, things being what they are. Looks like the Ryder is going to get towed to the club. We unload it and the Ryder folks are going to try to work on it at the club. I'm just hanging around. This day has been suffocating.

12.26.84 EDMONTON CANADA: At the hall. Got here last night. Took us about 24 hours of straight driving to get here. Still freezing cold outside. Maybe tomorrow will be warmer. The show in Winnipeg was okay. Lots of "We have been waiting years to see you. You assholes better be good," and shit from the audience.

It's hard to find quiet anywhere. I'm constantly around people that talk a lot, but say nothing. A sad case — the singer in St. Vitus brought his woman on tour. I asked her what she does for a living. She said she "watches the house." She said that it's okay because Scotty makes enough for them both. She doesn't want Scotty to go on tour because she doesn't like it. What kind of shit is that? She wants him to quit. What a drag. It's no real concern of mine. But still, what a drag to go out with a ball-and-chain woman. Tonight we're playing in a roller rink. It's cold in here. Load-in highlights: I carried in the soundboard — an all metal case. My hands froze to it like a popsicle. Oh man, that shit hurt.

   Show was so-so last night. Lots of stupid punkers at the show. I told them that Jello was a narc, a government-paid agent. That bummed their lives real bad. Some people beat up the van, busted out the headlights, ripped off the windshield wipers and side view mirrors. That's why I don't like you. That's why I don't answer your letters. That's why I don't want anything to do with you. I'm getting sick of Canada. I don't like stupid drunks and sub-zero temperatures. After tonight there's only one more show in Vancouver. Vancouver is Drunkville. People make me sick. I am burning out. I'm getting the lumps in my throat again. I ran out of the medicine that the doctor gave me. I'm having trouble sleeping. I can only manage about four or five hours at a time. Something will give at some point.

That's all the journal left from 1984. After completing the shows in Northeastern Canada we drove to Vancouver. We played the last show of the year there and that was it. I went down to Seattle and did a spoken gig on New Year's and then flew down to LA. It sure was great to get out of that cold. It was one hell of a year.

   One thing that Bill the drummer said to me in a restaurant a few days before we hit Canada. I was saying that this was pretty fucked. He said, "Yeah, but it beats working at Burger King — flat out." He was right. If you ever want to do anything that amounts to anything, then you're going to have to go hard.

MUGGER'S SURFBOARD (GLEN E. FRIEDMAN)

BOSTON, MA / 6.30.85 (CHRISTIAN WILSON)

KIRA ROESSLER / 1985

1.3.85: Yeah, on a plane. The rest of the tour went okay. Lots of cold, but what the hell. The Lhasa Club show was real cool. That was last night. Have not slept as of yet. LA was warm. Got almost a pound of coffee, my filters and my plastic thing. The temperature in Madison was +7. Luxury. I don't really feel like writing.

1.22.85 SHED: It's been almost three weeks since I wrote in this book. I finished the spoken word tour. It was cool. People were great. I have been here about a week now. Book almost done. This girl Staci is going to help me proofread and type out some of the pieces. Not much to tell. All I do is practice, work out, and work on stuff at the Ginns'. I am feeling okay these days. Working hard on my stuff. My mind is a blank. Nothing worth writing down. I wish there was. I really like writing here.

1.27.85 AT DEIRDRE'S: Saw X last night. Their new songs sound good. People bothered me. I missed a few songs because people would not leave me alone. I hate going out. Almost every show I go to that's not one I am playing at is the same trip. The Black Flag instrumental set at Fender's was real cool. Those guys really blaze. Kira went into the bathroom and this big old woman beat her up and smashed her hand into one of the stalls. Kira's hand was all fucked up, but she played the gig anyway. She's tough. I don't like her very much, but I sure respect her.

1.30.85: I watch Pettibon a lot. He does so many drawings. He's my favorite artist. He's brilliant. He makes no phone calls. I wish I didn't have to make phone calls. I don't want to talk to anybody except for a few. I got a letter from some guy in Kansas who said that it must be nice to get to tell everyone what I think and get "$$$." Fuck. I guess I do it because I'm a "$$$" hungry, bloated, self-centered bastard. Oh, it feels so good to come clean — to get it right out in the open!

RAYMOND PETTIBON (*ED COLVER*)

I walked to and from practice today. I walk down Artesia Boulevard and back. I always look inside the bars that litter the strip. The men inside are faceless. They don't move. They stand or sit at the bar — frozen. Some of the bars open at six in the morning. Drink to insulate. Drink to escape. Drink to get swallowed up. I guess it feels okay. The neon beer sign shines like a lover's eyes, an island, a watering hole. If every night is a Saturday night, when does the week end?

I think the Family Man's dog died. If he's still alive, he sure is quiet. Whenever I run by the house, I always make sure to spit on his driveway no matter how dry my mouth is. I wonder how many quarts I've laid on that driveway over the years. It might be cool if the spit all reconstituted at once and formed the sign of the cross or some cool holy type shit.

When my first girlfriend and I would have sex, her chest and neck would turn bright scarlet for some hours afterwards. Her mother would always know and tell her that God would strike us down. She used to say it with such conviction, she almost had me believing it. It would have been cool if she turned red, but have the red part in the shape of a cross on her chest. A sign! I bet that girl is married now and turns red all the time. Her mother thought I was a creep.

The lady that does the 8 to 4 shift at the 7-11 on Artesia and Prospect really bums when I come in at 2 or 3 in the morning. I always make sure to take my time and act like Jack Nicholson. She doesn't like this. We're always alone in the store. She always says, "Is that all for you?" I just stare at her. She always gives me back my change by putting the bills down first — the change on top. She pushes it forward and attends to some minor detail of the cash register as if there's someone right behind me. One of these days, she's going to blow my brains out. She's probably a cop. The guys who work the day shift are for sure. They probably get in real good with the kids at Mira Costa High School and try to bust them for pot or something. Come on, you go in there and tell me what you think. Maybe all 7-11's are headquarters for police surveillance all across the U.S.A. We are being watched as we play video games, cook in the microwave, and buy Rolling Stone magazine. Under those dopey orange and white smocks lies a badge and a chest to pin it on, fella. So watch it. Don't say I didn't warn you.

2.2.85 SHED: Saw *Maria's Lovers*. Yes, another Nastassia Kinski flick. You know, you get about twenty minutes in and you're saying this is awful. I'm trapped! I want to leave! The five dollars I paid, anchors me to my seat like a cement condom. So I sit, watching her lips, her nipples and her eyes. Meanwhile, my ears were pummeled by some of the dumbest dialogue imaginable. I watched the chubby guy in the leather pants in the row ahead of me maul his girlfriend. To keep my dinner in my stomach, I diverted my gaze back to the screen. Nastassia is masturbating. She sounds like someone is lancing her with punji sticks. The poor gal is in the fetal position and convulsing. Is this the way girls do it? Whoa.

Busted out of there and went to see Exene read at McCabe's. She was great. I watched from the control room and left right after so I wouldn't have to talk to anybody.

I took my book to the printer yesterday. The typesetting will be finished in about a week. Writing is nice, but I see how some people who do it for a living can slip and lose touch with what's going on around them. It can be very insulating — very isolating. The outside world is nasty, dirty, hostile and at the same time of course, very nice. All it takes is one person to turn a good day into a day in Philadelphia.

Things like going to McCabe's are what bring me down. I don't like idle conversation. I don't like handshakes, introductions, the same questions over and over. I don't like looking at pretty girls because it hurts and makes me lonely. So I bail back to my planet. It makes me wonder why I go out on stages in front of people. Maybe it's because it's the most alienating, humiliating, emptying thing I have found. I am a coward of course. In alienation, there is no pain. It's a drug. I will play in front of 800 people who all know my name, finish the show and feel so used up and lonely that I want to curl up and die. I start to hate the people who cheer for me. The more they like me, the lower I sink. I lie down alone on the floor of whatever hovel I'm sleeping in that night and I am empty. But I can feel it and this is good. It hurts good. The hurt feels good. You want more. You want to get more high, more gone — more pain. Goddamn right. More pain. In pain, there is no pain and that's the escape.

The story must be told. There is a house I pass by almost every day. On the balcony of the house there is a sign: *Forget the Dog, Beware of the Owner*. Underneath the writing is a drawing of a gun barrel and six slugs pointed right at your face. Occasionally I see the inhabitants. It's usually two to three men. They are big and muscular. They hang out on the balcony and sun themselves. They blast music real loud, stuff like Quiet Riot, Motley Crue, etc. They drink Coors. I see the empties in their trash cans when I walk back from 7-11. They're great. One of them has a Cadillac. The license plate says "BIG DOGG." I like walking by their house when they're partying down on the weekend. There's hot looking girls in bikinis lounging in deck chairs. BIG DOGG and his buddies have the bar-b-que going and the Coors Light flowin' and Quiet Riot riotin'. I remember walking by once and some of them laughing at me. I kept on walking, but I was thinking, "A bullet for you, fucker." Today I was walking past the house. BIG DOGG was out there putting a nice finish on that stylin' Caddy. A wide-eyed blonde haired girl was holding a rag for him. I loved how she watched him wax the BIG DOGG mobile. She looked at me. I kept moving before I started laughing. Today they were playing Jimi Hendrix. The song was "If Six Was Nine". I passed the house at the point where Hendrix says, *"White collared conservatives flashing down the street / Pointing their plastic finger at me / Hoping soon my kind will drop and die..."* BIG DOGG is singing along. I kept on walking as usual.

2.3.85 Shed: Just got back from seeing Deep Purple at the Long Beach Arena. They were real good. The high point of the show was seeing a girl with a shirt that said "Dad is God" across the front. The shed is cold. I am cold. People bum me out. About an hour ago, I was sitting in the house going through Pettibon's new work and I heard a girl outside saying stuff like, "Don't... Stop... Stop, you're hurting me!" Adrian and I peeked outside. It was the girl across the street and her father arguing. Yow! 21st Street wild life. I bet the Family Man has it all down on videotape.

2.4.85 Shed: Just got back from Al's Bar. Black Flag played an instrumental set. It was great. I sang on two jams. Billy Bragg played after. Not bad, seemed like a cool guy. I don't like going to shows anymore. Can't have a good time. People don't leave me alone. I walked offstage and stood in a corner. Black Flag went on for another jam. This girl came up to me and said, "I have to talk to you about a few things." I just stared at her. "You and I have a lot of mutual friends." I said, "That's impossible." I mean I have less friends than fingers on my left hand. "How come you're not up there?" she said, pointing to the stage. I just stared at her. She repeated the question. I just stared. She walked away. What am I supposed to say? I don't have anything to say to this girl. I don't fit. I get at a loss for words. I don't read the papers. I don't read magazines. I can't understand these people. I like the shed. Nobody here. Nobody yelling my name. I have something to say. I write. I "sing" songs. That's all people need to hear from me. They don't even need that. People come up and talk to me about real nowhere stuff like, "How's DC?", "What's up?" or "Do you know this girl? She says you tried to rape her." You've got the wrong guy. Go have another Bud, bud. Be cool and leave me alone. I don't think I am better than anyone. I am tired of people treating me like I was something off a shelf.

People can think anything they want about me. I care less than anyone could believe. I read about myself in magazines. They don't have a clue. It's good comedy material. If they knew what they were talking about, they wouldn't have to write about it. Whoa, how profound. My inability to be social is purely my own fault. I can't care about hairstyles after seeing some lady's brains splattered all over a wall from the shotgun she put to her head. The gossip column of the LA Weekly is not the real world to me after being held down and beaten. Someone has problems with me because I'm a "rock star" for getting mentioned in Hit Parader. This isn't the real world to me. Of course, some guy who lives in his Mom's condo knows what's hip for me. I'm just lame. Don't bother, I'm hopeless. If you want to "get radical", if you're hardcore… if you are, spike up your hair, put your boots on and go take a walk in Watts. Go take a little trip to East LA. You'll get all the punk rock you want. Skip Al's Bar, La De Da and Club Lingerie. Go downtown and really thrash. You'll cancel your subscription to Flipside. Pray that some Crips don't decide to come to Melrose Avenue and party down. If anything like that happens, your pose will be burned to the ground. Imagine fifteen young males pulling a train on Siouxsee Sioux and her Banshees. Lord have mercy! At that point, the fun will really be over.

2.5.85: Back from practice. Went okay. My throat hurts from it. Got more letters today. I read them and threw them away. I have nothing to say. Sometimes I would like to stay in the shed and the back yard forever. It's nice here. Trees, sun, a nice big hunk of sky, hummingbirds, spiders… I like it here.

There is a distance from myself and the rest of the band and crew. I can feel it. I felt it tonight. That's alright. I mean, it's okay with me. Whatever they want is fine. I think they're cool folks. I don't care what they think of me. They don't live in my world. No one does. I'm glad of it. Not much went on today. Just one of those days I hate. My mind wanders like a bum with a rail pass. I have to get up in a few hours to go shoot this cable thing for TV. I should be back here before noon. Fine. I have to work out. I have nothing in my head. I sure wish I did. Ian told me that he wanted to come out and visit here. I guess he never got it together. I don't want to think about it. Things are dropping out of my life. I wonder when it will end and where I'll be.

2.7.85 SHED: Did a cable show with Brewer and Dukowski this morning. They were great. Practice was cool. Did "Modern Man" for the first time in a long time. I watched Ray tonight. He sat in his room with the lights off and the TV on. He doesn't say a word to anyone. I think he's really feeling low. Ms. Ginn asked me about him. She notices everything. Walked to and from practice today. It's the only time when I feel free. At the Ginns', the phone can find me. That's a drag sometimes. So I walk down Artesia toward the post office to check on my box. Someone yells my name out of a car window and I jump out of my skin. Jangles my nerves. I keep walking, never jaywalking. You don't want to do that

HENRY AND CHUCK, REDONDO BEACH, CA / 1985 *(NAOMI PETERSEN)*

around these parts. You can get nailed by pigs. I go to my box, some guy says, "Hi, Henry." I say nothing. I have nothing. This is my time. I'm not Henry. I'm nothing — no one.

I leave the post office and keep walking down Artesia Boulevard toward the practice place. Another car goes by and someone yells, "Hey, Henry!" It startles the shit out of me. I wish for the desert… the shed. I cross the street and go to the practice place. We practice the new songs. I like them. After practice, I walk back up Artesia toward the sea, back to the Ginns'. I look into all the bars as I walk by. I breathe in every doorway of every bar. They always smell the same. Like depression. Like loneliness. Like losers on a losing spree. Come on in. The lights are low and the losing's free. Our doors are open. We have a warm seat waiting for you. I pass by the market. No one inside except for the cashier and two Mexican men who are buying beer. I walk on. Not bad tonight. Not as cold as the night before. I wonder how many times I have walked this route and how many people I know are narcs. I don't know either figure. I cross Aviation Boulevard where the Denny's light always catches my eye. I eat at Denny's all over the US. I wonder what the special is this month.

After a while, I reach the Ginns'. I am tired. I got about an hour's sleep last night. My head is pounding. The last dose of aspirin must have worn off. If I don't take aspirin, I have a constant, drilling headache that drives me to distraction. I go into the shed. I turn on KCRW. Snap #201 is on. I read, write, think, play music and wait until I fall asleep.

2.8.85 SHED: Listening to the *Joe Frank at Midnight* show on KCRW. Very depressing. He really knows how to get you good. He's from Washington DC. I didn't practice tonight. Throat hurts pretty bad. Been in the shed most of the day and night. I don't even remember anything about today. The nights are bad. Every dream is a nightmare. They come one after the other. They make me wake up. I think they're real. I talk out loud. It takes me a while to realize that it's a dream. I sleep alone on the floor here in the shed. It's cold in here. I sleep in sweatpants, a sweatshirt and socks. I have two sheets, a blanket and a sleeping bag covering me. I just don't like the dreams — the voices. I dread sleep. I wish I could be awake all the time. I am finding that I can hardly deal with people anymore. Sometimes just the sight of them makes me want to hurt and destroy. I must hold on to myself. I must hold on. Sometimes I want to reach out to someone. A second later, I think of the futility of such an action. I think of the one fucking thing that's always there.

D.I.E. — Discipline, Insanity and Exile. That's what I see and it makes me smile. I laugh at myself. I laugh with myself. Fear and horror. Fear is a powerful blade in your mind. It's a motivation and a sensory enhancer. To succumb to fear is to be weakened. To make friends with fear is calming. Fear is a friend.

Walking down the streets. Walking among the handshakers. I don't want to shake hands. When someone extends their hand to shake yours, smile and keep your hand at your side. Watch the person's eyes. Something happens. Something becomes unsettled, unsure. This is good. In unsureness is awareness. Walking among the handshakers. Feeling them, feeling their lives. What do I fear? I fear the day I have no fear.

Saccharine Trust is playing and this huge guy with two Black Flag tattoos and a Black Flag shirt sees me and comes over. He's drunk. He yells over the music, spewing beer spit all over my face. We're supposed to be carrying on a conversation over the volume of the music. He tells me he is from Germany and all this other bullshit. I can barely understand him, and he's spitting on my face and his breath stinks. He won't leave me alone and I want to get the hell out of here because I just came to see the fucking bands play. Finally I just bail and go in the dressing room and my Deutsch friend comes busting in yelling, "Where is the rock star?" I don't like going out into the world of handshakers.

At least the bands were cool. The girl who was talking to me earlier ran up and hugged me. I pushed her away from me. There is a party tonight. Black Flag instrumental, SWA and Raszebrae are playing. I'm not there. I don't have the need to feel even more crummy than usual. The more I stay away from things like this, the more I want to. It feels nice to let go. I'll let the winners party down for me. I'll just stay here and lose on my own. I feel lonely when I'm on my own. But I feel even more lonely when I am in a room full of people. I feel the alienation. Here alone, there is nothing to make a comparison or contrast to. This is okay. I am not in the shed right now. It's been raining the last few days. The shed leaks water like a screen door. There are glasses, ashtrays and buckets in all the appropriate places. Pretty damp in there. Some of my tapes got it pretty good and so did the rug. I woke up last night in a big wet spot. It's like camping I guess. Played a tape of an old DC band called the Enzymes. This tape has a live cut on it from a club called Scandals. If you listen carefully, you can hear the singer/guitar player Dave Byers yell, "Bring back Henry, you motherfuckers!" That brought back memories.

Earlier that night, I was hanging out on Wisconsin Avenue with some people when two big bouncers from a strip joint down the street came up to us. They gave a "Wet T-Shirt Night" flyer to this girl Melissa. I thought that was pretty gross and I spat a mouthful of Coke and ice on one of them. The guy said, "We'll be back for you." Later on that night, I was dancing around as the Enzymes were playing. Two bouncers escorted me out in wristlocks. I thought they were bouncers from the club. Okay, fine — I'm being thrown out. So what. They took me outside and walked me around the corner. Oh yeah, *those* bouncers. They proceeded to work me over. I had a leather wristband on. They took it. As they were leaving, I told him to give it back to me. The one who had it said, "Come and get it." I did. This bouncer and I proceeded to beat the shit out of each other. That guy was big. He tore my pants open and tried to rip my balls off. I was pounding his face as best I could. Two people broke it up. The cops were coming. I split, ran down an alley and made it to Häagen-Dazs. I was pretty messed up. I pulled my pants down — my underwear was soaked in blood. I laughed. Shit, I don't use the parts much, but please let me remain intact until a fairly ripe age! I felt around. Okay, close enough. That was a pretty sound beating. My right nut swelled up to the size of a hen's egg. I walked rather funny for a couple of weeks. Just another Wednesday night in DC. It sure was cool hearing that tape.

2.13.85 SHED: Not much went on today. Got some interesting mail. I walked down Artesia Boulevard to practice. I use Artesia to monitor the world. Highlights: Walking past the Lucky Market, saw a man blow up at a phone booth. He tried to rip the receiver away from the cord. The cord wouldn't give. The man got even madder. He smashed the phone into the booth and stormed off. I was walking past the Gulf station at Artesia and Aviation. I was in the middle of the driveway when this car pulls in. The woman inside is mad because I won't move fast enough for her liking. She yells at me. I give her the old Hitler salute. She bums. Fine. Saw a kid rip off a Creem magazine at the 7-11 at Artesia and Phelton. Real slick mover, that kid. He bent down, wrapped it around his leg, rolled his sock over it and bailed out of the store. Kids in Iron Maiden shirts playing videos and hanging out.

Someday those kids will grow up and they will stand behind the counter. Now it's just a dream. But isn't it everybody's dream? To don that orange and white smock. To have your own little name tag. To stand with your feet planted solidly, facing front proudly. Only turning to fill an order for a Big Gulp or a Slurpee. "Oh, 7-11. Man, it's 4 a.m. and everything's closed. Who can I turn to, but you?" (Hey little lady, I'll help you with that microwave!) Have you ever looked into the cold drink section? Have you ever seen that familiar orange and white smock bobbing around back there? Bet you'd like to know what goes on back there. Always hoping that Channel 7 would do a behind-the-scene report. I bet. Hey! Me too! 7-11 is the pulse beat of America. I think that Bruce Springsteen should do a little number about a 7-11 in Asbury Park, but write it in such a way that the entire U.S.A. can identify and slurp along with Bruce. Suck for the Boss. Hail the Boss! Hail 7-11!

For the record, sleep is getting bad. The dreams are heavy. The dreams are real. I am a freakout. I have scales. I have feathers. I have fur. I have enlarged incisors. I have claws. I have escaped the crucifixion. Stepped aside. Let the parade pass me by and pass away. I have come to drop fire. I have come to bring them to fire — to unite them with fire. Confessions of the torch. I thought I was in the Salvation Army. The Salvation Army? No! Salvation's Soldiers — saints set on destroy. Purify! Make fire! Let it come down. The joke is killing me. Let's end the joke so I can get some sleep.

2.14.85 SHED: Took a ride on a Santa Monica bus today. The #3 that goes down Lincoln. "The Blue Bus" — the one that Jim Morrison sings about in "The End". Oh brother... Anyway, I'm on the bus doing my time, watching this blind lady crab at everybody. She was a trip. Her golden retriever seeing-eye dog stepped on her boot and she even bitched at the poor pooch. Maybe that dog will get wise and lead that babe onto the 405 Freeway at rush hour.

Read for *SNAP* on KCRW on my birthday. It was cool. You can do your thing and split and not even have to shake anybody's hand.

Walked down Artesia Boulevard to practice today. No good stuff happened on the way down. A guy in a car told me to fuck off. A girl said, "I'm a fan of you guys. I just wanted to say hi," as I passed her at a bus stop near the post office. No mail today.

2.17.85 SHED: Saw John Lee Hooker last night. He was cool. He told stories and played songs. The audience was real straight, like cops and students. John Lee Hooker is a very old man. He sure looked alone up there. When he would talk, you could understand about every third word or so. About halfway through his set, people started to leave. That kind of struck me as sad. By the time he finished, most of the place had cleared out. Maybe it was just late or something. The straight people seemed to laugh at him not with him. I've never been to a blues show before. One of the most reserved crowds I had ever seen. People kept staring at me. I guessed I was an outsider to their scene.

Yesterday, Staci and I were eating at a restaurant on Artesia Boulevard. This man came up to us and said, "Do you know what today is? Today is National Raccoon Day!" He whipped out these little raccoon puppets that were on his fingers and wiggled them a bit. I took my plastic fork and started making stabbing motions at his face while whispering, "Die. Die. Die." He said, "Okay... Well, keep smiling. Goodbye!" He bailed real fast. It was cool.

Another night of bad sleep. Dreams that won't stop. There are things living in me. I should stop fighting them. I should give myself over to them. My brain is full of napalm. Airstrike to airstrike. I imagine all the people I have killed in my thoughts. I imagine them swinging from nooses that drop down from the roof of my skull. Swinging and burning. No one knows that they're there except for me. I'm going to get tattooed tomorrow. I like getting tattoos. They seal off my pores from the world. It's like a coat to put on. You are showing less of yourself — giving less of yourself to them. Less for them, more for you. This is good. Most people don't like tattoos. They say stupid things like, "Won't you regret that in 20 years?" I'd regret a wife and kids more. Tattoos are permanent. They stay on for life. They make you say something. I am no longer a Caucasian. My skin is white, black, green, red, purple, yellow, etc. I am a minority. I didn't get any Valentine's Day cards this year. This is good. The heavens are smiling on me even though I didn't buy a copy of *Thriller*.

2.18.85 SHED: Tired, but can't sleep. Don't want to sleep. The walls of the shed are tightening a little tonight. I can feel it. The walls are breathing. That's why I get these headaches.

People are weird. They are the hurters. The dead are swinging from the rafters. There's an inferno in here. A secret within a secret. Laughing, walking, holding hands with a lie. They are the cause of this. They are the cause of me. I am to blame. There were no phone calls today. I'm glad. I don't like it when people call me. I have nothing to say. Yes, I do. I don't belong here. I don't belong anywhere. I'm here. Why? The thing to do is to keep moving. Maybe the world will go away. If the world was the size of an orange, you would be holding a ball of dirt with a bunch of little parasitic creatures running all over it. You would say, "Fleas," and throw it away.

2.20.85 SHED: Speaking to you from the bottom of the well. Not much going on for the last few days. Not a lot to do right now. Got some flyers of me and Exene. Exene looks good. I look bad as usual. Walked down to the post office today. The line was too long so I bailed. I walked back up Artesia. Mira Costa High School had just gotten out and all these kids were walking down the street. They stared at me. I guess I look like a freak. I sure feel like one.

The Family Man had his station wagon in the driveway yesterday. I spat on it as I sauntered back from the printer.

Last night I had a dream that I was with my first girlfriend. We were in a car. I was driving. I was telling her what I had been up to. She just stared out the window and said nothing. I don't remember how the story went, but I remember I was feeling sad for her. That's all I remember. She seemed pathetic. I was a jerk for going out with her as long as I did. I guess I deserved the unhappiness and frustration I felt at that time. She was pretty. She told me that she was a virgin. I remember this meant nothing to me at the time. Found out she was lying anyhow. If I was late to pick her up, she wouldn't talk to me for part of the night. Like I said, she was very nice looking. My schoolmates saw her and were blown away. The school freak? Out with a girl?... A girl who looked like that? That felt good to see their mouths shut for once. She really hated the music I liked. I went out with her for sixteen

HENRY AND EXENE CERVENKA *(SUZAN CARSON)*

months. Man, that was a long time. I have never gone out with a girl nearly that long since.

I remember when her period was ten days late. I hardly ate, slept or anything else. Finally, the flood came. I was never so happy to hear that someone was bleeding before or since. After I broke up with her is when the fun started anyhow.

Imagine seeing the Damned and the Bad Brains together on one bill. It was the summer of 1979. I was still going out with her. That was the year I graduated from high school. That was one of the best nights of my life. My girlfriend wasn't around. I was hanging out with Ian. What a show. Waiting in line to get in, I saw Captain Sensible lean out of the window of the club's dressing room and tell underage kids to shimmy up the side and crawl in the window. It was great. Ian was not of age yet so we made a fake I.D. that day. It worked perfectly.

That was the first time I had ever seen the Bad Brains play. They were scary onstage. The fact that they were black blew away most of the crowd. They were great. The Damned had just put out the *Love Song* EP. I thought they were great. They did songs from the first and second album and stuff. Ian's sister, Katie got hit on the head with a bottle. She was bleeding like crazy. Rat Scabies, the Damned's drummer, dragged her up onstage and took her away. After the set, Ian, Rat, Katie and I hung out in the kitchen of the place. We eventually split and took Katie to the hospital. I remember Dave Vanian, the Damned's singer, pounding Ian on the head with the microphone in time with "New Rose". A good night.

I hate nights now. They drive me nuts. I lose my grounding. I float. My feet don't touch. I wallow in myself. I write myself to sleep. I feel like walking to the beach and disappearing under the waves. The nights are stifling. Through the window I can hear the wind whipping through the palms on 21st Street. I wish I was somewhere else. Anywhere else. Anyone else. I should go down to that bar near the shore. I could pull up a stool, get a Coors Lite and become nothing. No one.

Neutralization. Neutralize. Kill the pain. Drown the hurt. Desensitize. Embrace the non-pain. The palm fronds are slapping together. I am waiting for sleep. I sleep alone. Sleep alone, wake up alone, and so on. Pettibon is in the front room with me. I heard him say about four words today. Three of them were, "I don't care." I know how he feels. I feel like it's 1982 again. 1982 was not the greatest on my end. Felt like I'm feeling now. Nowhere with the desire to always be doing something at all times. Sleep is a disturbing experience that conjures up guilt and bad feelings. Like waking up after eight hours of sleep, slapping yourself and saying, "I could have had a V-8!"

2.22.85 SHED: Call me Mr. Rock Video. I shot a thing for cable TV today. It's called Video 22. Nice enough people, I guess. I don't like this kind of thing usually, but this was relatively painless. I got a tape of the new Nick Cave and the Bad Seeds LP and the new Einsturzende Neubauten EP. I don't know — the Bad Seeds thing is good. I guess I'll have to play it more. I have played it twice and it still has not grabbed me yet. The new Einsturzende Neubauten is great.

Walked down to Global to be driven to the interview. The people at the studio were so straight. They really glad-handed me. I see how those people do their thing. Pretty sanitized. The girl who was interviewed before me looked like Chrissie Hynde. Oh yes, I must write a thing about Vince Neil going to jail and getting fucked in the ass by all his newly-found friends.

2.23.85 SHED: Did about twelve hours of video shooting of spoken word and interviews today. I feel shitty, used up, exhausted and stupid. I did a lot of stuff in the street. All these people were watching me. I don't like being the center of attention. That's all I was today. I'm not cut out for this activity. I go out in about nine hours to start the whole thing over again. I am in such a fucked up mood, I can hardly write. I don't like it. I don't like going outside anymore. The fuckers — looking at me, pointing at me, taking from me. I don't like them. Never again. It's a sellout. It's a fucking washout. I want to wear sunglasses for the rest of my life. They can't have my eyes. The fuckers. The pigs. The fucking pigs. Never again. I swear. Just got back a few hours ago. I'm exhausted, but I can't sleep. I feel more stupid than usual.

No good, no bad — it's all okay. It's not fire and forget. It's fire and don't even bother to acknowledge. Don't even talk to them. No smile, frown, nothing except impact they must reckon with. Hitler is just the same as the fucking pig that takes from you. You think to yourself, "I'd like to kill that guy." You killed him in your mind already. Probably tortured, maimed and killed the person over and over and over in your mind. How can you think yourself better than someone who does it for real?

Show me a happily married man who works at TRW and I'll show you a man that sees a hot looking girl on the street and dreams about eating pussy.

I'm writing to cover my tracks. I'm writing an arsenal. I'm writing a coat of armor. I'm writing to get to the numbness that I crave. I can't sleep now. I never want to sleep again. I can't take my mind off wanting to cut myself up. I want it so bad. It would feel so good to bleed, but I know I should not. Sometimes I think about the cuts and how they feel — and the blood... It's almost irresistible. One of these days soon, I'll wreck myself again. I want it so bad, I can taste it.

2.24.85 SHED: Back from the last day of shooting. Today went pretty good, I think. I came home tonight and I got a letter from Diamanda Galas. She wrote me back finally. She said to call her and come on down anytime. I would like to meet her. Her voice is incredible. I am spent. I don't have anything to write down. My brain and body have had it for today. I just drank two cups of strong coffee, but I still feel like I'm dead. I hope I did okay for Randy and the crew. They worked real hard to make it happen. I hope I can return the favor at some point.

2.25.85 SHED: I go into the studio tomorrow night to start vocals for the new album. I am running out of time. I will probably be doing a spoken gig at Cal Arts on March 7. That's cool. It will be good to do some shows in different places. Greg just came in. He said that I go into the studio Wednesday night not tomorrow night. Okay, fine. I wish it was tomorrow night. I would like to start as soon as I could. When the record is finished, I will breathe a bit easier. All that video stuff I did this weekend left me feeling shallow and burned out. It sucks to have to look at yourself that hard all the time.

Later: I fell asleep. I am filled with all these bad trips. It's been going on for weeks. I walked down to my P.O. box today. Picked up my mail and walked back to the shed. Nobody bothered me. I feel spaced out. I hardly know where I am now. I don't know what I need. To move — to stay still, I don't know. I hate it. I'm starting to feel like a fucking shut-in. I don't like to be in the same place for any amount of time. I work out real hard to try to take my mind off my mind. I make me sick. Fallout shelter to fallout shelter.

She said it's pain for pain. Another sick trip, another needle in the vein. Heating up the dope in a silver spoon from your parents' kitchen. You shoot up like you fuck — like a pro. Moving down the trail, past the fuckers and the lovers and the dead things that can't get any deader, I look into the mirror and see two dead swamp eyes. In the dead swamp, the water does not flow. It hasn't for years. Stagnation, still and silent. The water is black, the bottom is nowhere in sight. The water. The dead black water is teeming with life — creatures, larvae, monsters and friends. It's not as dead as you think. My swamp is overflowing with life.

I saw a picture of a huge pile of bodies at the Belsen Death camp. All these bodies tangled up in obscene and beautiful contortions — twisted limbs and emaciated genitalia. Looked like an orgy of sorts. They moved them around with bulldozers. If they all got up at once, I wonder what kind of dance they would do.

River of ruin. In the privacy of my damnation I wait. Dry on the outside, sweating on the inside. Waiting for the summer. Waiting for the rumble to fill my ears. The mad dog summer. I'm going to be there, pressed against the window looking at you. Fallout shelter to fallout shelter. Life is a fool's game. Genocide is a walk in the park. I wonder what the dreams will be like tonight. Last night was Sadie. I dreamt of a girl named Sadie. I don't know anyone by that name. I don't remember what happened in the dream. I just remember the name Sadie. On another trail, in another fallout shelter, I wait in darkness. I wait for her. I know she will come. She'll walk right in through the wall — right to me. I can hear the roar of her wheel. I can hear the scraping of my shoes as I shuffle down Death Row. I can hear everything. Every orgasm. Every car crash. Everything.

2.26.85: At the Ginns'. Went to K-Disc today. Listened to the mastering of the October Faction LP. Sounds good. We drove through Hollywood. Lots of boy hookers — muscled out ones, girlish ones — all kinds. Anything you want. It's right there.

This girl called me tonight. She and I were hired on the same day at Haagen-Dazs years ago. She now goes to college in New York City. She told me how things are going in DC. I try to isolate myself from conversations like this. I don't want to hear about Washington DC. The news is never good. It just makes me look over my shoulder and feel crummy. I just remember the last time Black Flag played in DC. A member of the band I used to be in, gave me a lot of shit for leaving DC and doing what I'm doing. He told me I used to be cool and now I'm nothing but a rock star. That didn't make me feel guilty or anything — just hateful. I don't need that shit. He couldn't pull my workload for a week straight. So fuck him. He didn't have to lay a boatload of shit on me. Talking with him makes me never want to go back there again. People want to make you feel bad for doing anything it seems. That's fine with me. They don't understand me. They don't do anything except sit and talk and slag and grow old gracefully. I am always ready to say goodbye. Always. If you have problems with me, goodbye, okay? I'll go back home. I'll get a job. I'll get in an unambitious band. I'll practice twice a week. I won't go on tour. I won't do anything. Then will you like me? Fuck that. Fuck you. If you do what you want then people burn you. I'm charcoal-broiled.

I just saw part of the Grammy Awards. The people who got their trophies for music should have brought their briefcases with them. They thanked their managers and their costume coordinators and shit. They're not musicians. They're businessmen, stock watchers, pleasers — them.

Fuck the daughters and kill the fathers. Drive in cars. Go to the movies. Disruption is honest. It's okay to fall short. It's okay to blow it. It's okay to fuck the daughters and kill the fathers. If my father saw me, he would disown me on the spot. That is the verb they use. You are *disowned*. That is to say that you are no longer owned. Why do people fear freedom? I call it freedom not abandonment. When I say disowned, that means the chains are off. If that's the case, my father can never disown me. You can't push away what was never that close to begin with.

In a different sewer system. Nobody can hurt me as good as I can. I like it when it hurts because it's real. Breathing does not pass for living anymore. The distant summer is making a low, powerful hum. Rolling toward this town — gentle and true. It's the kind hand that will break your spine. It's the warm eyes that will break your heart. Killers smile. There is nothing but safety out there. All they can do to you is rape you, rob you, kill you, maim you, mutilate you, disfigure you and call you nasty names. But that's about it.

2.27.85 SHED: I was walking on Artesia Boulevard today. I was crossing the intersection of Artesia and Aviation. Crossing the other side was a blond haired, blue-eyed youth with a McDonald's uniform on. He was perfect. He had the steady hand and the alertness of a meat flipper for certain. He passed me and sneered. It was easy to see that I don't have what it takes to be in the ranks of the Golden Arches. I felt lowered and humiliated. I turned and watched him march down Artesia Boulevard, his cap jauntily pushed to one side. He entered the McDonald's recruiting office (the office has a poster of Mayor McCheese pointing straight ahead with the caption, "I McWant YOU!" posted on the door). That's the last I saw of him.

I walked over to the 7-11 this evening. I don't like it out there. I was walking point on Prospect Street. I saw three young girls up ahead of me, walking my way. They could have been VC. I could imagine them smiling and saying, "Hi Joe! Want to come to a party on 23rd?" And then one says, "Hey Joe, have a Coors Lite!" She reaches into her bag, pulls out a bomb and blows me up right there on Prospect. I feel a lot more comfortable when I have my M-16 with me.

I'm still thinking about that girl calling me last night. Whenever I hear about people back in Washington DC, it always makes me feel confused. I start to thinking about people back there and it makes my feet drag a bit. I lose concentration on things I really have to work hard on. I don't like the downtime — the time we are not on the road. I know that we have a lot of stuff to do, but still. I stay here and I lose my edge. I don't like being here. I'd rather be there. Wherever that is.

I can remember having sex with this one girl. I felt empty afterwards. I thought of her tonight. I wish I didn't. I don't like feeling weakened. Every day I'm here I lose a little. I can barely tell, but I can tell all the same. I go crazy being around here. I go crazy anywhere, but I need to get out of here. I could live here forever and nothing would happen. Thirty years in the shed.

Going down the trail…. Her boyfriend thinks of sex — always. He has sex on the goddamned brain! Always pawing her, messing up her makeup. He's an animal. She thinks of needles. She's always thinking of that needle. If they were in a comic strip, the drawing would depict the two walking down the street with those thought-balloons over their heads. In his balloon: a naked female from the belly button to the upper thigh. In hers: a syringe with bright white light radiating from it. *Needles and pussy*. Walking down the street — itching, sweating and going crazy.

2.28.85 SHED: I just talked to Diamanda Galas on the phone. She was real cool. She's going to call me tomorrow. She had to split to go to a singing lesson. She just got back from Europe. She will be going back soon. I can't believe that I had the guts to call her up. I sat and looked at her letter for a long time before I could do it. She was so cool to me though. I don't know what I expecting, but it was a relief to find out that she is friendly. I like her even better now.

3.1.85: I'm in the living room. I did four songs in the studio last night. That's a good night's work. That's the most I have ever done in one night. Another Friday night at the Ginns'. Today was a worthless day. I hardly did anything. I wrote — read some Edgar Allen Poe. I want to do something, but there's really nothing to do.

I was really hoping that Bruce Springsteen would die, die, die. I thought it happened in the late 70's. I said fine, okay. No more high school girls having "Bruce" parties where they all sit at one girl's house, play Bruce Springsteen records and cry. What a fucking drag that must have been for the guys. But he's back and more people than ever are bending over for the Boss. I can't imagine Americanism as a hip trend. Do you use it as a pick-up line? "Hey honey, I was born in the USA. Let's party." The Boss is a letdown. No booze, no drugs, no spandex, no pyrotechnics onstage. Your parents would like him. What a fucking bore.

I can see the troops now. Bounding over the fields in a war, singing "Born In The USA" while they catch bullets. Young males will copy Bruce's "look" — boots, blue jeans with a red handkerchief hanging out of the back pocket and a white t-shirt. The Boss looks like a stock gay boy. This is good. These kids will go downtown and get it good — the hard way — *the American way*.

This is sickness. Rock music breeds soldiers and killers. It's okay until Bruce Youth chases you with a crowbar screaming the Iyrics to "Dancing in the Dark". That's when I get a little inflamed. Whatever happened to Jackson Browne, earth shoes, corduroys and stupid belt buckles?

3.5.85 Shed: Have been real busy. Some cool stuff happened in the last few days. This guy came to the door, trying to get votes for his contest. One of those guys... you never can figure out what they're running for, how they win, what they win or who put them up to such an absurd task. Usually some kind of religious trip going down. Going door to door wanting to talk to people? That's a very risky activity in this country. Must have been a Christian. They're used to it by now. Imagine having a bunch of your relatives ending up as lion's food. Anyhow, this guy is explaining himself to Ms. Ginn. Ms. Ginn has infinite patience and politeness. I don't. I was in the kitchen making some coffee, watching this guy trying to come in and talk. I grabbed a steak knife, made stabbing motions at his face and said, "Die, die, die!" Ms. Ginn tried to make light of it by saying I was an actor. I told him he had nice legs and if he took a shower with me, I'd vote for him. He really bummed on that one. Finally I told him that if he won and didn't let me in on the money, I was going cut him up. That one was a bit too much for Ms. Ginn. She just slammed the door in his face. She bummed at first, but after a while, she thought it was funny. Ms. Ginn is awesome.

Last Sunday I went down to San Diego and hung out with Diamanda Galas. She's really great. I have been a fan of hers for years so it was cool to meet her. She and I talked about all kinds of stuff. She lent me some records. She had to split to Europe that day so we didn't have time to do much except hang out while she packed her bags. I saw the SST gig that night — SWA, Saccharine Trust, Meat Puppets, Minutemen. Really good show. The best Meat Puppets show I have ever seen. Their new material is excellent. They encored with "Little Wing" by Jimi Hendrix. Amazing...

The Cutting Edge called me today. They asked if I wanted to shoot some stuff tomorrow. I said okay.

I went out amongst the pigs today. I went to 7-11. The guy at the counter always talks to me. The high school students hanging out, playing videos, leafing through rock magazines, always stare at me. They watch what I buy and watch me leave.

People will put you down for being into what you're into. They want to stop you. They want to just talk about it, talk about it, talk about it. But when someone "does it", then it's bad news.

She's a cancer carryin' Marlboro puffin' Budweiser suckin' kind of a gal. Mildly brain-damaged from PCP and glue. Fucked up from being handled by her father. She relives those times in her dreams. They send her crying and groping for Budweiser and Marlboro. She's sitting across from me at the laundromat. She's smoking, waiting for her clothes to come out of the dryer. She hates her job. She hates her skin. She hates the tattoos on her arm and breast. She hates the self-inflicted burns from the red hot bowl of a pot pipe that mark her hands and wrists. So high — no pain. She is beautiful. She is absolute in her self-hatred. No money, no brains, no energy to care. No hope. No way in, out, up or otherwise.

Car crash to car crash. Every day a little Death. A Highway Patrol officer dead. Body burning on the 405 South. Hot pig cookin'. A couple drives by. KMET-FM blaring the Beach Boys out of the window.

The husband says, "God hates policemen. I thought everybody knew that."

"Not policemen dear," replies his wife. "The word is pig. God does not hate pigs. He just tries to make them good. A good pig is a dead pig. The Lord never gets a moment's rest keeping his eyes on his pigs and his pigs' sty."

I have dreams of the most beautiful girl in the world. In my dream, she looks at me with worry and apprehension. I tell her not to cry when she sees the blood. If you run away, then run away and don't look back — ever. Allow me my insanity and I will stay in your heart with the tenacity of a crab louse.

3.10.85 SHED: So I come back from doing the show at the Lhasa Club. I'm in the shed. The electric heater is on to take the chill off the air. I am playing a tape of Strauss' Zarathustra — a guy Mr. Ginn refers to as "Dick" Strauss. So I did the show with Exene. People were pretty neat. I thought I did okay, not that good. Sure is strange. One minute, you're up onstage with all these people that are real nice to you. Hour and a half later, you're sitting alone in the shed with a bunch of spiders and moist air. This girl came up to me. She told me that I used to "kill" her. She said I didn't do that anymore. I suggested that she "kill" herself. It's a drag here in the shed. I don't like doing those shows sometimes. I mean, the people are real cool and all. But it hurts to be all alone after it's over.

Exene was real cool. I like her stuff. I don't like going out — not even to my own shows. I know that these people wouldn't give me the time of day on the street.

3.12.85 SHED: I walked down Artesia Boulevard today to go to the post office. I always pass the nursery school. There's always these little kids playing and yelling. Today as I passed them, I thought about how those ladies are on trial for child molestation. If it was my nursery, I would start a new policy right away. Rubber gloves on all the teachers. Instead of them touching the little brats, they prod them with pointed sticks. There... No more little kids saying they were raped and shit. No human contact whatsoever. This is cool. You want to get rid of problems? Then get rid of them.

HARVEY KUBERNIK AND HENRY *(SUZAN CARSON)*

Some lady called me from USC today. She's going to interview me on Friday. The Cutting Edge show called up Harvey the other day and said they want to run me every month now. I finished this article for Spin magazine tonight. Spin is a new magazine. They asked me to do an article for them. I said okay. I went down to the 7-11 to get a cup of coffee and think of what I should write the article about. I came back to the shed and did a thing on 7-11. I didn't have the money to xerox it so I sent the original. I hope it gets there and I hope it's good enough. I go into the studio this week.

Two little girls had a table out in front of the post office today. They were trying to sell Girl Scout cookies. They asked me and I said, "Heil Hitler." I saw a thing on the news — an aerobic class for pregnant ladies. These bloated ladies in leotards. Life is full of bad trips. It's 2:30 a.m., I don't want to go to sleep. I never want to sleep again. I really liked talking with Diamanda last week. The sound is driving that woman insane. There is no doubt. That woman is getting consumed. I like people who play for themselves. I have dehumanized myself to the point of no return. When I go outside, I feel like a gun. I want to chew them up. They don't hear the wheel. They don't feel the blood in their veins. That's why I can't relate to them and they can't relate to me. I can't hear them because they don't say anything. Through pain, I find extreme clarity. I can see in total darkness.

3.18.85 TOTAL ACCESS STUDIO, HERMOSA BEACH: Today has been long. I did a photo session with Ed Colver for my article in Spin magazine. That took a long time. Now I'm at the studio trying to get going on some songs. There seems to be problems with the board. I did a reading thing at Cal Arts the other night (3.14.85). That was relatively painless. Tried to take pictures in the 7-11 on Artesia and Phelton, but they said that it was illegal. Some freedom. I have not worked out for a couple of days, been too busy. I have a lot of work to do. I did the vocals on "Loose Nut". I'm glad I did okay. That song is real hard for me to sing.

3.19.85 SHED: Studio was long last night. Sounds good though. Chuck was running this summer's tour plans down to me today. Sounds real cool. We are going to be real busy.

I saw Star Trek tonight. These android people were going to take over the galaxy. They were built to serve mankind, but they got wise and wanted to take over. The one main android said that they were going to "serve man, take care of him and control him." I thought this was great. Just like cops. Protect, serve and control. Staci was drunk today. I told her that booze is a tool to control the masses. That's why they sell it over the counter. Booze keeps you stumbling, fuzzy and dependent. It makes you easy to control. Booze keeps you down. That's why it's so easy to get. I'm no fool. I'll wait for you to be drunk and stupid. I'll take your money, your car, your everything. You'll belong to me!

Imagine a Twilight Zone episode where a guy becomes so paranoid that he thinks that everyone is a robot. He thinks he's the last man on earth. He gets a pistol and goes into the streets, shooting people down and screaming, "You're not real! You're monsters!" He sees that he cannot possibly wipe out all the robots. With no one to help him, the last man on earth runs back into his apartment and puts the gun in his mouth and pulls the trigger. Smoke, wire, screws and circuitry all over the place. The body slumps over onto the table. A little smoke still trails from the burnt wires.

I saw a guy walking his dog on Artesia Boulevard. The man didn't even give the dog a second to take a leak. Every time the dog would raise his leg, the guy would just keep right on walking. The dog would make a choking sound from the leash grabbing at his throat and kept moving.

3.20.85 SHED: I was thinking about the UK Subs the other day. What a band. They had a song called "I Live in a Car". That was my anthem in the summer of 1980. Some people would call my car a 1968 blue Volkswagen fastback, but I called it home. I would get off work at Haagen-Dazs, have a wonderful dinner at the 7-11 on Wisconsin Ave. and then I would drive to a nice quiet place and fall out. I had some interesting experiences. One night I parked at St. Luke's Church at Wisconsin & Calvert. Imagine being woken up at dawn by a priest all dressed in black. He's screaming at you and pounding on the window. I don't know man, it scared the living shit out of me. Another night a week later was the strangest and to this day, I can't figure out what happened. I was parked in the parking lot of a very high class condominium. I parked in the darkest corner. The air was hot and it was hard to sleep. Around three or four in the morning, I heard footsteps outside the car. Hard shoes — probably male. I sunk down real low in the back seat so I couldn't see out. The footsteps went around the car. I caught a breath of tobacco smoke. The shoes stopped making noise. He was close. I knew if he tried to come in, it would be through the driver's side because the window was open. I was ready to grab a hand or an arm or something. Then I heard some glass break right next to the car. Not a lot of glass, just a small piece. At this point, I jumped out of the back seat. Nothing. Not a soul around. I never heard whoever it was leave. I was listening so closely that I almost forgot to breathe. I jumped into the front seat, started up the engine and peeled out of there. I drove back to the 7-11, got some coffee and tried to figure the whole thing out. I couldn't then and I can't now. Why was I sleeping in my car? Because I had no place to live. That's just the way it worked out. I caught showers here and there. I did okay.

She would get all her boyfriend's names tattooed on her breast — the left breast. They would come and go. At one point, she had three men's names tattooed on her. That's when she decided she hated men forever. Bastards. You give your love, your time, money, body and soul to a man and the bastard laughs in your face and leaves you. She came to the conclusion that men are pigs. She burned the names off with her lit cigarette letter by letter. The room stank of burning flesh. Pier Avenue fuckup. Now she has deep circular scars on her breast. Who would get a man's name tattooed on them? She would burn the letters off one by one. Each time she sunk the hot coal into her flesh, she would stare at the wall and think of his eyes and how they lit up when he saw that she had gotten his name on her. She hated herself for ever having loved anyone. The burns made her bleed. The burns made her remember. Never again. She wanted it sewn shut. Never again would there be such a vile intrusion. It was like someone jabbing a broomstick in you. Never again. She was no longer alive. No more pain. She was dead inside. Burned out. Sewn shut.

3.24.85: Sunday afternoon. I hate Sundays. No shit. It's probably school damage. Sunday meant Monday. Monday meant school, uniform, teachers and my classmates. It was like swallowing big hunks of dirt.

Now there's no school, there's the same shit as always. Tomorrow I'm supposed to pick up my books from the binders. This will be cool. I started work on this project in mid-January. It only took eight weeks to print 1,000 books. Isn't that amazing? I can play about 50 shows in that time, travel about 11,000 miles. 1,000 books take a lot longer. It's easy to fuck with me because I have no money and I get no respect.

Friday night, Black Flag played at the Music Machine. I sang three songs. Sure was good to play, even if it was just for about 10 minutes or so. I hate Sundays. I like it in here though. No one to bother me.

3.26.85: Did the initial outline of the back piece tattoo. That felt pretty tender. When the needle would my spine, I would flinch uncontrollably. Got my books the other day. They look real swell. I hope I can s

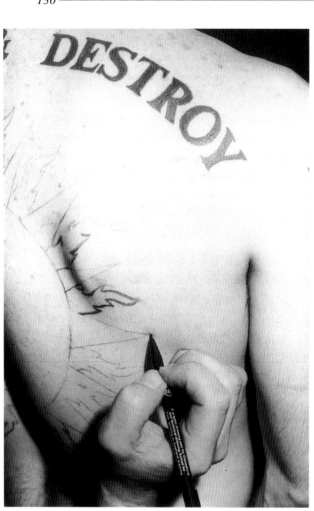

RICK SPELLMAN'S STUDIO *(SUZAN CARSON)*

them all. If not, I can build a doghouse with them or something. I'm sore and tired, but I can't sleep yet. I can't remember the last time I relaxed. My brain won't quit. I am the gun. I am the bullets. If I don't do this, no one else will. This is what I must remember. Every time I feel weak (a lapse in discipline), I must remember this. I could sit in this shed for the rest of my life or I can push it. Sitting behind a closed door does not cut it. I must see what I am made of. Even if it means ripping out my guts. Death is not the issue here. That's just another trip. It takes nothing to be here. This is what I must remember. There are people who will cut you up and down for sticking your head above water. It's so easy to drown. That needle got me good tonight. I could feel it in the chest and stomach. I guess that's where the nerve endings connect. The needles were going through me like lightning bolts.

It's raining outside tonight. I like that smell. I wish I could go for a walk. I am pretty tired. Still can't sleep. I must reach the point of self-discipline to relax myself. If my back wasn't so sore, I'd do another workout like I did earlier today. I've got a meeting with Harvey tomorrow. I have a lot of phone calls to make.

3.27.85: Climbing the thread. Looking up. Always climbing up. Up to the sewer of my soul. They couldn't understand the loss. They will never lose. I can lose no more. Climbing up the glowing thread. The soul burns and shines like the sun. I want to blister and cook there. They understand my scars as animal. They understand stupid animal pain. When the flesh is torn open, the brain discovers new parts of itself. The brain works independently of itself. Climbing the glowing thread. I am madly in love with my pain and the incineration of rational feeling toward common effects of pain. Imagine an army of men, strengthened through their pain. They would be tender, merciless and totally immune to ailment. Eyes of steel. Death will never come. I will never die.

The dislocated man. Out of touch with himself. Looking for something to bring back with him. Why look? The earth needs some new animals. I want to be a new animal. A disciple of the sun.

3.29.85 SHED: It's 3:30 a.m. I can't sleep. I feel like I will never sleep again. I'm sitting in the shed. Classical music playing on the radio. I remember sitting at my desk in my old apartment in Washington DC in spring and early summer of 1980. Yeah, I would have just gotten off work. Too uptight to sleep. The apartment was hot — no moving air. I got thirsty and drank Coke. Fine. Not much help on the sleep situation. I remember — the small cubicle — all dark except for the desk light. Nothing on my desk. The occasional letter. Many years before, my mother bought the desk in the vain hope that it might inspire me to be more diligent in my studies. Sitting in my cubicle. Smelled like roach spray and dirty socks. Listening to the Damned's *Black Album*. Razor blade slashes on my arms. Four years later, I'm in the shed — alone, unable to sleep — still confused by everything that moves, smiles or smells good.

3.30.85: Saturday night, another depression rolls in. I cannot control it. I can feel when one is coming on. It stalks me slowly. I worked out real hard today. I like to work out when I'm mad. I can concentrate on the reps real well. I walked to 7-11 tonight. I saw a police cruiser parked outside one of the apartment complexes. There was nobody inside it. I wished I had a stick of dynamite.

I have got to shoot a video tomorrow at the Lhasa Club. I have no idea how the fuck I'm going to get out there. What a drag. I hate not being able to pick myself up from the pits. I feel like I'm trying to punch my way out of a paper bag. Paralyzed. I'd rather be a chicken without a head.

I went to the Anti-Club last night. I saw Dog, Faction and Saccharine Trust. All three were real good. I don't know why, but hardly anyone was there. I sat in the yard today and talked with Pettibon for a while. He's real cool — real smart. I got the Birthday Party live album today. It's pretty good — vocals go in and out. Sandra Goode refused the terms of her parole. She wants to stay in prison if she can't be with Manson. That's pretty loyal. What balls. He said that if you don't put a value on something then it has no value. Human life? I'm living the human life. Doing the human thing.

If I step on a bug with purpose — if I mean to kill it and go through with it, how is that much different from going across the street and taking that little boy and bashing his skull against the curb until he's dead? I wake up at night screaming, "Turn on the gas! Turn on the gas!" Nuns with flamethrowers going into Palos Verdes — reading from the telephone book, torching men, women and children, masturbating and reciting numbers and names from the white pages — the clean white pages — annihilating and rubbing themselves furiously. This is the salvation — this is the plague. This is the salvation — this is the divine punishment. Raise your wings. Prepare to meet.

3.31.85 SHED: Another Sunday afternoon. I used to have some pretty good Sundays when I worked at the ice cream store. The store was cool. I could turn my mind off when I punched in. The night shift had to defrost the freezers after closing. I had to be there most of the time to make sure it was done correctly. I signed on for Sunday shifts because I would do anything not to be in my apartment on a Sunday. I would work at the ice cream store on Saturdays too. Saturday was something like 4 p.m. until 3 or 4 a.m. Wake up the next day and go back in for the Sunday shift. I wouldn't be on shift all the time. I would just be around, making sure everything went okay. That was better than the apartment — better than having to think. The shed makes me feel dead.

I was supposed to go into the studio tonight, but the studio broke again. Greg called me and said we'll try again later this week.

He made a suicide pact with God. He jumped off the roof of a Holiday Inn in Bakersfield. God chickened out. I heard on the news that two policemen were gunned down today. Not bad. I hardly spoke to anyone today. Spent a lot of time in the back yard, trying to read Henry Miller. I have to be in a good mood to read Miller. He's always happy — even when he's bumming out.

Diamanda Galas sent me a letter from Berlin, Germany. She said that she's doing okay and her Berlin show was real good. She said she told the guys in Einsturzende Neubauten about my tattoo. That's cool

She also went on to ask me, "How are the waves?" etc. Your basic burn, I guess. I played a record that she lent me — this guy named Iannis Xenakis. Collages of sound with real interesting structure. Oh yes — she also wanted me to look up the word *cretino* to see what it meant. She's my favorite all-female band.

4.1.85 SHED: Hot out tonight. Killer in the house tonight. Fucker in the house tonight. House of flesh. Kick it, suck it, bite it, burn it down, melt it, end it, stop it. I have twisted cats' necks until they died — I have. Entire litters. Pet shop — slaughterhouse. Flesh house — meat house. Feed it, clean it, sell it, kill it. Pets, animals, flesh, whores. Bought, sold, fed, killed. They'll always tell you that to hate is worse than to love. Worse? No, let me try that again. They'll always tell you that it is better to love than to hate. Okay, then why is it bad to love Adolf Hitler or some other "bad guy"? Is it better to hate them? I thought hate was bad. Well, I don't care because I don't hate. Hot out tonight. Makes me hot and fucked up. Warm nights make me think of Washington DC. Makes me think of the East Village in New York. Rooftops, loneliness. Beating off in the hot bathroom. Going to sleep above the covers. Feeling like you're soaking in warm water. Always damp. Face always greasy. Always thinking about some girl. All hung up. All torn up. All messed up. All fucked up. Spaced out. Frustration, heat, sleepless nights, smoldering. Hot air. Sweating alone. Oh man, that's when I sink the blade. Murder the flesh. Destroy it. Get even. Show yourself who's boss. Master your pain. Pain is better than love — less depleting, more satisfying. Anyone who doesn't agree isn't wrong. They just don't understand where I'm coming from.

They said, "Anything that's defenseless shouldn't be here." That's when I left. Swallowed a whole vial of hot solitary nights. Slashed my wrists with a rusty "I don't live here anymore" and waited for the fucking world to subside. It didn't work. I got the scars, but I'm still breathing. Breathing my last — over and over.

4.2.85: Just got back from another installment on my tattoo. Tonight was fill-in. Wasn't that bad. Some parts were real tender — the needle in your back. You feel it in your stomach. Needles — lots. Drinking coffee, dropped three Tylenol Extra Strength. I could use some Extra Strength.

Another hot day — another warm night, spent alone in the shed. Summer's coming. I'll be all over the United States this summer. Plenty of hot nights in the Ryder. Summer makes me think that all the girls look alright. Last summer I was in England, riding on subway trains, sweating, wearing the same shorts I'm wearing now. I looked like a psycho slob.

I saw *Desperately Seeking Susan* last night. This is the movie with Madonna in it. It was a pretty good movie I thought. Madonna was good. She reminds me of this girl I know. Fuck, she really does. It makes me think of her and the jerk I made out of myself. I've said it before and I'll say it again, "A man's got to do what a brainless idiot's got to do." Yeah, I guess that's my problem.

The Tylenols are kicking in just fine. My back no longer feels like it's on fire. An hour ago, I couldn't stand up straight — now I feel alright. I worked out hard today. Felt good. It's time to move. Nothing happens here — nothing. I'm going into the studio tomorrow during the day. I haven't done that since the *Damaged* sessions in 1981. Starting to wake up. 1:03 a.m. Fine.

The heat rises in waves — shimmering. August of my 10th year: Saw a big dog get hit by a car down in the Adams Morgan district of DC. It was so hot out in the street that the pavement was soft. The dog, with half his guts laid out in the street, rolled around howling. No one did anything except sit on their front porches and watch. Imagine yourself writhing on the street, guts all over the place. So hot... so fucking hot. You're dying. Disemboweled. A bunch of people watch you die. Finally, you stop writhing. You stop kicking and you're dead all the way. Small children — the kind that just stare at you but don't make a sound — poke your eyes with sticks and break off your teeth with rocks. Your mouth is bleeding. The children poke you and jab you, but they can't hurt you anymore. For me, summer means a lot of grease, sweat, beating off and feeling like they can't hurt me anymore. But then she smiles and I start to find ways to make it hurt some. You can always make it hurt if you try. If it doesn't hurt, then you're not trying. And if you're not dead, then you're just dying.

RICK SPELLMAN'S STUDIO *(SUZAN CARSON)*

I defile myself — permanently. Scars... tattoos. I know there is no way I can win with all this. I can play the outcast game real good. It's easier than trying. I take the easy way out. I defile and disfigure myself. I don't want to succeed. I'm down in the sewer. Always looking up. Always hungry — clawing. It's easier than trying. I think of new and inventive obstacles. How can I fuck myself over this time?

Being petty. You get to be sullen, quiet, nasty and deprived. It's cool. You "suffer" for your "art" like a good little tortured genius. That's what we are, right? Even if only we know it. This is what I am. This is what I do. It's easier than trying. You can't lose at losing. You can't fail if you succeed at failure — unless you win. Anyone who tried and didn't fail is a sellout — a lightweight piece of shit. Anyone who tried and failed is okay after a while because he's back down in the sewer with you. Anyone who never tried and never failed is totally bitchin'.

4.4.85 SHED: Did a lot of stuff today. Did an interview with Jeff Spurrier of the LA Times. Did a talking show at some university in Pasadena with some people who sucked hard.

Those people are not the type I would like to do any shows with at all. The whole night was a lot of people patting each other on the back and talking just to hear themselves make noise. It had to be done. Now I understand more things. I like learning experiences. I learn. The alienation is where it's at. Listening to them talk, sip beers and make their comments. I can feel my teeth sharpening — grinding together. Sitting in a chair in this room, listening to these people spew out their in-scene chatter. I know for certain that this sure as hell is not my scene. I like that feeling. I just sat there and stared at them. People are funny people. I don't get it.

4.6.85 SHED: I got a phone call from Diamanda Galas last night. We talked for a good while. She is very cool. She's pretty tired from the shows she's been doing. I feel pretty burned out too. Tonight has been very long. I have been thinking of killing myself — not in some kind of romantic sense, just quietly dying. No big deal. I'd just like to slip away. I sure am not happy here. I don't want to think like this. I don't think it's cool at all. I don't want to feel like this. But when something makes plain good sense, I can't help but agree with myself. It's just not good to be here. I've been sitting in the shed all day. I went out to get some rubber cement at the store but that's about it. I'd like to bury myself in here. That's a good idea. Pound through the floor, dig out some dirt, lay down in the hole and slip away. There is not a fucking thing here for me and it makes me feel numb — seals me off. Living in a bubble with spikes on the inside.

It's 11:15. I'm not tired. I wish I was. Maybe I could sleep this off. Even assholes — even macho, self-serving chauvinist pigs get the blues. We do — we really do. I've got the heater on. I've got the radio tuned to a classical station. Fine. I was going to do a tour of speaking dates this fall, but I think I just canceled it in my head. I don't want to make trouble or raise eyebrows. I want everything to be cool in our camp. I don't need to do any of that stuff anyway really. I just thought it was a good way to communicate and do something constructive, but it's not vital that I do this. I'd rather have a good situation in the band. The others in the band get so bent out of shape when I do talking shows. Greg does really bad. I don't see what the problem is. The clock just struck midnight. I don't remember the last time I was asleep before 3:00 a.m. I've got at least three or four more hours to go before I sleep.

I had this dream the other night. I was talking to this girl. I think she was supposed to like me or something. She started talking very matter-of-factly about how she really didn't like me much at all. I asked her, "You don't like me much, do you?" She smiled and said something to the effect of "No." That dream made me feel so crummy. I was glad when I woke up. I remember a few girls who were like that. I remember this one girl. She said all kinds of nasty stuff about me to people. Luckily for me, I'm subhuman so this kind of thing just rolls off. But still, I never had much luck with girls. I guess I have a crummy personality. If I didn't, I would probably not be alone so much of the time. What a fucked up dream. What a car crash. What a letdown. The people at Spin magazine called me the other day. They really liked the article I wrote for them. They want me to write another one for an upcoming issue. I'm playing ZZ Top's First Album. Sounds good. I never want to leave the shed sometimes — like right now.

I killed this cat — the last cat I killed. I remember... About a year and a half ago, I was in this car parked outside of SST. I was hanging out with this girl. Anyhow, this cat comes walking across the street toward our car. Another car was passing by and it squashed part of the cat's guts out. The cat rolled underneath our car and started to flail around. The girl started to really bum out. I got out of the car and grabbed the bloody, writhing cat out from underneath. I snapped its neck with my hands. I recognized the cat. It belonged to some rednecks across the street. I took the cat over to the house and knocked on the door. This big guy answered. I said that his cat was hit by a car and here it was, pretty much all in one steaming piece. The guy didn't take it too well. His woman came to the door and started freaking out pretty bad. He said, "Get it out of here!" I just smiled and said okay. I dumped it on the front lawn of their apartment complex. I walked into the bathroom at SST and washed the blood, guts and cat hair off me. I hate the South Bay.

Wiping guts off my hands. Reminds me of Lincoln, Nebraska. I checked out a place where a woman had shot herself in the head a day earlier. I had my hands covered with brain tissue, slime, dirt and dead grass. I wiped my hands off on Ratman's van and on my t-shirt. I remember pulling the brains to my nose to see what they smelled like. It didn't smell like much. I thought about tasting it. I did not. I should have. I still have some of that lady's brains wrapped up in tinfoil. I should break some off and eat it. That will probably be my only chance to eat some human flesh. What a trip.

Eat some of the brains from a lady that blew her skull apart. What would that make me? What would you think?

Your god is a mushroom cloud. The Church of the Nuclear Christ. Mushroom Cloud Messiah. The fallout mission. That would put the real fear in you. Yes, forget this Christ guy. He died for you. Now you die for me. That would be real cool to see you praying to an ICBM missile. Watching you on television, kneeling to a perfect, gleaming warhead. Now that's a real idea. Guaranteed destruction. Forget the second coming. You give me the missiles and I'll melt heaven. I'll blow your saints to Lawndale. That would be great to see you grovel in front of a god that you could see, that you could touch. Only an idiot would believe that some god in the sky is going to wreck the place. Let me give you something that you could really believe in. Don't you want — don't you really need something to believe in? Something solid? Something to calm your nerves? Yes, look to me. Let me supply you with your faith. The Church of the Real Deal. Have mercy? Why? You're into destruction. Forget needles and suicide. I am offering you something better. You love to be controlled. You dig ownership and control inflicted upon you. Now you can kneel and confess and pray and grovel to something that offers you ultimate carnage without judgment or concession. Isn't that what you want? Yeah, it is.

4.11.85 Shed: Went to the Doors video thing at the Roxy tonight. Ray Manzarek invited me +1. It was an invite only thing. I walked through the door and Danny Sugarman was there. He waved me and Staci through. He said, "That's Henry Rollins. Let him in." Sounded like I was some hot shit. I didn't recognize many people there. I saw Rodney Bingenheimer and a few others. The Doors video thing was cool. All these people stared at me. I was not dressed up. I guess that tattoos trip people out.

Tomorrow I'm going to San Diego to do a talking show with Exene. I am going down a day early to hang out with Diamanda. That should be cool. Going to that thing tonight made my mind spin. Seeing all those people and shit. There were free drinks care of MCA and everybody was getting wasted. The guy next to me drank all this shit and by the end of the film he could hardly clap. After the lights came up, Manzarek, Krieger and Densmore came out on the stage and thanked everyone for coming. Danny Sugarman came out and talked about how this video "ships today" and the Doors producer Paul Rothchild came out and talked about how the stuff was all done digitally and shit. Manzarek told everyone to drink up because MCA was paying for it. I didn't have anything to drink. I left.

4.12.85: I'm sitting in Diamanda's car outside her singing teacher's place. The weather is beautiful — lots of hot looking girls all over the place. Diamanda's voice is coming out of the window, mixing with the ocean, the wind in the trees, birds and these drunk rednecks. Sounds real cool. People walk by the car and stare at me. Two cop cars check me out. A van load of girls singing "Follow the Yellow Brick Road" drives by. The rednecks are whooping it up. I can't see them, but I can hear them clearly. They're talking about "the game" and they're cussing a lot. I'm having a good time. It's good to be out of LA for a while. I am in La Jolla. La Jolla looks like Beverly Hills parked next to the ocean. Kids in wetsuits: "I can almost do a 360!" — "No way, dude!" — "Yes way!"

Diamanda is doing some scales. She is easy to hear. Sounds pretty haunting. The air is getting cooler and the light is beginning to fade.

4.14.85 Shed: I got back from San Diego at about 3 a.m. this morning. I had a real good time. I thought the show went real good. Exene was great. A lot of people showed up. The in-store thing at Off the Record went real cool. People were alright. I signed stuff and hung out. I had a great time hanging out wi

Diamanda. We went out to dinner, hung out, played some records and stuff.

I'm feeling very depressed. A good combination of Sunday and having done one of those shows and being here alone.

Yesterday at the record store, this pretty girl came up to me and gave me a rose. I left the store to go eat and I was sitting in the car waiting to go. The girl came out and gave me the rose again. I had left it in the store. I felt real bad. What a fuckup. I thought, okay, she'll probably be at the show tonight. I'll apologize onstage to her. I even forgot to do that. What a fuckup.

This girl gave me this thing she wrote about her mother killing herself. I thought it was really good. I put it in a book so I wouldn't lose it. I sold the book. What a fuckup.

I played the tape of the show last night. I need lots of work. I found lots of errors and mispronunciations — talking too fast. The flow needs strengthening. The whole all-around thing could be improved a lot. I guess I wasn't as good as I thought I was. I need to work on my voice. Singing, speaking, etc. — I must work. What I just heard on that tape was weak. Bad pauses, lots of bad shit. Damn, I thought I was okay. I was not.

Much later: I am here in the shed. I wish I was somewhere else. I called Ian's house tonight. He wasn't home. I'll try him later on this week if I get the chance. I bought Diamanda a copy of *Fun House* while I was in San Diego. Everybody should have a copy of that album.

This anti-nuclear war guy started to lecture me about whatever bullshit he thinks he's into. I told him I wanted to blow the world up to get rid of the bullshit. I made him very aggravated. I fuck with anybody that comes on with a line.

I'd like to have a string of ears around my neck. Ears I cut off the policemen and policewomen that I killed.

Policemen should put little skulls on the side of their car for every person they've shot just to shake things up a bit.

All laws should have the same penalty for being broken. I'm tired of all this court bullshit. Tons of law books, bullshit processes, time consuming, money wasting. Put a uniform penalty on everything. Either you give them the gas chamber for a parking violation or make homicide a misdemeanor. I'm tired of all this jumping around.

I can't respect people who don't respect the laws they made and pay money to support. They, them, you — are all liars. I cannot have any remorse when you are shot, raped and mistreated. I laugh at dead cops. I hope their families understand that Daddy or Mommy was a pig and was asking for it. How can I not laugh when the Marines die? I've seen their bodies on the cover of Newsweek. Imagine that, a stiff making the cover of a magazine. I thought Rolling Stone was the only one still doing that. The Marine puts on his uniform, goes to some country and gets his entrails rolled in the dirt. What did you expect? I laugh. I remember being chased and teased and threatened by Marines. Of course I am into them dying! And me not going to jail for it! Well alright!

Abusing corpses. Dress them up. Put them in busses. Load them into cars and drive them downtown. Put them behind their desks. Make sure to prop them up — they might fall over. At around 8 p.m., drag the bodies back into the suburbs. Porters will put them in body bags and number them. Their mates will come, identify the body and drag it home. Cook it dinner, prop it up in front of the TV set and drag it off to bed. Next morning, the process will be repeated. This is the way life is around these parts.

4.15.85 SHED: Another day. I got a dark cloud above me — two days now. I don't know what the matter is, I think I do, but.... I did my workout today. It was like swallowing dirt. Probably the worst one in a long time. I can't find anyone around that I can identify with. I feel that I need to. I do... at least a little. I can take humiliation and loneliness. I do every day. But the depression and frustration just kick the shit out of me.

There was a car accident. Somebody's son, in the middle of the intersection. The steering wheel pins him to the front seat. The car explodes in flames. People stop to watch the man burn to Death. We don't have witch trials anymore so this is as close as we come to a public burning. People stop what they're doing to see the incineration in the street. The man in the car is burning to Death. His flesh is curling back and hissing. The man in the car is burning. Smells like Burger King at lunch time. Cooking meat is cooking meat. He is covering his arm with A-1 sauce and chewing his flesh before it becomes too well done. He has no hair on his head. He is the man in the car. Burning for you. Ripping his own flesh away from the bone and eating it. The people on the street applaud and cheer. Yes, this has been a good burning. The summer is coming — closing in. There will be more burning, more flesh eating parties, people jumping off buildings, abortions and pigs dying in the streets.

When I was in the sixth grade, I was taking a bus home from school. About a mile before my stop, the bus had to pull over. We couldn't continue down Wisconsin Avenue because a car had knocked a cop off his bike. The pig was sprawled out in the intersection and it was blocked off. I got out and walked home. I should have walked over, kicked him hard in the ribs and yelled, "Fuck you, pig meat! Get the fuck up!" Making me go out of my way. I hope some cop gets shot tonight. Fuck that. Even better, I hope a cop's kid gets abducted, raped, dismembered and UPSed back to his house.

The summer slithers closer. White hot. Never threatening. Just delivering more of what cannot be "new and improved". More heroin addictions, child and wife beatings, crushed and mutilated bodies trapped in burning cars. More pain and more desperation.

I think about that girl and my heart just wants to... keep beating. And it's a good thing too. I think of how she used to laugh real loud and how she used to tell me about fucking all these guys. I lost sleep over that girl. All I wanted to do was to be a good dog. Now I know more. I never learned any new tricks. I just got a lot of mileage from the old ones.

4.16.85 SHED: Got back from the needles. Tylenol numbing my back. I could feel them bounce off the spine. Getting close to being finished.

Tired. Tattoo work wears me out. Trauma to the nervous system. Bandages pulling at my neck. When the needles go in, my hands swell slightly. I think about the meaning of pain. Pain is personal. It really belongs to the one feeling it. Probably the only thing that is your own. I like mine.

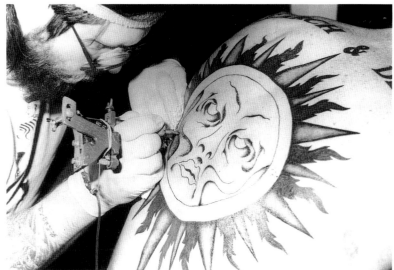

RICK SPELLMAN'S STUDIO *(SUZAN C RSON)*

A story about a guy who lined up ten shotglasses. He poured a shot of Jack Daniels, a shot of Clorox. Jack, Clorox, Jack, Clorox... ten shots lined up. Downed them all, one after the other. Went out to the garage and dropped dead. No note, just ten empty shotglasses. Tired, depressed and one day closer to the end. Been eating dirt for three days now. Can't shake this depression. Lonely, hollow. Feeling ready to lay down. You know what I mean? Like a dog. Sitting in the shed, eating dirt. Thinking of some other place — a warm place, a ring of glittering water — someplace.

4.17.85: Took the bandages off my back. Feels good not to have that shit on me. I go tomorrow for more work. I can't wait for this to be over. There's this big gray cat who lives in the back yard of the Ginns' house. Ms. Ginn calls it "gray cat." Gray now hangs out at the shed from time to time. Old Gray is here now, sleeping in front of the heater.

I am infected. I am lucky. I am stricken. I am alive. I choose to pursue my infection, to bring it to a rabid boil. I want to shake my flesh. Everything can be true. I think of killing myself sometimes. When I go to sleep at night, I think about my Death and how I will die someday. I think about killing myself sometimes, like the other night. I never come close. I just think about it. I am the infection. Hungry. Burning. Crawling forward. I am my end. I am the infection. Today I was relieved to find that I do not want to cure myself. I thought that was the reason I was writing, singing and carrying on so. I am not wrong.

I think about killing myself sometimes. Blowing my head all over the place. Laughing, getting up, picking my head up and patching it into place. Wiping my hands off on my pants, relieved and saying, "Okay, what's next?"

I went to mail a letter. A pig stopped me on Prospect Street. He asked me where I was going. He told me I looked like I was "dragged through a knothole." I told him that these were my clothes and I liked them. He let me go. I hope he has some kids. I hope the kids get hit by a bus tomorrow. I couldn't enjoy my walk. I was too busy looking around for that fucking pig. I hate pigs. Their wives should be destroyed. So should their offspring — they might have some of their father's traits. This is what I call *crime prevention*.

I get frustrated when I can't break through to my thoughts. I am full of thoughts on the infection, the consumption and the surrender to them. I was thinking of other people and how they stare at me now, wherever I go. I'm getting used to it, but I don't see that I have a choice. I wonder what they see. I know what I see when I look in the mirror or at a photograph of myself. Would I recognize myself through someone else's eyes?

No one would understand that I see the jungle on Prospect Street. Always jungle. Napalm falling through the polluted sunset. A village up ahead. People have been poisoned. Something was stolen from them in the night. Their insanity replaced by hope. Their vision destroyed by the thirst for security. They will always tell me that this is a street, a sidewalk — that this is civilization. I know better. I always will. I see jungle, fire, black water, blank stares. They see "streets". I know better.

There was a big, shiny green fly perched on top of a box on one of the shelves above me. I took a magazine and swatted him. The fly sat straight up, stuck to the box by its guts. The abdomen of the fly was crushed. I watched the fly for a while. Its legs would kick and crawl at the air. The fly couldn't move. The fly was anchored by its own entrails. It's only a fly. What if it was a cop? What if it was some kid? Imagine some kid... imagine yourself nailed to the floor by your lower intestines. That sure would be a "crime" wouldn't it? No one saw me maim this fly. I did not kill it. I'm just letting it sit there, glued to the box. No police will come. I am torturing and killing inside this shed. No one will hear the fly's screams. I am going to get away with this crime. I can learn from this. I can move on to bigger and better murders. Many people kill without learning or gaining from it. Think of when you step on a female roach, full of eggs (heavy with child). You kill a mother and her children. I go out and I blow away a pregnant woman coming out of the market. We have both killed. I go to jail and you go free and we are both "guilty". Do we both feel the same way? I am a "killer". What are you?

The fly is still alive. I'm gonna stick it with pins and think of someone I don't like. I'm going to torture the fly, pluck his little red eyes. Pull his legs off one by one. I am pulling legs of a helpless victim. All they see are trees and sidewalks.

4.18.85 SHED: More needles tonight. Didn't hurt that bad. I am glad it's done with. A night of this always leaves me tired and vacant upstairs. The fly died. I checked on it this morning. It's getting hot outside now. Makes me think of touring.

I wonder if there are people who destroy themselves without anyone else around to see them do it. Of course there are. People who cry alone. People who sit in silence with the lights off, silently burning, not seeking attention but falling apart on their own. These people are heroes to me. Someone with enough stuff in them to just take it and not seek attention. I'm not saying that waving one's arms for help is bad or weak. I'm sure there are thousands holed up in hot or freezing apartments, tool sheds, basements, just simmering. Ready to explode or cave in. Pressing their eyes to the keyhole. Scratching a clear space on a dirty window to have a look outside. Going to work. Waiters, dishwashers — grinding through shifts, punching out. Walking to a fast food place for dinner then going home. Living in a custom-tailored hell.

I imagine a view out of an apartment window. The apartment is on 18th and Columbia Road in Washington DC. I used to live in that area from time to time. The same dirty window, the same intersection. It's always hot as shit. Hot everywhere. The streets are gummy. The heat waves coming off the asphalt make it look like the street is a river — a shimmering body of water. The cars are like hydrofoils skating on top. All the people on the street — uptight white boys walking fast, groups of black girls walking to the McDonald's — talking loud, laughing. They pass my window. They don't see me.

I can't wait to leave. There's nothing here at all of course. There's practice and all that stuff and that's good, but my brain doesn't like it here. Whenever I'm in a place that I don't like, I think about places that are far away, especially at night, here in the shed.

I remember hearing about this trip that went down at the McDonald's at 18th and Columbia. This guy worked behind the counter. His brother also worked there as a security guard. The two of them got in an argument at the McDonald's. The security guard sibling shot his brother in the leg. What a story. That was about 1980. Of course, it was in the summer. The heat drives people to distraction.

I caught another fly last night. I put him under a glass beaker. He's sitting there, waiting around. I am not going to let the fly go free. The fly will starve to Death inside its prison. It's only a fly. It's only your sister. What's the difference?

4.21.85 SHED: I went to the Anti-Club last night to see SWA, Saccharine Trust and Black Flag Instrumental. Lots of drunks in my face, talking to me and being assholes. Don't worry, I was a good dog. I just smiled back and shook their hands like a good rock star. I didn't break some loud, obnoxious drunk's jaw because I am not allowed human rights. I have to take this bullshit. I know. That's why I go out to these clubs. I don't want to see the bands. I want to be given lectures by drunk fuckups. I'm glad I came out in the open about that one! I hate drunks. The bouncer at the door was drunk. These punkers who were drunk came up to me and told me to write lyrics for their band. I politely suggested that maybe they should write their own. They acted like I was some asshole. Later during Saccharine Trust's set, one of the drunks came up and said, "These guys suck." I said, "You suck." I hate drunks. They seem to be everywhere.

I know this house where this drunk guy lives. He gets wrecked and he comes home and lies on the couch for 12 to 15 hours at a time. He cusses at his parents. This guy is a pathetic pig. His friends come up to me and tell me that he's so wasted he can't even walk. They want me to do something about it. I say that I'm sorry, but I don't give a fuck about drunks and maybe they should throw him into the street.

I have got to get out of here. Every day I build myself up into fits that keep me up until dawn. Tonight is one of those nights. I sat here for two hours. I keep having to unclench my jaw because my teeth are grinding together. I went out and ran a couple of miles to blow off some steam. Didn't help much. I don't know what I'm so wound up about, but I wish I would cool out. I'd beat off, but I am afraid I'd rip my cock off. I feel like burning something down. I was in the living room of the Ginns' today. I saw a couple of beer commercials. Fuck, they must have a lot of idiots watching. Those ads were really gross. They make being a drunk slob look cool. Why can't they have Hitler ads? Ads with mushroom clouds going up with people riding motorcycles and drinking beers? That sounds nice and gross — just as gross as the ones on the box today.

Here is my rationale: You get to go buy beer, get drunk and waste my time. I get to smack you with a pool ball and take your money and clothes. This is a good deal to me. At least it's fair. What a cool way to spend an evening. Wait around for a drunk asshole to fuck with you — and you and a lot of your friends kick the drunk to Death with steel cap boots.

4.24.85 SHED: No practice today. I have two shows coming up this weekend. It's getting late. Hot as shit outside tonight. Wind blowing all over the place. I hate it here. I worked out today. Didn't do a whole lot else. I haven't been writing much lately. Too scattered from the heat and practice.

The dreams and the voices are coming back again. Something is going to happen soon. I sit in the shed and I get the feeling that I'm waiting, waiting, waiting. Sweating. Thinking of the dirt. Thinking of that apartment on 18th and Columbia Road. Thinking about the hallway, pulling me toward the bathroom. The bathroom is where the suicide lives. Coiling at my feet. The suicide feeds on insanity and the vacuum of the hallway pulls me down. The insanity is autumn. Leaves falling — making no sound, falling upon you, spiraling, funnel, vacuum, Death, suicide, insanity. Burning brightly. Burning to ash.

The DNA in his semen could automatically encode with any animal he put it into. Didn't matter what he mated with, it would bear his children. He built an army of beasts — half-human, half-whatever. He led them into the city. They put on clothes and blended in. No one seemed to notice until the moon was full.

I am waiting. Time is dripping on my forehead with steady, unwavering rhythm. I have developed rings under my eyes. I look in the mirror now and I see them quite clearly. They have been there for a while now. I don't want to talk to people. I did tonight on the telephone. They always ask me what I am doing. I just tell them I'm working and playing and I leave it at that. I'm so wired on coffee now that I'll probably never get to sleep. I hate having to maintain. I'm no good at it.

We will never know the feeling of napalm and that makes me sad. I am losing my human values. The can that holds my humanity has been shot full of holes. Two years ago, I was different. Every waking moment is such a dehumanizing experience. I will not struggle to keep it. I choose not to resist the draining. And in this draining, a new animal will be born. Rational thought is just so ridiculous to me now. I hear them talk and I cannot understand. I used to feel bad that I did not fit in because I thought that it was a failing on my part. Now I understand that no one is wrong, including me. Drinking beer and sticking a screwdriver in someone's head are the same thing. One is no worse than the other. If they can go fly a kite, then I can dismember children and throw the amputated limbs on people's front lawns. This is what I understand. This is true. People would argue that this activity is against the law, therefore wrong. I cannot respect that. A law book is just a bunch of words that someone wrote down. I could write one of my own if I wanted to. It's my word against theirs. Knowing this makes life a lot easier for me. I can go with the flow. I don't respect the law and the people that live under it. Cops are men and women with guns. That's why I stay away from them not because they have the law on their side. I think it would be fun to change the law every week but not to tell anybody. People would be getting shot for doing laundry, arrested for eating. It sure would put some excitement into things around here. Some motherfuckers would try to bust the sun for coming up in the morning.

4.28.85: Sitting in the living room of the Ginns'. I don't feel like sitting in the shed right now. So I am here in the living room with Pettibon. Bill and Greg don't get along. Yesterday, Bill quit Black Flag. Yet another lineup change. When this happens, I feel like the rug has been pulled out from under me. I had to go out and do a talking show in Huntington Beach yesterday. It was one of the hardest things I've ever done. I couldn't concentrate too well. I had to drive down there about twenty minutes after he quit. We had a tour starting up May 8. I don't think that will go down now. I don't know what's going to happen. It's a terrible feeling. I feel totally worthless. I don't even want to go outside. I don't want to talk to anyone. People recognized me on the street yesterday. I just stared at the ground. I have just finished two books and an album. I feel like shit. I won't feel better until we have a new drummer and some kind of game plan. I'm not going to go into the reason for the split. I know the trips that went down. I saw this coming. I'm glad in some ways, but only some. There was a lot of people who were depending on us to tour right now. Ratman, who scraped every last penny together to construct a new PA system, now has to eat it. When I think of that, I want to die. I don't care about me. I feel awful that people around us have to suffer now. Tom, Davo, St. Vitus, DC-3, the Minutemen and SWA now have to rearrange their lives because we will not be able to come through. I feel amputated, phony and illegitimate.

I have so much shit to do this week it's unreal. San Francisco on Thursday, Boston on Saturday. I couldn't muster the get up and go to even work out today. Now I feel lazy and lame, like I should throw myself off a building.

I talked to Ed at Spin on Friday. They want the new thing I sent them a couple of weeks ago. They also want me to list the five albums I would want to have should I be stranded on a desert island. The only one I can think of is *Fun House*, the second album by the Stooges. After that, I can think of a lot of others. Maybe *White Light/White Heat* by the Velvet Underground. But then the avalanche ensues — Swans, Einsturzende Neubauten, Birthday Party, Bad Seeds, MC-5, Diamanda Galas, The Damned, Black Sabbath, Jimi Hendrix, etc.

I was on the Cutting Edge show tonight. I didn't see it. I can't really see myself on a screen without wincing a bit. To think that I am on television in front of people is nice, but that is about as far as my interest goes on that.

All I can think about now is playing. That's all I want to do. Playing in Black Flag has become a very big part of me. Without doing it a lot, I don't feel complete and this is awful.

Diamanda called me today from Chicago. She said that her shows went real well and she'll be back in California in a few days.

Today was miserable and lonely — real lonely. Fuck, I was really planning on getting out of here. But now, it looks like I will be here for a while. Right now I feel very selfish. I think to myself that I am not getting any younger. I feel that I'm wasting my life away. I am wasting my life — the only one I have. I realize that every day is one day closer to my Death. I cannot relax, not even close. When I write, my face hurts sometimes because I am grinding my teeth so fucking hard. Sometimes I put a cassette box between my upper and lower rows to stop this. I must look stupid sitting there with this cassette box in my mouth.

I cannot derive satisfaction from anything that does not cause physical pain. I think in terms of my body. I think through my body. Sex is an exception. Even sex causes me great torment so I guess it is not an exception. I cannot escape my mind. I try. Have been for a long time. What is beyond my mind? Insanity? Sometimes I can almost separate myself from my thoughts and almost stand beside myself. This causes me to have a lot of problems relaxing or even sleeping much at all.

Last night, I had this dream that I was walking down this street and I was saying, "This is the most beautiful block in the world!" Then I looked over and all the houses were gray cinder blocks with no windows. I'm still trying to figure that one out. Now I don't know if I'm thinking or thinking of thinking. Is it pure thought or thought inspired by sound or something I saw? Is it possible to have an explosion in your head like something out of the black space? When will I see myself walking down the other side of the street or passing me on the highway? What would it be like to come home and see your own body on the floor, brains all blown apart, gun in your hand? You're standing there looking at this corpse and it's you splattered all over the room. Maybe sometime that will happen to me. I'll come into the shed and I'll trip over my own corpse. I cannot understand from where all this torment comes from.

Once I saw my life, I saw the lie. Colonel Kurtz said that the middle word in life is 'if'. Take the "f" out of life. That's what I see. The lie blinds me. The lie makes me see the blindness. The lie turns me inward against myself. If I win, I lose. If I lose, I lose. I see no truth — just the inability to face the lie.

4.29.85 SHED: Saw *Apocalypse Now* earlier tonight. I don't know how many times I have watched that movie now. I couldn't even guess. Makes me feel old. My pal Chris Haskett sent me some pictures of the new Bad Seeds lineup featuring Nick, Mick, and Rowland S. Howard and two guys from Die Haut. That's three quarters of the Birthday Party. This will be very interesting. Chris said they were real good when he saw them.

5.5.85: In a plane en route to Los Angeles. Whenever I'm on a plane, the Jim Morrison quote "I don't know about you, but I want to get my kicks before the whole shithouse goes up in flames" always runs through my head. The last few days have been pretty busy. Thursday I flew up to San Francisco to do a show with Exene at the Stone. Diamanda, who was also in LA, flew up to SF with me. The show with me and Exene was real good. I was a bit worried that the people who came would be nasty and stuff, but they were great. Exene was great. Exene and I spent the night at Systematic Records. Joe from Angst put us up. Angst is now on SST. I think that's great. They went on after Exene and I had done our thing. They were great as usual.

Friday, I flew down to LA. Staci was nice enough to pick me up at LAX. Staci got her job at IRS records. She was invited to this party they were having to celebrate IRS moving into MCA and I went with her. Free food is good food. I talked with all the people who work with the Cutting Edge. The Lords of the New Church were there. They all looked like they were going to fall over and die. Stiv Bators has legs about as thick as your arm. He looked like a concentration camp prisoner. I was sitting at this table telling these people how happy I was that I could provide this nice spread for them and how I came up with the idea of IRS in the first place. The Cutting Edge people filmed me while I was doing it. I hope it came out okay. Late Friday night, I flew to Boston to be on the US Rock Seminar panel for multimedia artists. I got a hotel and everything. I hate these planes. If I make it home from this one, I'll never go up in one again, I swear. A lot of great airplane stories though. There's hardly anyone on this 747. I have an entire middle lane to myself. There's a man and a woman in front of me. At first, she was in one row and he was in another. But now they're sitting next to each other in her row. She is a strange woman, that's for sure. One minute she has her head in his lap and the next minute she has her walkman headphones on and is sitting a seat away from him. He walks up the aisle and gets a cup of coffee. Now they're sitting next to each other, drinking lite beer. We must be going to California. Every ten minutes or so there's a lot of turbulence. The last one was the worst I've ever experienced. Stuff was falling off trays and people were making noise. Scared the shit out of me. I hate planes. I feel stupid for having set myself up in a situation where I cannot see the driver — where I could fall to my Death, crash, burn and choke in gasoline fumes. But here I am... trapped. Two more hours to go... maybe. After the turbulence cooled out, I sat still listening to my heart pounding fast, aching as it did. I smelled my sweat as it wafted up from my shirt. I felt mad, like I should go kick one of the stewardesses in the stomach or something, but the feeling passed. The movie *Starman* is playing on the movie screen. Unfortunately, the movie's audio portion does not work and the flight attendants have to refund the money to the people who forked out for it. I have been watching it from time to time as I monitor the lite beer love affair in the seats ahead of me. What a drag. That Martian guy didn't even get it happening with the girl. I guess the Martians don't fuck or something. Back to the romance ahead of me. He makes little advances. He tries to put his arm around her, but he chickens out when he's about six inches away. I don't think she's really into it. When she's lying down, occasionally he will dip his head below the edge of the seat. I can't see what he's doing. But whatever it is, I don't think she's interested. She responds by sitting up, moving a chair away and slipping on the headphones.

The Boston trip was pretty cool. I met the bass player in Aerosmith. He was cool. The best part of the whole day was the guy from Raven. He had dyed black hair and a red leather suit on. He said something like, "Right now I'm calm. But onstage and in our videos, I'm a bloody wild man, right?" Just like something out of Spinal Tap. I nearly laughed in the guy's face. I've got to check that band out sometime. I did a talking show a few hours later in a disco type club called Man Ray's.

A lot of people recognized me at the airport in Boston. One girl hid next to the telephone booth when I was calling someone. When I said, "Hello, this is Henry." The girl ran over to her friends and watched me talk on the phone. Two people have talked to me on this plane ride. Makes me feel funny.

If you're an atheist or whatever the name is for someone who does not believe in a god, then who are your talking to when you are sitting on an airplane grinding your teeth saying, "Please don't crash!" Yourself? I asked myself that the other day when I was flying to Boston. The guy who is scamming on the girl in the row ahead of me just came back from the men's room. I see him sitting down gingerly as to not wake up Sleeping Beauty. He looks like a cop, complete with mustache and beer gut. My hand is falling off. If I make it off this plane alive, oh Lord, I'll never play surf music again.

5.8.85: I have been back in LA a few days. The plane did not crash. A lot has been going on. Our new drummer's name is Anthony — a real cool guy. He's a hot drummer. He sounds great with the band.

I have been busy the last few days with practice and business. Last night, I got the face of my back tattoo done — almost. That was by far the hardest sitting so far. The last 40 minutes, I was ready to throw up. It was hard to keep my eyes open, they kept wanting to shut on me. Practice wears me out. I can barely keep my eyes open.

SIMI VALLEY, MAY 1985. L-R: HENRY (w/snake), GREG, KIRA, ANTHONY MARTINEZ. (*NAOMI PETERSEN*)

The tour starts on May 19 in Arizona. Jessamy called me today. She's with Einsturzende Neubauten in Chicago right now. They will be here on the 18th and on the 19th they fly to Tokyo, Japan. I wonder how they will be accepted there.

Tour starts next weekend. I don't want to come back from this one. I never want to come back from these trips. When I do, then I feel like I have let myself down.

5.12.85: Junk. Needles. Junkies. Whores. Fucking a junked-out girl: Stick your needle into the most attractive gash you can find. As you fuck, study the needle marks on her arms. You think you can help her. She doesn't care how hard you fuck her. She's not there. Moist sheets. Clammy skin. The prettiest girls always seem to look like they are going so fast. When a batch of bad shit hits the streets, they drop like flies. The street cleaners wish the sewers were a little wider so they could kick the bodies down and not have to fill out those stupid reports all the time.

I finished a vocal for the *In My Head* LP yesterday night. About nine more songs to go. The album will be released late this coming summer. Hardly slept last night.

Recovering from suicide. Cards and letters come in: "Better luck next time!" — "If at first you don't succeed, try, try again!" — "Don't stop tryin'!"

Black pool. Drowning in my soul. I am okay. My soul has gone insane. Convoluted, flagellating — my soul has gone insane. Drowning in a black well. Twisting in a sea of glass. Sinking to avoid the guilt of surviving. Felt good. Ghetto fire. Purify. My soul has gone insane. My eyes spiraling upwards. I can't go home. I burned it down.

5.14.85 HIT CITY WEST STUDIOS IN LA: Sitting at one of those Pac Man machines. The table has a glass top. I wonder how many miles of coke have been snorted on this surface. Greg and Chuck are in the next room mixing the SWA album. I'm here because I will be doing vocals. The sounds are different here than in Total Access, the studio I'm used to working in. I will be here for a pretty long while before I do any singing. I was here this morning, several hours ago. It's interesting to watch Greg mix. He'll put the mix on a cassette and play it though his Walkman headset to see how it sounds in there. I am looking forward to taking off for tour. I never expect to come home from any tour — ever. I always do though. Black Flag just released a new record called *Loose Nut*. Sounds real good I think. *Loose Nut* will be a good, strong record to go out and tour on. That's about all I can think about — leaving here and getting there.

This has been a real busy week. I have studio work until I leave. Between practice and workout last night, I could barely think. I fell asleep before midnight. I have to find time to squeeze in one more tattoo session before I go. I hope Rick can get me in this week, otherwise it will be September.

I had a dream last night. I was in this apartment and I was looking out the window. In the apartment below, I could hear the laughter of these little kids. I could see them in the reflection of the window somehow. They were throwing food at each other. One child leaned a ladder against my window and climbed up. He stood on the ladder and grinned at me. I told him that he had better climb down the ladder or he might fall. He did. He climbed down and stood on the roof of a smaller apartment building. All of a sudden, the child began to sway and then he fell off the ledge. It seemed like he fell forever. Finally, his body swept around the corner of the apartment. I never saw him hit the ground. I went down the street to find the body. I found him. The boy was dead. He was in the gutter with all his blood caked around his mouth. I flagged down a policeman and showed him the body and asked him what to do. He just shrugged and said, "Just leave him." That was about the extent of the dream.

Diamanda called me from San Francisco yesterday. She has been up there since she and I flew up there last week. She will probably go to England soon to work on some new material. Einsturzende Neubauten should be here in a couple of days. I hope Jessamy contacts me.

This is torture. There is some band mixing down with the door open. I have been hearing this one stupid, boring song for about an hour now. One of those typical lyrics: "Woman, let's make some dreams that we can share." Oh yeah, and this one: "It's only a weekend, but we can make it last forever."

Later: Still at the studio. I'm in the front room. On the walls of the lobby are these real gross paintings — woodsy scenes and such. They have real slick silver frames around them. They remind me of the shit on the walls of the basement office at Haagen-Dazs. I used to spend a lot of time down there — counting money, writing up inventories and minding the store.

I'll never forget the pictures my boss Steve had on the walls there. He had a portrait of himself done in pencil by some street artist and he had a picture of this sailboat on the open sea. There was a caption on the picture and it read, "Who am I, under this sky, with the wind upon my face?" One night, Chris Edwards (aka Chris Fucking Edwards, aka C.F.E.) and I were down in the office counting money on a Saturday night. Chris decided that the "art" on the walls were too much to bear. He took a pen and drew a small army of shark fins heading toward the boat. To the portrait of Steve, he carefully added some overgrown nose hairs. We worked on the portrait of Steve for months, dotting in stubble, plaque and more nose hairs. I don't know if he ever found out. The sharks did get washed off. But after a while, they surfaced and started making trails toward the boat once more. I never got any flack about that. But I did get a lecture about putting a beard and a mustache on the picture of Steve's daughter that hung on the wall behind the counter. I was creative with my subversion. I would take down the picture of what's her name and paint on a beard, mustache and big eyebrows with chocolate syrup. I would let the syrup dry a little and then I would press the picture face down in the chocolate sprinkles. When I pulled it out, the four year old girl looked like a girl trying to be Fidel Castro. I hung it back up and pretended I never saw anything.

5.19.85 PHOENIX AZ: At the club. Hot as shit inside and outside. I don't think I have slept more than 12 hours since Tuesday. Feel strange. Headache. Yesterday was real cool. Einsturzende Neubauten flew to LA en route to Japan. Diamanda flew down from San Francisco. We all hung out at the Tropicana. Saw Jessamy and the band. Had a real cool time. They had a dub deck with them. I went to Tower Records and got some tapes and copied about five or six hours of great stuff of them live as well as the new Einsturzende

Neubauten album. I left the Tropicana and went to the studio to see how Greg was doing in there. He has been in there about two days straight now. He has to fly out here to make the show. I slept about an hour today. Today is the first of about four months of shows in the US and Canada.

5.20.85 PHOENIX AZ: At the Meat Puppets house. The band is out on tour but we are staying here. Slept in the Ryder last night. Got about three or four hours of sleep. I woke up at about 8 a.m. to a few flies trying to crawl down my throat. The show last night was not too good on my part. The first show is always the hardest. I guess I played okay considering I had one or two hours of sleep the night before. I am on the front porch, looking onto a beautiful cactus garden which is on the front lawn of the house. I was last here in November when we played about 100 miles from here. We are going to leave here fairly soon to go to Tucson to buy some drum cases.

Later: At a Denny's. Talked to a newspaper in Dallas, Texas. They wanted to talk to me about 7-11 since they read my thing in Spin. I spent most of the morning in the front yard with the cactus and the birds. The weather is beautiful. Very hot outside. I am looking forward to going to Tucson. Neck aches. I scratched my chest up last night while we were playing. Felt good.

Much later: Now in Tucson. Sitting on the back porch of the club, writing on a Budweiser box. I went to a 7-11 here. The man behind the counter says he really liked my thing in Spin. That's cool. We don't have a show tomorrow. We have a drive to Salt Lake City. The sun is setting, the air is warm. Makes me feel tired.

5.22.85: In a plane headed toward Denver, Colorado. Yesterday, Greg and I flew to LA to finish up the *In My Head* sessions. I did two more vocals, one song called "Black Love" and another one that I have not put a name on as of yet. Greg remixed two songs and mixed the other two. It was very strange being in LA again. I had made such an effort to leave and then... Bang! Back in the Ginns' back yard. Was in the studio from 6:00 p.m. until 7:00 this morning. I have slept about two or three hours total. This makes a week straight of four hours or less of sleep a night.

The show in Tucson was good. Some guy scratched my stomach up with his nails. I tried to sleep in the Ryder after the show, but the heat woke me up by 7:30 a.m. or so. I need sleep. I have forgotten what it's like.

Last night, I lay on the floor of the studio and tried to sleep. My stomach kept knotting up. I crawl inside myself so far sometimes that I cannot grasp rational thought. These states come and go. I have problems shutting my brain off. There I was, totally exhausted and all I could think of was giving birth to rats and how the plane was going to crash. I have a note pad that I write in. On the cover, I have glued on pictures of mutilated bodies in car wrecks. I like looking at the pictures. They take my mind off girls.

Black and white pictures of car crashes always have shorthaired men covered with blood. The blood is always black. Sometimes it looks like the guy was tarred but not feathered. They are always missing one or both of their shoes. They should have contests to see who can wreck the best. Decapitations would be optimum. There could be single or tandem contestants.

Car crash sex: The man removes his Florsheim shoes and takes his slacks off. His white, pudgy thighs and uncircumcised cock are exposed. The woman — his "partner" — removes her polyester pantsuit, briefs and panty liner, and straddles the man. She puts her chin on his shoulder and stares out the rear windshield. With his cock firmly established inside her, the man starts the engine and they take off down the road. The smell of the radiator, the hum of the engine turns the team on. The woman bounces on his lap. The car hurtles down the road toward the rising sun. Minutes go by... the team is reaching orgasm. Through months of testing and practice, the team can reach orgasm simultaneously. When one or the other is getting close, they will signal the other with a password such as "Roger Wilco" or "Big Mac Attack." The other will speed up or slow down accordingly. When orgasm takes place, the partners will yell "Geronimo!" in unison. The man will then drive into the nearest object and attempt to kill them both. Contestants will be judged in the following categories: mutilation of bodies (dismemberment, impaling, decapitation, etc.), mutilation of the automobile and lastly, the degree of satisfaction on the corpses' faces. A crash and burn is a disqualification. Contestants will be allowed to do dry runs, (i.e., clothes on, dry humping and no collision). This will give the contestants a "feel" for the course. I have seen some teams walking the course, looking for the optimum place for collision/orgasm. They will then drive the course "dry" and start practicing their "run". The "winners" will get a mention in Car & Driver.

5.23.85 SALT LAKE CITY UT: At a Denny's. Last night's show was real cool. People were into the new material even though the record is not out yet. Girls were all around me. It was weird. I talked to this girl whose father beats her fairly often. She and I hung out backstage for a while and talked. She was 15 or 16 I guess. She said that her father treats her like a car. "He thinks he owns me. Since he owns me, he thinks he can wreck me or dent me anytime he wants. I'm not a car." What a girl. Tough. I told her to keep it together and get through school so she can get the fuck out of her house. She fears that her father may rape her.

Parents are such a trip. What a thing for a young girl to have to think about. She rebels by getting wasted. I told her that she is just playing into her father's hands. The only way for her to get out of that situation is to get it together and not let it fall apart.

5.24.85 DENVER CO: At the Rainbow. Arrived here about 3:30 a.m. Slept in the parking lot. Jerry Garcia played here last night. There are portable toilets in the parking lot. I guess to handle the crowd that camped out for the show. All the employees are talking about the Garcia show, mumbling about Deadheads.

Went and did a video interview for some local station out here. Went okay. Hungry, tired. I wonder how many people will come tonight. I wish we could stay and play in Boulder or something.

Much later: I heard the security staff getting briefed. "There have been 700 or so advance tickets sold. The walk-up may make over one thousand. This will be the hardest night you will have. These people have no respect for authority. If you take one out, you will have to take out his friends also because they stick together. At the door, watch for spikes, fireworks, bottles — whatever. These people are our patrons, just as if we were having any other band playing. Usually, we let things slide, but tonight is Black Flag and we are going to be hard-line all the way. Remember, just because they are slamming into each other doesn't mean that they're fighting. That's how these people show they love each other. The doors open in ten minutes. Are there any questions?"

"What's the difference between a skinhead and a punker?"

"Okay, a punker is a person who has funny hair. This person is a leftist. A skinhead has no hair and is into neo-fascism. Okay, is there anything else?"

I went and got a Coke at a liquor store across the street. I think I got my picture taken ten times in a minute. One kid ran up to me waving a plastic machine gun.

Much later: At a Denny's in Colorado. I liked the show tonight. I played real hard. The Minutemen were real good. Talked to some girls who were "sent for the band." Yow! Ten to twelve hours to go until we hit New Mexico. I need to sleep.

5.25.85 ALBUQUERQUE NM: Got into town about two hours ago. I went by Living Batch Books where I did the talking show last January. Ate at the Frontier, bought a tape of *Master of Reality* by Black Sabbath. That's one of the best records I've ever heard.

This morning in Las Vegas, we stopped to get gas. Across from the gas station was this convenience store. The sign said 7-11. Could it be? Could I have stumbled upon the first 7-11? I dropped to my knees in front of the door. The rising sun burned my back. I heard angels singing. At last, I had reached Mecca...

Inside, there was a woman who looked like a pig — a real pig. There was something wrong with her nose. Behind the counter with her was a Nevada cop. I saw his mud-caked car outside. A pig and a pig — male and female. Perfect.

sed an overturned Chevy Blazer on the side of the road. There was nothing around it. I don't know how it tipped over. There was a bunch of people standing in a semicircle around it.

I am sitting on the steps of where we play tonight. Same place as last time. Your basic slum — broken down houses, mud, Madonna blaring out of someone's window. Clear day — hot and lots of clouds and mountains.

When I was in the bookstore today, I was looking through this book about Vietnam. Lots of color pictures. My favorite picture was one of this Vietnamese boy looking into a pickup truck. He is crying. In the bed of the truck is a dead girl — all shot up, covered with blood. There were flies all over her body. The flies seemed to be most interested in her face. The flies were all over her face, eating dried blood. I know what there is. There is nothing. There is no one. I love no one. I love you, no one.

Last night, I stared at all those people staring at me. It always trips me out. They look like little fish swimming around. My friend is no one. A drained body, hollowed out. No guts, no blood, no mind, no problems. I wish she would bleed me, but she always leaves

ALBUQUERQUE, NM / 5.25.85 *(D.D.W.)*

me alone. I can drain myself. I can spoon out my brain into a ziplock bag and put it away. Take it out when I think I can cope. Maybe be able to get some sleep. I don't want to dream anymore... at least for a little while.

Dream in a dark room: I saw this thing on television the other night. Cheryl Ladd starred in it. She has this high forehead. It looked like it was made out of porcelain, like the side of a piggy bank. There was this one scene where she's getting raped and the studio light reflects off that big, fat forehead of hers. I wanted to take a bite out of it, like taking a bite out of the side of a chocolate creme-filled Easter bunny. Yeah, I take a big bite out of her head. Flesh, skull and brain are in my mouth. I eat it. Cheryl Ladd's brains and heck, she's so darned pretty that any part of her would be nice. I stick my cock in the hole. I fuck her brains out. I grab a handful of her hair and fuck her brains out.

5.28.85 OKLAHOMA CITY: Waiting outside the club to get in. Shows have been going well. Last night was Lubbock, Texas. We drove all night to get here.

Met an interesting guy in Albuquerque. I was loading equipment out and this Mexican guy starts talking to me. He had all these tattoos he got "in the joint." He pointed to a rolling eight ball on his forearm. He told me that meant cocaine. On the underside of his wrist, he had "Killer Loco." He told me that was his name. He asked if I wanted some heroin.

I was in this diner in Santa Rosa, New Mexico the other day. I got an iced tea and just watche eat. It was disgusting. This one guy cut his food all up until it was one big mess and then he laid into it. He smoked between bites.

I spent several hours in the back of the Ryder the other night. Pitch black. I like it. I sit in there and do nothing but think. There is nothing to inspire the eye and nothing but rattling and motor noise for the ears. It is the dark room. I am sealed off from their world. I have my own. I like darkness.

The other night I lay on the floor of the truck as it went down the road and I wondered how I was going to die when the Ryder crashed. I cannot see outside. I have no idea what's happening out there. I had two different scenes very well planned out, but I cannot remember them now. It's very hard for me to write. I think maybe the playing burns me out to the point to where I have nothing to think about for hours at a time. Loneliness and fatigue burns me out to a great extent. I looked back at page one of this journal. I started this one here at this club on 2.6.84. Some lady just walked up and asked if she could interview me. I said okay. I might as well. All I have done for the last twenty minutes is write a bunch of boring drivel. I had such good ideas in the truck the other night. Where are they now? That man at the diner was so repulsive. But now, I cannot hardly remember him at all. What a letdown.

You walk into the diner. You go up to the counter to sit down. You notice that there's only one stool. The rest of the counter is taken up by gynecological stirrups. You sit on the stool and await service. Two large, naked women get into the stirrups on either side of you. There is a large, infected vagina on either side of you. You notice a jar of what looks like pickled pigs knuckles in front of you. You look closely. You see that they are human fingers. Still no service. You look around for a waiter. Finally, a man appears from the kitchen. He is corpulent and covered with running sores. He is naked, save for surgeon's gloves and a greasy pink t-shirt that says, "Warm Polio Flesh". You ask him, "Are those really human fingers in there?" He grins and pulls one out of the jar and eats the entire thing, bone and all. He burps and says, "Yes." He points to the two women and says, "Are these broads with you?" You tell him no. You check out the menu and order the "Squirming Fetus." He yells, "One lowlife coming up!" He sticks his arm into the woman on your left and pulls out a blue, writhing fetus and throws it on a plate and slaps it down in front of you. He asks you if you want garlic toast or dinner roll. You choose garlic bread. You eat. You pay the man. You say goodbye to the girls and leave.

5.29.85 OKLAHOMA CITY OK: At a Village Inn, waiting to eat. Last night was two sets. No one told me, but it was cool anyhow. The first set was okay, but the second set was real good. Slept in the Ryder last night. Hot and sticky. Me and Cancer Man. Slept next to a school. Woke up to all these screaming kids.

The Madonna clone who was at the last show we played here was there last night. Belly button exposed and everything. She watched me and her boyfriend watched her watch me.

Later: Now in Tulsa. It's nearing 5:00 p.m. and the club is still not open. This does not give us a lot of time to set up.

Later: Loaded in. Didn't take a lot of time. Everybody pitched in for a change. Well, almost everybody. I have noticed that there is a mutual disregard for others here in our crew. To deny it would be lying. It's kind of cool actually. It keeps you on your toes. Everybody puts themselves first and at least none of us are too chickenshit to admit it.

When I was sitting on the sidewalk earlier today, this couple parked their Bronco and got out. The man — a pot-bellied cowboy — stared at me hard. Silly redneck. I just stared right back. He bummed, took his wife by the arm and whisked her off. I can't wait to play tonight. It's the only good thing I do the whole day. It's a high — takes my mind off Cancer Man. I am Cancer Man. I infect myself. I paralyze my own thoughts. Strangulation, but I can't figure out why.

Summer is here — right now. I am steaming. My skin is always moist. I can smell myself. I like that. Lets me know that I am alive. My eyes can see for hundreds of miles. I live in alienation eyes. I hear people talk to my face and I know that I'm not there with them.

People say funny things. Last night was funny. Not that funny, mostly just depressing. I'd rather hurt them than make them smile. Have been depressed for the last week or so. The only one I can stand is myself. I'm starting to really enjoy being alone. When the truck pulls in and I can get out and go somewhere, I feel like I have triumphed or something. Not gotten over anybody or anything, but just gotten something for myself. I have tried and tried, but I cannot identify with anyone but myself. I can under-

stand and identify with the sun and darkness and insanity. Humans just don't make me feel good. There is not one person I feel I understand. What is NOT alienating? How many circles do you have to spin until you see where you are? I am here. But I don't know where that is.

5.31.85 AUSTIN TX: At the Ritz. It's near 10:00 p.m. and still it's hot and muggy outside. Rode from Dallas to Austin inside the Ryder. Over one hundred degrees inside — no moving air. I felt like a saint. Last night was crazy. Good show, but real crazy. Girls backstage, onstage — everywhere. One girl passed out when she met me.

Texas is depressing. A few more days and we will be somewhere else. I am dripping sweat as I am writing. I feel shapeless, empty of myself. I don't feel burned out so much as empty. Like running down a road with no end in sight. Can't see why or where I'm going. Did two interviews this evening. I sure do a lot of those.

Tomorrow we play in Houston. Two sets plus an in-store appearance at some record store. There's no escape from the heat. Everywhere is hot. The heat wears the body out. Hard to sleep at night. In these situations, I usually get about three to five hours a night and consider myself lucky. The best thing I saw today was this fat lady going into the ladies room here at the club. She opened the door and bent over real far to see if there was anyone in the stall. There she was, all bent over, huge ass looming into the air. She cut a nice profile against the pink tile.

Everything in Texas is big. The guys on the street all look like football players — Bud Lite-fueled shitkickers. The pigs here really look like pigs. Heard one at the liquor store today talking about how he goes sparring every weekend. He was sporting a black eye.

6.2.85 San Antonio TX: At the club. Have not checked in for a couple of days. Austin show was a drag. Some girl dumped a cup of hot piss on me while we were playing. Nothing like a mouthful of some girl's piss to put a damper on your mood. The show turned into an exercise after that. The show started real late. By the time we had loaded all the equipment into the truck, it was almost five in the morning.

I was in the alley loading up and this drunk guy started bothering us. He came up and tried to kiss me. I punched him in the throat. He flew into the side of a dumpster.

Slept at some creepy skinhead girl's house. She was on speed so she was up rattling around all night. I "slept" on the floor of her room. Some of the crew slept in the living room. There was this girl sleeping on the couch. She got happening with one of our crew. When I left in the morning to go to the truck, I saw these ugly women, naked and lounging in a hot tub in the courtyard. It looked surreal. Steam rising all around these nude women. I thought I was hallucinating. I got about one hour of sleep. Got a couple more on the way to Houston. We did two sets in Houston last night. I did this in-store appearance at a record store called Infinite Records. Great place. I bought some cool John Lee Hooker records.

The two sets went okay. The second set I had to take a breather because I started to see double. It was so hot in the club that our drummer had to take a break. I thought he was going to fall off his stool from the way he looked. I don't know how we make it through sets like that. When I'm playing, I never think about it. But when I'm loading out the equipment back into the truck, I'm amazed that we keep pulling it off year after year. When we were playing "My War" in the first set, I concentrated on a single spot. The spot started to take shape and color. It was cool. We have two sets tonight.

Oh man, the place we played yesterday was located on Westheimer Street. What a trip. The street was bumper to bumper young people, cruising in everything from low riders to pickup trucks. Hundreds — literally hundreds of people on the street. People all over the place. Everywhere I went, I could hear people calling my name or saying, "Look, it's Henry Rollins!" Fine. I still sleep alone. Saw some male prostitutes on a corner. One said to the other, "Let's call it a night. Let's get up early tomorrow and go fishing." I got about four hours of sleep last night.

This club has air conditioning. I feel very cool, temperature wise, that's it. I'm sitting at the bar. A portrait of Jim Morrison stares right back at me. The local paper has compared me to Jim Morrison and Henry Miller.

I must never forget what I am. Not for a second. I know what I am. Yes, I am denied certain things and that's okay. In the place of the things I have denied myself, I have things that mean more to me than sex, fun and happiness ever could. I can hear the sun rise. The wind talks to me. I know the language of the stillness and the silence of my mind.

Whenever girls talk to me, I feel dirty — ugly. I want to touch them. I feel like a monster. I talked to a girl yesterday that made me feel almost human. I looked into her eyes and I could feel the lead in my veins. I felt the wall build itself. All of a sudden, I was talking to her from a million miles away. I went cold. I stared at the ground. In the dark, alone and imprisoned. I didn't want to talk anymore — to anyone, anywhere. That's my mind right now. That's what my brain told me. I slept on the floor of this apartment last night. Cancer Man spoke to me as I lay there. Cancer Man never lies to me. I trust Cancer Man. Last night, Cancer Man told me to turn inside — that no one can understand. Turn inward. Turn your flesh to stone. He is always right. The truth hurts. May I never grow numb to the pain of truth. The pain hurts. But the hurt feels good.

Later: Played the first set. I focused on the red exit sign over the front door. People were very still. Why two sets? I don't understand. Feel pretty low. Don't feel like shaking hands and signing autographs. I'm back at the bar with the picture of ol' Jim. I don't think we're playing tomorrow night. That might be a good thing for me right now.

I touch her hair. Her shoulders clench together and she stares at the ground. She looks like a stone bird. I am an iceberg. Everyday I float farther and farther out to sea. But that can't be. An iceberg feels no pain. An iceberg doesn't feel cold. I feel cold. I feel distant. There is no one. There is nothing. That's where I am. She won't look me in the eye anymore since I asked if I could kiss her. Even wanting to turns her cold. I feel like a greasy newspaper. I feel dirty. I feel like I should not be allowed these feelings. They are okay for everyone else though.

Been on the trail too long. I don't know how to deal with earthlings. Cancer Man is standing to my left. He is reading this and nodding. "Everything seems to be in order," he says. When I listen to him, I'm okay. I remain untouched, unharmed. My blood is leaden. My soul turns to cold steel and I understand everybody's everything. When I stray or don't listen, he gets me good. He punishes me with truth. Heroin probably feels good — like lies. I hate the memories and thoughts that feel like I'm swallowing glass. Your stomach is all cut up. But what do you do to kill the pain? You swallow more glass. I ask myself, "How stupid can you get?" The answer is always the same.

Much later: Second set over. Some motherfucker stole my shorts. I don't have shorts because someone stole them from me. They are gone. We are staying at this club tonight. A lot of the crew are drunk or getting there. Great. Now I have to listen to it all night. That's fine. I didn't like playing tonight. I'm glad we're not playing tomorrow.

I saw the new Spin with my second article in it. This issue has Nick Cave in it. The interview was done by Kristine McKenna. She never seems to get anything interesting out of anyone. I miss Nick. He's a good man. The Spin editors rearranged my article and messed up a few words but it still looks good. They mentioned me on the cover. That's cool. A photographer from Spin has been with us for two days now. He will be with us for a few more.

6.5.85 LAFAYETTE LA: At the club — the Jefferson Street Cafe. Slept in a hotel last night. Didn't sleep too well, just tossed and turned a lot. Too horny to sleep. Every girl I have seen walking past this place has looked hot. I wrote Nick Cave a letter today. I sent it c/o Mute Records in London.

The last time we played here, we played a transvestite bar. It was cool, but I like this place better.

Had bad dreams last night. I'm starting to notice changes in myself in the night before and the night of a full moon. The last time sent me into a spin that is still tripping me out. I can feel myself slipping away. It does not scare me anymore. I welcome dark hands. Powerful, slow moving river taking me under. I can feel it. Cancer Man is insane. His eyes never close. I have stared into the sun too long. The music is bright. The music is deafening. Pulling me under. Making me see everything.

6.7.85 MEMPHIS TN: At the Antenna Club again. Hanging out on the sidewalk because the air conditioner in the club is cold as hell and I got shorts on. Outside here, the weather is real nice, not anything at all like Texas. People keep bothering me out here. I did an in-store today. Not bad. A lot of real young people who will not be able to get in the show tonight. Sometimes I get nervous. I sure as hell feel pretentious going in there all by myself and standing around. It's good for me. Keeps me in touch with people. The vibe at a record store is a lot different than at a gig.

We played in New Orleans last night. A lot of people came. More than the last two times we played there put together. The cops busted the show about five or six songs from the end. Now people are hovering around me like mosquitoes. I guess it's time to go in.

6.8.85 NASHVILLE TN: Outside of Cantrell's. Good show last night. Slept at a truck stop. There was a real good restroom at the place. Every urinal had an ashtray. That's class. No butts in the bowl. I can see some guy in there now — cock in one hand, cigar in the other, staring into space.

Went to a used record and book store. Picked up a copy of *Tropic of Capricorn* by Henry Miller. I already have a copy but it's really torn up. I gave my copy to Brian from the sound company.

There are people standing all around me asking me questions. I feel like saying, "I know it looks like I'm busy, but I'm not. Really." But I don't say that. I answer the questions like a good guy. I watched a little boy play alone on the front porch of his house that faces the front of the club. The way the house looked and the way the boy was dressed, you would have thought it was a scene from *Tom Sawyer*. The neon sign on the building next to the house fucked that up though. He kept picking up rocks and throwing them up at the roof. Finally, a hornet's nest fell to the ground. The boy leaped on it and stomped it flat. After he destroyed it, he kicked the remains into the street.

6.11.85 ATHENS GA: At a diner. Slept in the truck last night. The show last night was okay. Not great, but good. Athens is a very nice looking town. I took a walk around the area of the club. Some stupid college guys gave me some shit about long hair. I just stared at them and smiled.

Last night some guy spat on me so I dumped a pitcher of water on him and cracked him on the head with the pitcher. Oh yeah, some college boy spat on me and I clipped him in the teeth with the microphone.

The show in Knoxville was real cool, but a bit alienating. I hate drunk women who try to pick up on me. I get confused. I like women a lot and all the time but I don't know when some wobbling thing comes up to me and says, "Russell, I'm here for the band!" She gets mad when I don't talk to her. She can't understand that I don't want my cheek covered with booze-infested saliva. She feels rejected when I push her away from me, and she walks away and trips and her head slams into the wall.

We are on our way to Birmingham, Alabama. Back to the Nick, the same place as before. I wonder if that same girl is there — the one who had a U2 shirt and a headset blasting Prince — a real champ.

I got this place rocking. I put three Madonna songs and a Cyndi Lauper song on the jukebox. Pretty swell. People are squirming left and right. Someone just put on some Rod Stewart. It's time to go.

6.13.85 St. Petersburg FL: Yesterday was a bit busy. Played Atlanta — the 688 Club. Did two sets, two interviews, a video interview and an in-store thing at a record store. Packed up and drove all night to get here. I slept in the back of the Ryder. At one point, the fumes got so heavy that I started hallucinating. I saw red and pink triangles dissolving and twisting into different shapes. The fumes stung my nose and throat. I kept repeating the phrase, "Disintegrating into Christ" over and over.

The night before last was Birmingham, AL. When I got to the club, some guy came up and told me that it was time for me to go to the "reading". What reading? No one told me about a reading. Off I went, not knowing what I was going to do. We pulled up to the place. It was a public park. All these people were there waiting for me. I felt ill... I pulled it off. I sat down and talked to these people for about an hour. I did the best I could.

The people here at this club are all cokeheads. I heard them talking earlier today. A guy telling his bro about how he went to this party and got his "nose froze." His friend says, "Yeah, there's nothing like downhill skiing, nose first." I saw a lot of gross, fat people here today. Even the kids are fat, waddling around, sunburned and greasy.

At this shitty breakfast place this morning. Lots of fat people, lots of old people gumming eggs and buying tourist paraphernalia. Saw a sign on the side of the road. It depicted a piece of meat on a spit. The lettering underneath it read, "Flame Kist." *Kissed by flame.* Yes, I can see it now. The family station wagon with an entire set of Samsonite luggage, the car is engulfed in flames. I can see the father, strapped into the front seat behind the wheel, hair burning off. Polyester Hawaiian shirt burning into his flesh. Eyes staring straight ahead, hands on the wheel. The wife and the two kids are writhing and turning, covering their burning, smoking bodies with melting plastic from the seats. Black, choking smoke curls and rises through the palmettos. *Kissed by flame.* The firemen put the fire out. The paramedics pull the bodies out of the car, load them into body bags and haul them to the swamps. Just tourists... No one will miss them. *Kissed by flame.*

Reminds me of the time I torched this fat kid because his father was a cop. As I was pouring the gasoline on his head, I told him that I sometimes eat the kids I kill. But he was pig meat — inedible.

I was talking to this girl the other day. She is currently in school. In one of her classes, she works with dead bodies. Not just normal cadavers, she works with bodies that have been found in rivers and car trunks. She says the only thing that bothers her is looking at dead children. Her most recent study is a male body found in the woods. Arms, legs, head and groin all chain-sawed off. She drove me by the place where the body was dragged from. Looks like a nice patch of woods to me.

I can see her now. Her beautiful hands cutting into rotted human flesh with sharp blades. Anything is possible. I imagine her putting jars of blue flies on the flesh to see how fast they lay eggs (to test how long the body has been dead). She stares at cold, rancid bloated corpses and hopes to get an "A".

Much later: Did the show. Thought it went real well. I played real hard. Workout and ginseng really happening for the set. Driving all night to Miami.

Pretty drained. Brain pretty tired. The waitress at the restaurant I'm in now is laughing because everyone is all split off in different corners. Everyone in the crew gets along real well. But still, people need their space. So far things have been going pretty damned good considering the workload and the new faces.

Pretty friendly crowd for Florida. Floridians are not famous for their warmth. That's fine with me. As long as I know where everyone is at, then that's cool. I can barely keep my eyes open enough to write. I hope I get some sleep tonight. I can use it. My body is tired. But my mind is awake now.

The fat people. Blue/white flesh. Varicose veins. Bloated abdomens and sunglasses. Ankle socks. Inquiring to the location of the restrooms. Holed up in motels. Maybe the gators will snap them up.

6.15.85 TAMPA FL: Yesterday was Miami. Pretty busy — college radio interview, in-store talking thing. Place so hot that we had to take a break two-thirds of the way through. A girl up front passed out and was carried out. There was one boy in the bathroom who was real wasted. He just stared into the sink and played with the water. People were snorting some kind of shit in the stalls. I don't know what. I asked one of the guys who was snorting. He didn't know what it was either.

Drove all night to Tampa. Woke up sweating — clothes and blankets wet, a bowl of something dumped in my shoes. I got out of the Ryder and pissed in the road. I walked around, trying to figure out where I was. I walked down an alley — rats darting for cover, garbage and old cars. Playing in another slum.

All of the places I go in Florida are slums. I took a walk around today. Most of the places are boarded up and closed down. Blacks and Cubans on the street. When I am on the street walking around, I always hear Madonna blasting out of a car or a store. Madonna's everywhere. She is a celestial body. In the big cities and slums, Madonna is there, just like Sister Theresa, making our day just a little brighter. Making us forget about the rats and the garbage. I stink. I am sitting here in my wet, greasy clothes and I can smell myself. I have no friends besides myself. None. I made that decision today. People turn, pull attitudes, lie, don't come through. I see it all. Every fucking second of it and I hate it.

I know some great people, some of whom I trust. They are okay by me. I always watch them to see when they will betray me. I have only one friend — Myself. I am always amused and amazed at how hostile and abusive people can be. When it happens at Black Flag shows, that's the strangest. There are all these people there to see you and they will give you shit, try to hurt you and try to rip you off. This shit used to turn me off from playing, but now... Shit, I can handle it because I know where these people are at. That's cool. I don't trust them an inch and I never have problems with them. But it's a lonely place I have put myself in. Why? Because I am sick of letdowns, lies, deceit and betrayal. I will maintain and support Fort Rollins forever.

6.16.85 TALLAHASSEE FL: Played okay last night. Throat very sore. Now inside the club — air conditioned. Drove last night to get here.

Lots of rain. Picked up a few nice fly-bites. It was dawn. My bladder was going to explode. The Ryder was parked somewhere so I slithered out of the back and looked for a place to piss. I didn't look far. I just stood next to the Ryder and let it fly. So there I was, pissing like a goddamned racehorse in the moist Floridian dawn, when good ol' Reggie comes walking around the Ryder right into the path of the stream. I tried to steer clear, but it was too late. Sorry, Reg. Of course I didn't mean to piss on Reggie. But seeing him jump up and down and yell a lot was kind of cool. He was so mad, he chased me around the truck three times.

This is not the same place as our last show here. Last time, we played two sets to about 50-60 people total. Well, whatever. Maybe since this is the state capitol of Florida, there won't be so much shitty trash everywhere. I don't mind ghettos and stupid, ignorant and violent people. But a week's worth of different ones is sensory overload.

I was walking in Tampa yesterday, looking for some food. I was walking past these tract homes. I was the only white boy I could see. I kept thinking to myself, "What the fuck am I doing here?" I heard these guys talking about "kicking his goddamned chest in." Great... Nobody bothered me. I probably looked like I didn't have any money. Tomorrow is a day off. Drive to South Carolina.

6.17.85 SOME BEACH IN FLORIDA: We have been here all day. I ran, swam and read a lot of *Tropic of Capricorn*. Images on the beach: I'm sitting on this rock. I look from my left to my right — an empty pack of Marlboros and an empty can of Bud. Perfect! Marlboros 'n' Bud — my buddies. I run on the beach. Fat white girls giggle as I pass. A lifeguard who looks like Madonna smiles at me. A little kid carries a large dead crab to his parents. Three people walk together on the beach, all hand-in-hand. A mother with her husband and son — mother in the middle. The Father: Tired walk, dull eyes, dragging feet. Son: Early teens, slightly embarrassed, bored, eyes roving back and forth. Mother: In the middle, looking calm, happy, radiant.

6.19.85 COLUMBIA SC: We played a new place last night. Pretty good show. We had to load the PA up these stairs. We parked the truck on the sidewalk and proceeded to load the PA. A cop came and told us to move the truck. We moved it. The pig bailed and we moved the truck back on the sidewalk and continued loading in. Another pig came and said move. We asked him to let us keep the truck there so we would not have to load in all day. He told us that a store owner called and complained about the truck. The second pig was going to let us slide. That was — until the first pig came back and started to chew us out. We all just stood there and laughed in his face. It was great. The pig blew a fuse. He started telling us that we were all going to jail if the truck went on the sidewalk again. We were all saying, "Fuck you" in high pitched voices. It was cool. After we loaded in, I went to the gun store and asked if they were the ones that called the pigs. The people said it was the Levi's place next door. Fine.

WASHINGTON, DC / JUNE 1985

To make a long story short, we got a seven dollar ticket from the pig — a ticket we won't pay. As we were leaving, I noticed that someone had spray painted "Fuck You" and a swastika all over the front of the Levi's store and the piece of sidewalk in front. I bet it will cost the city some money to get that off. Whoever did that was probably angry and just expressing themselves.

6.22.85: In a diner somewhere in West Virginia. The last few days, let's see... played in Charlotte at the Milestone. Another show at the Milestone. Did a long photo session with this lady from Spin. She had taken all these pictures of Sting and people like that. She told me that I was very handsome and stuff. She made me work. I never did a photo session like that before. I felt like some kind of model or something. Pretty stupid. The next night was two sets in Raleigh, NC. Nothing special — good shows, cool people and everything.

Last night was two sets in Richmond — same club as the 1982 tour. Sore throat. Some guy jumped onstage and kicked me in the head real hard with his boot. I grabbed him and punched him in the face. Don't hit the singer in the head because he will try to punch your lights out.

Now at the club in Morgantown, West Virginia. Drove all night from Richmond. At 6:48 this morning, I was sitting in the back of the Ryder. I was unable to sleep because of the bumpy road. We were passing through the mountains and I was looking at the terrain as we drove, when we hit a very sharp curve. I watched out the back and it occurred to me that we were going way too fast. All of a sudden, the truck started to lean to one side and I could smell the tires burning. The truck kept leaning and shit was flying around. *We were on two wheels*. I thought I was going to die. The truck came down and went up on the other set of wheels and nearly rolled over. If it had, I think that Davo and I would have been killed for certain. Two humans with two tons of equipment on top of them. Thanks, Reggie... I will not ride with him again ever. He nearly killed me. That was such a weird view. Watching the world turn sideways through the crack in the door.

The shot to my head has left me groggy and dull today. My throat is swollen. I have to keep the Tylenol going so I can think straight. Whatever it takes.

Went to a used bookstore today. Found some good books for cheap. Driving tonight for DC. Called Ian today. We will be around for the next few days in the DC area.

6.23.85 DISCHORD: Went here and there today. Got some records. Saw some people I recognized. Very late.

6.26.85: In Ian's room, sitting on the floor. Played two nights at the 9:30 Club. I didn't like the sets. People were great. I didn't like my performance. I never do here. I cannot concentrate. I felt very frustrated and empty. I want to leave so I can think of nothing but playing. The distractions here are not good for my playing. Otherwise, things are fine. Fuck it. I'm exhausted and full of shit.

6.27.85: In Ian's room. Raining outside. The smell of ozone sets my mind to wander. With each breath, I think. My thoughts are like moths around a street lamp at night. They flit and hover around the glow but never land. This puts me in a spin.

Went downtown today to go to the dentist. I wonder how many people feel like their neckties are strangling them to Death. Thirty-five year old Death. Dog tag necktie. I walked on those streets thanking myself over and over that I didn't fall for that lie. Damn... Whenever I'm here in Washington, I get paralyzed. I can't write. I just think about it. Ideas and memories fly through my head like a shitstorm. I am too busy listening, smelling, looking, wanting to see something, not wanting to miss a second. I didn't like those shows in DC. If I ever play like that again, I will flog myself until I bleed. I think I should leave here. I don't like what being here makes me do. It weakens my concentration. I no longer relate to the town. I don't feel alienated. I just feel like it's time to go and go and go until I drop. When I die, the world dies.

I went to the dumping ground and saw the bodies stacked high. A dead, cold mountain. My soul is a dumping ground. I bring the bodies to the pit. I try to dance with them while they are still warm. Dance with me. Hold me, please. They do for a while, then they turn stiff and cold and I dump the dead on the heap. All stiffs are the same to me. That's the way they are. The people — warm in your heart for a short while and then they turn cold, alien and dead. You wonder what ever made you notice them in the first place.

ANTHONY MARTINEZ, NEW YORK, NY / 6.29.85

6.29.85 NYC: In front of Irving Plaza. Last night was Dover, NJ. Not the greatest day I ever had. Got to the club and went to a Friendly's to eat. Every person around there looked like someone from a Bruce Springsteen video. Got whisked off to do an in-store. Lots of people there even though I was late. A few assholes — people trying to get me to sign Jim Morrison pictures and shit. I just told them what I always do. I tell them what they are. After that, I did a college radio interview for some place. Drove back to the show. People didn't like St. Vitus. They threw things and jeered. I didn't like our set last night. Real stiff on my part. I asked people not to get onstage, but they did anyway. I bashed two guys in the head with the microphone. I enjoyed that very much. Reggie got dragged into the crowd and got kicked around. I pulled people off as best I could. He smashed his elbow and is now at the hospital getting himself checked out.

Spent the night at this guy's house. This stoner — his mom was out of town and we had the run of the place. Imagine a large house that looks like a tornado ripped through it. Beer cans everywhere. I slept in his mother's dressing room. Shoes, dresses, cheap jewelry and trash everywhere. Sink all clogged up with puke. Slept okay except when the stoner guys would come in and sing Black Flag songs at the top of their lungs.

So now I'm in the Village. In an hour, I'm supposed to be at Bleecker Bob's for an in-store thing. Not looking forward to that much. I guess if you lived here long enough, you might learn to really like it. The streets, the buildings — you could like it I suppose.

NEW YORK, NY / 6.29.85

When I was here last August, I didn't have the greatest time. Got burned out on burned out people. The Village is a world away from reality. I think the "artists" here don't really see outside. The trip seems so insular. Like the skinheads with their tattoos. These skinhead children get a skinhead nailed to a cross, tattooed on their arm. That blows me away. They are the kings of the Village? That makes me think of a bunch of flies fighting over a big lump of shit.

6.30.85: In the basement of some guy's house — Quiet. Played New York last night at Irving Plaza. Ran into Danzig there. Played hard. Today was busy — in-store at Newbury Comics, signed stuff until my hand got stiff. Cool people though. We are on the cover of Boston Rock. *Loose Nut* is number one on their chart. There's this big picture of me on the inside that says "Henry Rollins Thinks" and has an interview with me. Did the show. Wiped out. Did an interview on WBCN with Oedipus. They sent a van to come and get me. Did an interview for the Herald also. Feel a bit burnt. Did a photo session with Rock magazine yesterday. Apparently, they are doing a thing on me.

I am watching Scotty from Vitus sleeping across from me. He's sleeping with his arm around his clothes bag. I guess he misses his girlfriend. I don't miss anyone or anything. I feel the alienation running through my veins. I see the bread and water in my eyes. I think my flesh is turning to scar tissue. My brain is twitching, budding, singeing. I have outdistanced their lying shallow lives. I have escaped their prisons, their nooses, their graves. I have not reached their mountain tops. But I have been dragged through their slums more than a few times. I stand on my own road — totally alone. The sun rises, warming my back. I am mine. I am the crawling king snake. I am my end. I am standing on the edge of my world, looking into my desert brain, listening to the dull roars and car crash sounds. I see the twisted bodies, the dead snakes — severed, gutted and piled high. I opened my eyes and their world fell away.

7.2.85 KATAUSQUA PA: Played last night at the Living Room in Providence, RI. Did an in-store thing. Nothing remarkable about it. Good though. The show went okay. I got popped in the mouth, but what else is new. Some guy asked me what "Search & Destroy" meant. I told him it was from the military term. He couldn't believe that I meant that. That man asking me about Search & Destroy got me to thinking about this crazy guy who used to hang out on Wisconsin Avenue when I was young. His name was Rocky. Rocky was huge, about 6 foot 6. Rocky was a Vietnam vet. He was crazy as hell. He used to tell me stories about search and destroy missions he went on. I'll never forget the story about the kid.

He went into a village to check it for VC. There was a lady with what looked like a baby wrapped up in a blanket. Rocky grabbed the bundle and checked it. The bundle was a child. Rocky threw the child into the air and bayoneted it as it fell downward. When he told me this, he started to cry, then he started to scream. He grabbed me around the neck and started to choke me. He was screaming and spitting Southern Comfort all over my face. Somehow I got free and I ran away. Days later, I talked to him. He didn't even remember.

Yesterday, I was eating at this diner. The waitress looked at the tattoos on my arm and said, "You're a busy little beaver, aren't you?" She remarked that I had no tattoos of Jesus Christ. She said, "If you found Christ, you wouldn't need those things." I said that I had already found him and passed him by. She said, "Christ makes life simple. You don't have to search anymore."

I hope the world burns down today. Tobacco drenched homeboys telling me what I am. I laugh and brush them off my shoulder like lice.

There is a store down the street called *My Father's Meats*. That's great. I could see a guy behind the counter, selling slices of his father's flesh to customers. There might even be a cult of father eaters.

My brain is in a vacuum. If I could fly, I would. I am in the summer. I am encased in the belly of a large black wolf. It's hot in here — hot and dark. I am alone

— finally alone. I have found my strength in the alone. That's what some will never understand. They are trapped in their houses. They are chained to their lovers. I have made the decision to... No! The decision was made for me by their faces, their lives, their tragedies, their shallow, lying mentality. They made me see. They made up my mind for me. I will never surrender to the velvet coffin. Never. Hate me, ostracize me, call me insane, call me whatever. But remember that I can see through you every moment of the day. I can close my eyes and write this.

My pen knows what to do. I close my eyes and I see this girl who glows. A girl who radiates. When she smiles, she beams. She warms my heart. I open my eyes with a feeling of floating past all the garbage around me. I will emerge from this unscathed because I will not endeavor to hide myself from whatever is coming. Bring on the worst. I welcome it with open arms. I think of that lady telling me that her life is simple now because she no longer has to search. She looks and acts pretty fucking simple.

7.3.85 ENFIELD CT: Playing in a roller rink. Drove all night. Got here at about 8 o'clock in the morning. I got some good sleep underneath a pine tree.

7.7.85 TRENTON NJ: Did the show at the City Gardens. Our fifth time there in three years. There were a lot of people at this one. After the set, I felt so weak that I could barely walk offstage. I found a chair and kind of fell into it. My head was pounding so hard I thought I had broke something in my brain. These people came up and immediately started talking to me. I couldn't make out what they were trying to say to me. They sounded real weird. I felt like I was tripping or something. I didn't even have the energy to tell them to leave me alone. It's hours later and my head is still ringing. Playing is starting to lock me in. Every set I do now, I kick myself farther and farther away from them, their lives, their minds — their everything. I cannot think anymore.

7.8.85 BALTIMORE MD: At the club. Got good sleep last night. Feel okay. I hate being at these clubs when they're in the middle of nowhere. The guy who runs this place just gave me some mail that I left here last time. A postcard of Henry Miller. Also enclosed is a picture of a pretty girl standing on the beach. I don't remember her. The guy probably made a mistake. Maybe I am plowing through so many women now that I don't even remember her!......... I think not.

Much later: At Denny's. We're going to drive all night to Adams, Mass. We have a day to travel to Vermont. We're going to drive tonight so we can cool out in Adams tomorrow.

7.9.85 ADAMS MA: A long all night drive. I got a few hours sleep. I was woken up by a silly conversation between Scotty and Kira. Kira was mad at Scotty because he didn't keep in touch on his days off. The conversation took some odd direction and they started talking about some shit and Scotty started asking Kira if she would step in front of a bullet for certain people. When it got to me, Kira said she would not do it for me because I had shit on her in the past. Things can get kind of boring around here so I guess you have to find ways to keep yourself amused. But you're cool, Kira. Keep out of the path of those bullets and remember — look both ways before you cross a two-way street or you just might get run over.

I was thinking about this girl I used to go out with today as I was in the shower. When someone betrays me, I almost want to thank them. Why? It's an educational experience. You can push yourself forward immeasurable distances in understanding. In the last week, I have learned a lot about myself and the people I work with. One must find the difference between paranoia and what I call "intensified awareness". I think I am finding out the difference.

7.11.85 SOMEWHERE IN NEW YORK: We drove from Vermont last night. We parked in a public park by a polluted river. The water is real dirty looking. There are apartment buildings all around. The hostile looking ones — dark blue-red bricks, tall, square — look more like factories or insane asylums than apartments. So much of New York looks like a war zone — dirty, bombed out, torn apart. Try as I might, I can never see myself living here.

Later: At the club. This will be an interesting night. This is a total homo joint. The staff is all gay. There are pictures of men all over the walls and shit. I am in one of those states where I feel totally thoughtless, numb — paralyzed from the neck up. This bathroom stinks. It reeks of insecticide and rotting food. This place is a hovel, like so many places I find myself in. I am totally alone in this group of people I work with. I feel no closeness with anyone here. I have nothing against any of them. They are all okay folks. I know what Kira thinks of me. She broadcasted it loud and clear the other day. That's cool with me. I don't really care what she thinks of me. Why should I? Just as long as she plays her bass. I seemed to have done something to bum Greg out. Still, I think that these are all good people. I am on the outside. I am not looking in. I don't want in. I don't. I understand all of this in my own way. This club is depressing, stinking in a junked out part of town. Nothing around here but cab drivers and stores with bulletproof glass. This is one of those days that I don't remember after it goes by. I am glad of it too.

Today, I tore up her picture. I had one picture of her that I carry with me. I tore it in half and then I tore off little bits as walked down the streets. I sat and looked at it for a long time before I tore it up. I looked at her mouth, her nose, her eyes. I remember how I used to feel when I looked at it. Today, I looked at it and I felt nothing. Her name is just not important, her face is not important. The memories of her are loaded in the trunk of a car that is speeding away into the sea. Bye bye. I feel no sadness, no relief. I feel nothing. My eyes were opened a little further. Thank you and goodbye.

7.12.85 ALBANY NY: In a VFW hall. Raining and cold outside. Just came back from a record store thing. The show last night was real cool. Played real hard. Slept in the van last night. This guy got me to sign his back. He wanted me to write a note to his boyfriend Bill. I wrote "Bill, rock out, you back-door man." After I signed his back, the guy asked for a kiss. No thanks.

Much later: At a Denny's. Show over. Went pretty well. Got smacked in the head. The guy didn't mean it, just one of those things. Went backstage after the show. People just poured in. Reggie tried to stop them, but they got in anyway. It's hard to deal with people when your brain is gone and you're sweaty and out of it. I usually hide for ten to twenty minutes to get myself together. I feel very anti-human after shows. People have no respect for your efforts and will yell at you and grab at you even when you're slumped over in a heap. Tonight was one of those nights. As soon as Reggie cleared the room, I had to do a video interview and some radio ID's. I pulled off the interview, but just barely. I was very out of it. I tried something new tonight. I took two Tylenol right before I played. I did this to see if this would help the intense headaches I get after shows. It worked. I can feel the Tylenol wearing off now. The headache is starting up. Maybe I can beat it with sleep.

7.13.85 BUFFALO NY: Woke up in a park again. I think we are near a zoo because all I can smell is shit. I'm sitting at a park bench trying not to move because it all hurts this morning. I would like to take a piss, but I can't with all these kids and their parents around. They'd probably call a pig.

This park reminds me of Washington DC. I spent a lot of time there this summer. As I walked down the streets, one thought kept going through my head. I looked at all the trees and the houses and I just kept thinking that if I stayed, all this could be mine. All of it — the streets, the air, the people. I could wake up to it every day for the rest of my life if I wanted to. That really made

me spin. When I am there, I know I will be leaving soon so I take everything in. I remember every detail. Every person I run into, every street I was on, every store I went into — I remember. I remember and absorb. Then one day when I was there last week, it all turned on me. All the houses, the streets — everything. It seemed like a velvet coffin — pulling me in, wanting to wrap me up and slowly choke me to Death. It was home. The familiarity, the gentle sameness that goes along with home. I felt like I was trapped in the belly of a cancerous, ageless shark. Swallowed up. The people I stay with when I am there are great people.

I watch them and I watch their lives. They don't see what I see. I don't think they could. If they heard me talk, they would probably call me an idiot.

The last day I was there, I went to my old job. I stared behind the counter — the place I spent hundreds of hours. Thought millions of thoughts. What if I was still there? I would probably have bored a trench into the pavement from work to my apartment. Key Bridge would sag on one side from the wear and tear I would have put on it walking on one side. All the clerks at the 7-11 on Wisconsin Avenue would probably have all invited me to their weddings since I was such a familiar face... I was there about a week ago. When I was there, I was thinking all of this. But I was unable to write down any of it due to the constriction of pen to paper I always suffer from when I'm there.

I must drive Ian crazy, making him drive me all over the place. He doesn't seem to mind. Ian is one of those types of people — genuinely nice and considerate of his pals. He always impresses me in that way as well as many others too. Ian is one of those rare types who takes time for others. He does it about 99% more than I do. I am one of the most inconsiderate people I have ever seen — ever. But back to the constriction, the suffocation. It's maddening. Only when I am miles away can I ever write about my home-town.

To my left, a man who looks like John Lee Hooker sits at a park bench and talks to a younger woman. In front of me, some kind of family configuration sets up a picnic. What an idea for a day. "Hey Honey, let's grab up the kids and have a picnic. The kids can run and scream and we can sit and breathe the shit-packed air and talk about some really boring shit." "Okay, let's go!" No thanks. I wonder when we will be leaving here for the show. It's 1:16. We should get going.

I talked to Dukowski yesterday. He says that several clubs in Los Angeles want me to do speaking dates at their place. He told me that my spoken tour for fall is almost all booked. I'll be leaving on the 15th of September. I will be on line until mid-October. I hope I make it okay. I hope I don't. To make it okay is not enough. I hope the next few months are a hard struggle. The hardest one I have ever encountered yet.

This family is disgusting. There is a woman with her child. She faces me. She eats with both of her hands. She pushes her child that sits in a stroller with her bare foot. Her legs open and close. Her shorts exposing her fatty, white flesh. Her legs open and close. She eats. She wipes her hands off and changes the kid's diapers at the table. How does baby shit stench mix with your potato salad, Pops? She now moves to the table next to the one occupied by the family and proceeds to breast-feed her kid. Oh shit, now another family at another table to my left — a husband and wife with their two kids in a stroller. The husband is setting up one of those propane cookers. What happens to young women after they have kids? They get that Mommy look about them. They walk funny. They gain weight. They just lose it. Imagine having to come home to that every day. Not me man, no thanks. Mommies are not my type. "Let's fuck." — "Okay, but first I have to change Junior." Yeah, that's cool. But make sure you wash your hands real good. I don't want any baby shit on me, thanks. Ooh... look at the cellulite on the wife's legs! Don't wear shorts, lady! Fuck, what a mess. Look at the husband just smiling away. Have a good time with all that cellulite tonight pal. Good luck. I will never go out with another girl who does not exercise and watch her diet. One girl I went out with told me how she hates exercise and likes being lazy. At first that didn't really bother me, but it started to after a while. No more out of shape girls for me, no matter how cool they are. They have to be fit or I'm not into it. That's cool. That's not too much to ask of someone. For some it is I guess. Not my problem.

7.18.85 MT. PLEASANT MI: Last night was Ann Arbor, MI. Yesterday was real busy. I did an in-store thing then I went to a radio station. Then I did a phone interview with the Chicago Sun and then I did some other interview. After we played, Greg and I did an interview with Creem magazine. I talked with Ron Asheton from the Stooges after the show. He told me that he was going to be recording soon and he will send me a tape. He said that he will be in LA in mid-October.

We spent the night at Mike Davis' house. Mike played bass in the band MC5. He was telling me some cool stories about playing with the Velvet Underground, Cream and Jimi Hendrix. He said that Hendrix would take off his Strat and put on a cheap guitar before he would start smashing it.

That was a loud house last night. I slept in the Ryder truck. I got about four hours of sleep. Getting up in the morning is really hard now. Neck will not move. I get up very slowly, take some aspirin and wait for the pain to subside. My head is aching constantly. I have not had any time to write. Some days I'm so busy with interviews and record store appearances that I don't even make soundcheck. We're doing a lot of press this time around and it's me who has to do most of it. The other night in Flint was real cool. I threw up during the middle of the set. There were all these girls up front, rubbing my cock and balls. Felt good, but it made it hard to concentrate on the music.

We have two sets today. The first one is over. We have two sets tomorrow in Detroit. I go on in about two hours time. I will have to take more aspirin soon. I can feel the last dose wearing off right now. I look up. People are staring at me as I write. Not many people on the street today. People either recognize me or they just stare. I am slipping away from them — a little farther each day. I understand them at times, but I can't relate. Last night they would not stop grabbing me, kissing me, biting me, hitting me. One girl started beating up another girl because she tried to touch my hand. Guys shaking my hand whenever they got the chance. Got kicked in the mouth fairly hard last night. Not bad though. This is the ninth week of the tour. I don't feel tired or exhausted. I am made weary by so much thought and understanding. I like darkened rooms. They calm me down. I see so many people now. I can see so many eyes. I can feel their eyes pounding on me. The headaches are growing more intense. Sometimes after shows, I cannot think straight for hours. The other day in the mirror — I'm sprouting more gray hair. Not so hot for twenty-four. When I'm agitated and distraught, I will think of water. Bodies of water. Water pouring out of pitchers. The stream of the water braiding and twisting like smooth glass muscle. The water falls and pours. It never hits the ground. The water falls silently, falls forever. I close my eyes and see a river lined with tall trees. It makes no sound as it flows. The only sound is the leaves rustling in the trees. The call of the wind is perfect and complete.

Later: Both sets done. Tomorrow is Detroit, two sets. Detroit is always hard. My head is pounding. People talking. They never seem to run out of boring shit to talk about. It's always the ones that don't have to play very hard. I wonder what that must be like — to not have every set be a guaranteed sweatout. I see these guys bust through the set so they can get to the Budweiser and the boring chitchat.

People were very "very" tonight. That's the only way to describe them. People shouting, "Henry, it's you. It's all you!" People grabbing me. All these girls were up front. I had a good time with them. They were biting and kissing me. All these boys want to shake my hand.

Reggie just came into the room and asked if I was going to sleep here. He wanted the room for him and his girlfriend since it's their last night together. I told him if he wants to be alone then go in the truck with her, it won't kill him. I've fucked in that truck before, it's fine. It won't crush his girlfriend's ass. He doesn't play two sets tomorrow. I do. He doesn't have a bunch of people screaming his name. I do. Goddamn right. He should fly home with her. He'll be back to his belligerent self as soon as she's not around to be his Mommy.

I've got all this mail in my backpack. Letters from all sorts of people. Some of it I actually want to answer. I'm too burned out from shaking hands, signing autographs. Two radio interviews today — one live and one taped. Tomorrow is two sets, three interviews and all the other shit.

7.19.85 Detroit MI: At Traxx. I have a tape of the Birthday Party playing here a couple of years ago. I always wondered what this place looked like.

The place is in one of those neighborhoods that are so fucked up that I'll eat at a McDonald's because the risk of food poisoning decreases somewhat. So there I was, eating at McDonald's — watching nervous whiteys eat, surrounded by blacks who didn't look nervous at all. Fat women with their noisy children eating, screaming and staring at me. I stare right back — right through them. I am bottomless. No guilt, no remorse. I am ugly. I looked at myself in the bathroom of this place today. I look bad. Haggard, spent, used up. So I stared right back and through as I ate my fish sandwich. I remember now how bad the food is. Woke up this morning at 8:30 or so. Headache. Couldn't move my neck much — still can't. Trying to cut down on my Tylenol intake.

Two sets last night, two sets tonight. I don't even know where we are playing tomorrow. I would bet Ohio or something.

7.22.85: In Kentucky at the Jockey Club again. The hunchback is still here, sitting in his chair, smoking cigarettes, staring at the floor. We have been playing every night. Detroit was hard. Two sets was a bit much for that day. I thought we played real good though. Got kicked in the mouth again. Found some cool Henry Miller books at a bookstore in Columbus this morning. I sent them to my P.O. box. I'm very burned out. I cannot remember the names of the books that I bought only two hours ago. I cannot even remember all the towns we've been playing lately. Just too much burnout. Last night, we played in Columbus, Ohio. I thought the show went real well. A girl bit me in the chest so hard that I bled. Now all that's left are bruises from her teeth.

I took a walk around town today. Went to the local shopping mall to look for some food. There was a store selling those gross, mass produced paintings. I stared at sailboats, misshapen nudes and all the other gross shit they had. The standout was a portrait of the guitar player in Kiss. People sure are gross. I walked on the streets with my shirt off. People stared at me hard. I am my own tribe. I don't look or act like them. I'm sitting in this dark, damp, stinking hall. The place smells like piss, shit, beer and mildew. Strange things happen to me these days — hallucinations, visions and wild thoughts of all kinds. I don't know if I understand what's happening anymore.

7.23.85: At some guy's house in Kentucky. Can't move my neck. Can hardly move anything. Headache. Just woke up. A lot of people at the show last night. A lot of stupid, drunk and ugly people — emphasis on stupid, drunk and ugly. This fat skinhead boy nearly bought himself a ticket. He fucked with me and then after the show, I was sitting in the alley and he comes up and acts all tough. He walked away muttering how he was going to break every bone in my body. I told him he better start breaking because fat skinhead talk is shit when there's only two of us in the alley. He still didn't deal. I wish he had been stupid enough to fuck with me. Fat boy, I would have kicked your ass so hard you wouldn't even know how to piss afterwards.

Last night, they threw beer cans, cups, ice, spit, fists — all of it. How can I respect them. Why would I treat any of them as human beings? I am losing my patience with these "people". A guy fucks with Greg all night, then comes backstage and wants to hang with us. I learned something last night. I now understand the "two-way street" concept. I hope the next asshole who wants to waste my time doesn't. Enough of this. I shouldn't let some belligerent drunk idiots get me in a sour mood. Not after 60 shows in 64 days.

7.26.85 CHICAGO IL: At the Metro as usual. Last night was Lansing, MI. I had bad luck at that one. The second song into the set, a kid and I smacked heads — hard. I nearly threw up. The rest of the show was a fuzzy dream. I took two more shots to the head before the show was finished. I was very out of it. I left my gym shorts in the dressing room. I would have left my head if it wasn't stuck on my neck. I have a lot on my mind, but my head hurts so much that I cannot connect. Not the best time to have a shiner and a lead head.

Chicago is a hard show. The last time we were here, people were throwing bottles which were smashing against the cymbal stands and glass was flying around. Greg and I hid behind his stack and waited it out.

Went to a supermarket today. Saw this stoner guy, reeking of pot and carrying a little kid around. Two young guys had this little kid and the kid was making a lot of noise. One of the guys says to him, "You better shut up or you're gonna get brain-damaged!" The kid shut right up.

Last night this guy was acting like an asshole. He handed me a dollar bill. I stuffed the bill in my shorts and kept playing. He asked for it back. I pulled down my shorts, wrapped the dollar around my cock and told him to come and get it. He didn't. Later, he was talking to me — telling me that he didn't like our t-shirts and he was upset that his band wasn't happening. I told him that I thought he was an asshole and he should leave me the fuck alone. He started to cry. What a trip. He stood there on the front lawn and started to cry. What a night. Got some sleep in this rundown slummed out house. At least I got a mattress. Took an ice cold shower this morning. That woke my ass up pronto. Talked to Ed at Spin. He said

MADISON, WI / 7.27.85 (*MURRAY KAPPEL*)

that they are going to use the new thing I wrote for them next month.

Much later: Somewhere in Wisconsin. We are playing in Madison tomorrow night. We decided to leave for there tonight. Tonight's show was pretty wild. We sold the place out. We've never done that before. There were about 900+ people in there. The head injury from last night is still giving me trouble. I have a black eye now. Some kind of badge.

7.27.85 MADISON WI: At my usual coffee shop. Bought a pot of Colombian. Sure has been a long time since I had some real coffee. I have a pain-snake crawling through my head. I take Tylenol and nothing changes. I combed all the local book stores. I couldn't find anything interesting. I am sitting in this coffee-house. The same crazy guy is behind the counter with that killer's gleam in his eye. The lady asked how many cups I wanted to accompany the pot. I told her, "One." She looked at me and said, "Have fun."

So many hot looking girls walking down the street. My eyes are aching from staring so hard. This is a nice break in the action. I have no name. I have no face. I'm sitting here in a room full of people. No one is looking at me. I am alone. It's Saturday. It's sunny out. I have totally forgotten my responsibilities to everything and everyone. I am floating. This is great. I could have been here for a few hours, I wouldn't know. The only drag is that Fleetwood Mac is playing on the stereo system and there is this idiot near me singing along.

Two guys stopped me in the street today and told me that some people have been talking of boycotting our show because we are fascist and sexist. I'm doing my best to understand this shit. A van full of filthy vegetarians. We're fascists? I don't get it. I understand them better now. I watch them run on their gerbil wheels — spinning, treading, running at breakneck speed to the liquor cabinet to free themselves from the grinding rut of their lives. One rut to another. Crashing their cars. Smashing their fists into each other — into walls — into the bottom. People talk so much shit. At the end of the day, they can all go get fucked.

Last night in Chicago, they were bottomless. People will drag you into the crowd, kick you, rip your hair out, and then pluck your eyes out like vultures. They will strip the flesh from your bones and then sell your skeleton if you let them. I understand. People who try to run and ruin your life. They get offended when you give them no respect. When you understand them is when you reflect them back at themselves.

Last night in that diner, I saw the model man. He came out of the men's room (I did not see him go in. I assume that he was born there). He was the driver of a beer truck. He was wearing work shoes, dark blue work pants and his work shirt. A Budweiser patch on his breast, a Bud Lite patch on his sleeve and a large Bud patch on his back. He was smoking a cigarette. He *was* beer and cigarettes. What a man.

This is the town my father came from. I think I can feel him on the streets. He needs a good kick. I got some brand new shoes.

Later: Now in a vegetarian restaurant waiting for my brown rice and vegetables to come. Did an in-store and a radio interview. Head is making me feel sick. Playing tonight is going to be hard.

7.28.85 AT A DINER EN ROUTE TO MILWAUKEE WI: Playing last night was no good. My head started to pound and freak out so bad that I couldn't remember the words. The people up front — all boys — all yelling the songs they want to hear. Not a very creative medium. Before the show, I was sitting outside trying to get some time to myself when this guy started talking to me. He was cool. He and I talked for a little while and then he split. After the show, he got hit by a car in the parking lot. I watched all the people as they crowded around him. He was laying on his back on the cement. His body was in the shape of a cross. He would turn red and blue as the siren light washed over his body. All these people put jackets on him to keep him warm I guess. He looked strange. Turning red and blue, all covered with leather jackets. They took him away and everyone went home.

Jesus Christ went downtown. Got fucked up on Scotch. When he got hit by that car, his guts flew like a shovel of mud hitting the fan. Fly guts. Red and blue Jesus clone doing his thing on the pavement. Saintdom is a slow and painful crawl. Never forget that rats can tread water for twenty-four hours straight. When the ship sinks, the rats will use your floating corpse for a life raft and food supply until you hit the beach.

I called Diamanda's mom today to try to find her. I got her manager's number up in San Francisco. Ms. Galas said not to call her until Tuesday because she has a very important show tomorrow. That's cool. I hope I get in touch with her at some point. I bought her this wolf's head pendant. It looks real cool. She'll dig it.

Much later: Show over. I'm sitting in the van with Greg. Good show tonight. Greg was excellent. When he plays, I think I will shake myself so hard that I will fly through the roof. I did an interview with a Japanese girl for a magazine in Japan. I cannot write any more. Pain in head and neck and exhaustion make it impossible.

7.29.85 CHAMPAIGN IL: No show tonight, show tomorrow. I found out that Adrian Belew lives here. Adrian Belew is pretty great on those Crimson and Bowie records. It's hot and moist here. I'm in the kitchen of some house. Nice of these people to put us up. Woke up this morning in Milwaukee unable to move my neck. That's a problem. Head and neck stiffening up. Brain solidifying — growing cold and dead.

Snakes. The sidewalks and the streets are bad snakes — man-made. The blood spilled on them gave them a soul. They have nothing of their own. They lay flat — dead and uninspired.

My heart is cold, but it will live forever in the discipline and the insanity. My friend is the end. The end never comes. The friend who never shows his face. In melting dreams, I wish for a glimpse of the end. That is what I need — reference. I keep crawling toward the sun, but I can't see an end. It's pain — an empty pain — hollow, carved out. Vacant soul. Spirit rising. Outside of the outside. So distant that I don't have a name. Crawling with a pain that has no name. Crawling with a pain that has no shame. Crawling with a pain that has no brain. Crawling along just the same. Spirit walking along the trail. This chain will never break. Sometimes, I must confess, I wish for the links to shatter into a million pieces. The crawl must end sometime. But how? When? Where?

7.30.85 CHAMPAIGN IL: At the club. We played here a long time ago. Sent my manuscript to Staci via express mail. I got in touch with Diamanda today in San Francisco. She said her show went well. It was good to talk to her. She's working out at Gold's five days a week. I haven't seen her in about two and a half months. Well, time flies. I'll see her in San Francisco at the end of August when we play there.

7.31.85 CHAMPAIGN IL: At a Denny's. Good show last night. Some bad luck for me though. During the third or fourth song, I was swinging one way and Greg was swinging the other. The tuning board of his guitar bashed me in the jaw. Hurt some after the show.

This morning, I woke up in the truck — hot and sweating, flies crawling on me — the works. I tried to yawn and nearly flew through the roof. I cannot open my mouth very wide. Side of my face is swollen. I must look pretty sad. Black eye and swollen jaw. What a combo.

Last night, this girl jumped onstage and we made out while the band jammed out "Slip It In". It was cool. Whenever that happens, guys will always flip you off and scream at you. Jealous? I don't think that I care. Diamanda told me that she is going to be in a fashion magazine in France called Elle. That woman has the most penetrating eyes I have ever seen. When you talk to her, they leap out at you and burn right through. She'll look at you and you think that she's gonna belt you one and then she breaks out in a big smile. Her manager said that her show at the I-Beam was videotaped. I'm going to try to get a copy. It's very cool that I got to meet her. It's strange to meet someone you admire so much. She is a good person. My head is pounding. Makes my brain dull. I want to fuck, I want to eat and I want to sleep.

8.1.85 ST. LOUIS MO: Played here last night. After the show, a girl offered us her parents' house to stay in. She said that her parents were out of town. We went. In the house now. The place is nice — a real rich home. This morning, plainclothes cops were all over the block, investigating our vehicles, talking into walkie-talkies. Davo went outside and the pigs landed on him. He smelled of pot and a pig said to him, "You're carrying a heavy smell there, fella." Davo just shrugged. The girl came out and told the pigs that we were her guests. I'm glad she did because by that time, pigs were all over the place — all plainclothes, shoulder holsters — the whole thing. I have not been outside all day. I want to go out but I'm scared of someone calling the pigs on me. This house is so clean and straight that it's making me uncomfortable. I don't like it here. Makes me feel trapped in. This girl showed me a picture of her boyfriend who works for the public defender. I thought it was her fucking dad! The house is full of paintings and antiques. She is a student at a university in Boston during the fall and winter. This place looks totally unlived in. The bedrooms are all antique and shit. She is kind of into us being here and kind of not. I think she is observing us. I wonder if there are any pigs outside watching us. My head is pounding. Jaw aching. Tylenol does not help anymore.

8.6.85 LINCOLN NE: I am now at the K-Mart next to the Drumstick Club. I am sitting on the spot where Katherine Arnold killed herself. I was right. The stain is gone, the grass is all grown up and it looks like a very normal place. I approximated just where her head was and I'm sitting right in that spot. I look straight ahead. There is a parting in the trees. Maybe she wanted someone to see her — maybe to try to talk her out of it. It is peaceful here. No one's around. Right below where I am sitting, I found a stone. I put it in my pocket. The odor that I smelled when I was here in October is now gone. Rain-washed, snow-washed, sun-dried... gone. I wish there was more here to get a hold of, but there is nothing.

8.7.85 OMAHA NE: Now in Omaha on a day off. I cannot believe some of the places that we end up in. Right now we're at the promoter's lake house. The place is huge. He has a boat and takes everybody water-skiing and stuff. Ratman and I have our own room. Not bad.

I broke my right wrist on a guy's head last night. I have broken this wrist about six or seven times before. This is fucked. I will not be able to do anything with my right hand for several weeks. What a fucking drag. My hand is hurting so much I can hardly think straight. I guess I won't be doing any load-ins for the rest of the tour. What a trip. I'm sitting on this big porch facing this big old lake. The sun is setting, the water-skiers are ripping by. It's like a scene out of a movie or something. I should have cracked that man upside the head with the microphone.

I talked to a kid who knows Katherine Arnold's brother. He told me the story of the events that led up to her suicide at K-Mart. Apparently, Katherine's husband beat her up a lot. They had a son whom he spoiled rotten. He would spend all the extra money on the child. One day, Katherine bought herself a new dress and was beaten severely for it. He had convinced the child to pay no attention to Katherine. This drove her crazy. She left to stay with her mother. Her mother urged her to leave him. She said that she still loved him and was going back to him. She did. More beatings... In reaction, Katherine went out and bought a whole bunch of new clothing. She came home and the husband told her to leave and never return. She went to K-Mart, bought a gun and killed herself.

Hopefully, this fellow I talked to will get me a picture of her and send it. I had a lot of cool stuff that was supposed to come in the mail but never did. People say that they're going to send me this or that and they rarely do. People will usually let you down. That's why I work with as few people as possible. Keep the circle small and neat. Less maintenance.

8.14.85 CALGARY CANADA: Just got here. There was a bit of a bad luck streak. Pouring rain upon arrival. Davo pulls out the loading ramp and slices his thumb from top to bottom, right to the bone. He looks at it. I look at it. Davo gets back in the truck and finishes the parking job. Finally, he is convinced to go to the hospital. Next, a person pours beer into the tape deck. The $250 tape deck is destroyed for good. We do the show. The promoter will not pay us what he promised. He owes us from the last time we were in these parts. He's sitting there — grinning, drinking beers and telling us how he'll pay us in September and how hopefully the check won't bounce. Reggie and I are pacing back and forth, wanting to beat him and his friend up. The asshole knows it. He wants it. He knows he can call the cops. So... not the greatest night.

So we get here and we are telling Todd, the guy whom we are staying with, about the gig and how the promoter had his front teeth knocked out and what a dick he was (the promoter told us how a biker jumped him). And Todd goes, "Yeah, he tried to rip off another band and I punched his teeth out, took the money and paid the band in full myself." Pretty great if you ask me. Fuckers always get it at some point. So we're stuck in Canada for the next while. I don't like it here. None of us do. We pulled into a Denny's this morning to eat. When we came out, there were cops in the parking lot checking out our vehicles. Fucking pigs.

8.17.85 VANCOUVER CANADA: Got here this morning. Took us about 20 hours to get here. This morning, there was a tearful little incident with Kira and Davo. Apparently, there was a small dispute over sleeping accommodations and Kira, who has a hard time handling reality, got all bent out of shape.

I think Kira hates everyone in this group and tells others what assholes we are, what a bastard Greg is, etc. She thinks that no one tells anyone anything. She lives in a dream world. She must be out of her weak little unbathed mind. She does all this, gives everyone shit and thinks everything is okay. Come September, we start looking for another bass player for the band. Kira is on the outs — has been for weeks. I never want to see her lying, rancid, fake self ever again. I wonder how she takes it. She goes and brags to people about further touring and all this assorted shit. I just smile because I know what's going down. She has been telling the road crew how she's going to quit mid-tour to try and fuck things up real good. I'm so glad she will be leaving our camp. There's other stuff I could say, but she's not worth the time it takes.

The world turns, the sun rises and falls burning. My sight crawls forth from the world that sits in my sockets. With each breath, an attempt at life... an attempt at Death.

8.18.85 VANCOUVER CANADA: Yesterday, we were on our way to Vancouver. Davo and I were driving in the Ryder truck. We saw a sign for the Stony Indian Trading Post. Davo really liked the idea of a "stoned Indian" so we pulled off onto the dirt road exit to go check it out. We came to an intersection and came to a full stop. There was a funeral procession turning right in front of us — Stony Indians. The hearse was a pickup truck. Behind it was a long line of pickup trucks packed with Indians. They were going into the hills, perhaps to some kind of burial ground. I thought about the ritual and how if it was a century ago, it would probably be done with horses and on foot. The train of pickups went on. I stared at the Indians. Many of the men were wearing black top hats. They sat in the cabs and stared straight ahead. It was very strange to see their noble, beautiful faces surrounded by such trappings as trucks and work clothes. There were four horses behind a fence at the opposite corner of the intersection. Davo and I simultaneously noticed their strange behavior. None of the horses moved, not a muscle. They all stood facing the same way in a line. They did this until the last truck in the procession had passed them and only then did they even twitch. The horses all at once started walking away into the middle of the field. We drove on.

I have not slept much yet. Head hurts too much. Tylenol really does not help. Nothing does any more. I have been in Canada for a while now — too long. I get tired of the shitty food and the cheats. Every show so far has been a burn. The promoter has burned us right to our face. Two more shows — Vancouver and Victoria tomorrow night, then on to Seattle.

8.19.85 SEATTLE WA: Finished all the Canadian shows. Show in Olympia blew out so we have the night off. The shows in Vancouver and Victoria went real well. I thought the playing was real hot. Not a lot of interesting stuff went on. The ferry ride to the island of Victoria is beautiful. I like traveling on boats a lot. They make me feel like I'm really traveling. I would like to do more traveling by boat. I have been on a few in Europe. I really enjoyed that. I remember the pull from Sweden to Germany last summer. I was nervous about Germany. The Germans can be really nasty and violent. They are some hard fuckers for certain.

8.21.85 SPOKANE WA: Last night was Seattle. Played two sets. Both shows were real good I thought. The second set was one of those that leaves me fucked up and incoherent. Before we played, this boy came up to me with this nice looking blonde haired girl. He gave me a Magic Marker, lifted her shirt and said, "Sign her." I looked at her body. She was very fine — perfectly muscled. I looked in her eyes and asked, "Where do you want it?" "Where do you want to put it?" she replied smiling. I gouged her in the face with the marker. She did not "want it" there. I moved to her stomach and drew a swastika with the word "fool" underneath. The boy walked away. She said, "Can I have a hug?" I told her to go off with her cute little boy. She went.

The front of the stage was pretty much girls. It's a trip to see girls push other girls out of the way to get to the stage. The feeling of three or four pairs of hands on me at once is one that I like. Last night, girls were grabbing my cock, my balls, my legs. Felt good. That stuff and this guy I cracked in the ear with the mic are the only things that I remember from the two sets. That guy had blood dripping down the side of his head. Oh yeah, this other guy pulled me into the crowd and I was chewing on his neck trying to tear off some meat. Felt good chewing hard on a living body. It drove me crazy. I had a mouthful of that muscle that goes down the side of the neck. I was thinking, "You wanted me. This is me."

There is no end to this trip. It just gets more insane and more twisted as it winds along. Last night, I lay on the rug of this hallway where the dressing rooms were. The sets were finished. My head was pounding so hard that I could hardly keep my eyes open. I felt like I was made of glass and if I breathed in too hard, I thought I might break. If I do a string of shows like that one, I think I will lose my mind. The trip is bottomless. You can go as deep as you want. You can go until the muscle tissue starts to dissolve and tear away. You can deplete the soul to the point at which the body will start to feed upon itself. The soul will remain, but it will declare mutiny on the body. There is no end to the trail. The soul can never be satiated once the door is opened. As I lay on the rug, I imagined so many scenes of depletion and deprivation, that I thought I was in another world. I thought maybe I had died and my spirit took me over completely. I don't know. All I know is that there is no bottom and there is no end to this trip. It is consumption. It is plague. It is possession on a circular two-way street.

Too many of them are victims of power. Some feel the need to gather it and exercise it on others and more still feel the need to be victimized by it. Both sides lose. I never want to lead. I play people into their own hands. I am merely a catalyst, a directional window, a directional mirror.

That boy and girl last night. Him coming up to me and handling her like a piece of meat. And her letting him. She stood there like a little lamb waiting to get its throat cut. I felt like spitting on them both. They probably would have liked that. I can't understand that way of thinking.

Some religious group was in front of the Seattle gig protesting our being in Seattle. It was great to walk through them and tell them that they were pigs and that I hoped that they would die.

Later: Show over. Played hard. We sounded good I think. People were real cool and seemed into our thing. It sure is cold out tonight — the air smells good. Tomorrow is Walla Walla. The last two days have wiped my brain clean of everything. I feel like a match that has been lit and burned. All burned out.

8.22.85 WALLA WALLA WA: Today I found a clothbound copy of Henry Miller's *To Paint Is To Love Again*. I recently finished his book *Tropic of Capricorn*. Finishing a Miller book is a grand occasion for me. It feels like the last day of school or something. It's as if he took you and put you in his coat pocket and carried you around for a while. At the end of *Tropic of Cancer, Black Spring* and *Tropic of Capricorn*, it's like he packs you a lunch and sends you on your way. I sat outside the show in Vancouver, Canada and finished *Capricorn*. I read the last page over and over again. I hated finishing the book. I felt as if I was saying goodbye to a friend. I felt lonely when I had finished it. The man is totally endearing to me. I always carry one of his books with me. It was a grand occasion. I felt like I had graduated from school, but without all the tension of the exams. If you're really alive, then you pass Miller's exam. I've never gotten this feeling from any writer.

8.23.85 PORTLAND OR: Last night was a hard deal. Playing is becoming more and more painful. My body is starting to break down. No matter how much I loosen up before a set, it makes no difference now. My neck doesn't move very well anymore. This happened around the three month mark. There were some cheap shit people at the Walla Walla gig. Just a handful, but that's all it takes. One of our road crew got pulled into the crowd. I watched about six people cheap shot him. I made sure to ID all of them. One came near the stage and I bashed him upside the head with the mic. I don't remember ever hitting someone that hard with a mic. He staggered and fell with his hands on his head. We finished the set. I walked out to the soundboard to get my clothes and I saw two of the cheap shot guys come in. I said, "Reggie, that's one of the guys." The two guys split up and they looked like they came inside to deal on us. I picked up a folding chair and went after one of the guys. He was smart. He ran fast. I chased him, but he made it out the door as the chair smashed right next to his head on the other door. If that piece of shit had hesitated a half-second longer, he would have been dead meat. Like I always say — disrespect is a two-way street. Not the greatest gig we ever did, but I thought it was good.

I am having problems with my body. I think it's saying, "Enough already!" Today is day 97 of this tour. My brain gets pounded to the point to where I can't even remember where we played five days before. I just checked my pockets for a phone number for an interview that I have to do and I found a note from a girl in Seattle. I have never seen it before and I don't know who the girl is. I guess she slipped it into my pocket. That happens every once in a while. I have never pursued one of the notes ever.

Later: I just got off the phone with Staci. I got a letter from Nick Cave. He wrote me from Berlin where he is living now. He said that he is working on his book and will send a manuscript when he hits the halfway point. I hope my books will be ready soon. I'd like to send Nick my new stuff to see what he thinks.

Tonight's show is being taped 16-track stereo for the *Live '85* record. I hope that my voice holds out. I think it will sound good. The last thirty or so shows have been the best playing this band has ever done. Anthony is a great drummer. I nicknamed him "Cosmo". Greg is the man. When Kira called him a bastard to Ratman, Rat lost all respect for the girl. If she ever said anything like that to me, I think I would crack her one. What a bitch. Last night, I was looking at these huge security bouncer guys. I noticed how they carry their upper body like luggage that does not belong to them. Like they were normal the night before and woke up with this hulk attached to them. Some of those guys are huge. One the guys last night looked like he could bend a crowbar with his ears.

Much later: Show over. I thought we played good. Lots of guys up front grabbing my face and hitting me. Makes it hard to really let loose. People in the crowd were yelling and telling me that I'm Charles Manson and shit. I walked into the bathroom after the show to wash my feet off. I play pretty much naked. It's the only way I can feel right. No shoes, no shirt, no service. I'm in the men's room. Smells like stale piss. The sink was filled with a bunch of paper towels soaked with blood. People prove to be harmful and a waste of time. When some guy comes up and all he does is smack me and scream what song he wants to hear, how the fuck am I going to want nothing else but to see the boy fuck off and die.

These two girls came backstage to meet me after the show. One was so worked up that her legs gave out and she hit the ground. Some boys came backstage and stood around looking totally useless. I don't see what they get out of it. I don't know where we are going to sleep tonight. I don't think tomorrow's drive is all that long. We will be in LA in a week. That's a drag. Not really much to come home to. LA is a lonely place for me. So is every place when I stay for more than a few days. If I don't keep moving, I get restless. When I keep moving, I grind myself into the pavement. I don't know what the middle ground is.

I hate this shit! I don't want another fucking boy to touch me again. These boys should just get down to it and start fucking each other and just get it over with. They always have their arms around each other and shit. They rub themselves all over each other. I'm not down on that shit at all. I just don't want to be included in male bonding rituals. And while I'm on the subject, I would prefer not to have to watch a bunch of males crawl all over each other and scream at me. Just do your thing off in the corner so the girls can come up front and we can get real. Boys don't even move with the music. No matter what you play, they do the same thing. The girls move with the music — always. I watch their hips and they watch mine. These boys should go join the Marine Corps so they can rock out.

8.24.85 EUGENE OR: From the top: We spent the night at this apartment. A girl told us it was her place. We find out later that the place isn't hers at all. The apartment building is a squat full of junkies. During the night, someone came in and ripped off a lot of our people's stuff. Greg got it the worst. He lost his bag containing his headset, practice amp, all the tapes of his new tunes, all his writing, his money, his tapes of music — everything. The girl obviously knew who did it but wouldn't give up any information. Some of our crew demolished the apartment — destroyed it, threw shit out of windows, etc. We bagged up what looked of any value and took it. We went downstairs to where this other junkie lived to try to get info. He said he knew nothing. Maybe he didn't. The guy's woman came into the hallway screaming, "That bitch (Kira) just spat on me! I'm going to kill her!" She ran past the guy and got a baseball bat. He stopped her before she could get to Kira. We left. Everyone is a junkie to me now. All of them want something. They don't care who they fuck over to get to their junk. There's a brutal beauty to that. The singleness of mind, the focus. A straight line. A one-way street.

Say a man has a lover who's a junkie. On the outside, he's calm. But inside, he burns knowing that he is second to the junk. What a drag. They're all junkies. The world is a junkie. I am a junkie. Life is my junk. Die junkie.

I am at the place we are playing. It's a house. We are playing in the living room of this fucked up house. It's like a house party I guess. I'm keeping all my stuff in sight. I don't trust any of these people. I remember the last time I was here. I was scheduled to do a video interview with this girl. I met the girl. What a knockout. She was beautiful. I hung out with her after the show. She was real nice to me, asking me how I was feeling and what I thought about. I told her a lot. At the time, I was having a series of dreams of car crashes. I had been seeing them a lot and they seemed to get closer and closer. The last one I had was in Seattle where I saw a head-on collision. A child lay sprawled out on the sidewalk, rain pouring all over him. He was screaming for his mother. The mother didn't know what to do. She ran around in circles, screaming and jerking spasmodically. I was certain that I was going to be next. I told her that I was lonely and that sometimes the crowds alienated me from them and from myself. I told her all kinds of stuff. It just kind of came rushing out of me all at once. Later that evening, she did the interview with me. I was sitting on a couch with her in a room full of people. She asked me questions that pertained to the stuff I had told her. I couldn't believe it. I felt like I was sitting there naked in a room full of people. What a nasty thing to do. I felt bad after that. Not betrayed, but used. I felt like a fool. Who was I to talk to someone? I got what

I deserved. Served me right. They're all junkies.

I am the shapeless man. I don't fit. I can't fit. I walk without form. I cannot translate into any language. I feel like a visitor that got left behind by his ride. There's no feeling in my limbs. I walk past them in a trance. I could be walking on hot coals and not even know. My keys don't fit. If I don't keep moving, I'll get evicted. I am the shapeless man. All that goes undefined gets attacked until it breaks down, wounded and bleeding. Out of loneliness and exhaustion, the unknown quantity picks up a title and a place on the shelf. They'll have to kill me first. That's what I've come to realize. Ten thousand nights in the gray, wasted desert of alienation and isolation is a joy compared to one filthy minute in their lifeless, Death-propelled incineration machine.

8.27.85 RENO NV: A fast rundown of our show in Reno. No frills or extras. Ready? Go! We arrived at the place — a skate rink in the middle of nowhere. Tom Troccoli's Dog goes on first. Near the end of the set, Tom is pulled offstage. He fell and broke his leg on the skate rink floor. Later on, Black Flag plays. Our set is stopped by the police. A boy was in the crowd with a knife and he stabbed two other boys. They are taken away. The boy with the knife is apprehended and taken away. The set resumed. Two songs later, the set is shut down for good by the pigs. I go to the dressing room. Two plainclothes pigs are in there with one of our road crew. I am told to stand against the wall. I do it. The male pig stares at me. I hold his stare without moving. Finally he squeals, "You better smile more when you come into my town." I just stare without changing my expression. The female pig asks me some questions. I ignore her. They both give our road crew guy a lecture about the pot they found on him. They tell him that pot is a felony in the state of Nevada. Finally they are called away. They get up to leave and the male pig says to me, "You better smile more or stay in LA." I just stared at him as he left. I hate pigs. I don't smoke and I don't need to get busted. Next time someone lights up some of that lame shit, I'm moving out of the room. This is the second near bust on tour and I'm sick of it. That's a night in Reno.

I overheard these boys talking in the men's room. They were doing crystal meth and tequila. They were talking about how all the boys are pussies because they don't do this or that or some bullshit. There is nothing. The world is a gross place.

We drove all night to Palo Alto, California. I did an interview with the local paper over the phone. SST called me and told me that the Village Voice wants me to write for them. I wonder what they want me to do. I am tired. I'm taking aspirin before I play now. It helps the aftershow headaches a little. The equipment is being loaded out and I am waiting to leave. I'm not much good for load-out with my broken wrist. This trail has no end. There is no one anywhere. I don't think I'm human anymore.

8.29.85 SANTA CRUZ CA: I'm sitting in a shopping plaza in Santa Cruz. The scene almost defies description. That's the way it has been for the last few days since we've been in Northern California. Yesterday I was in Palo Alto. It's strange to be in California again. Three and a half months away and you realize just how different it is from any other place anywhere. The streets of Palo Alto are well kept and the people dress very well. All the shops are modern and well lit — yet there is a very low undercurrent of paranoia that filled me for the entire time that I walked on University Avenue. The scenes were too perfect, almost surreal. I half expected to be dragged away by police at any moment. No one talked loud. No one jaywalked. No one did anything that even hinted at normal behavior.

The people at the show were okay. Some of the boys were telling me to get a haircut. Why? I know why. These kids are brought up in an unreal world. They are well kept by their parents — like pets, like investments. They don't see the real deal. I felt very removed from the crowd last night. I couldn't attach any human quality to them. It was hard to look at them when I was playing. They seemed like they were watching a video. There was no life there.

I walk into the men's room to piss. This guy is putting on makeup. He looks absolutely ridiculous. He says to me, "Hey dude, got a light?" I'm thinking to myself, "I gotta get out of here." What a creepy place.

Palo Alto is nothing compared to the trip that's going on in front of me right now. We pulled into Santa Cruz about an hour ago. Davo started the thing right by backing the truck into a traffic light pole and wiping out some of the lights. A man and a woman with a baby started to chew us out. We had upset their balance. Something broke and they didn't know how to handle it. I told them that they will be destroyed and asked if there was anyone behind us to run over. They didn't like that much. Empty lives. They stayed until a young blonde pig came over. The pig was drinking a bottle of orange juice. Too much. The man and woman, seeing that bloody chaos was quelled, walked away staring over their shoulders as they went down the street.

"See, it's him!" someone says as they pass me. I look up. Some people are staring at me. Santa Cruz is beyond belief. Almost every female I see is perfect. Reminds me of Sweden. The people here look to be for the most part either hippies, ex-hippies or Bob Weir clones. The women... I can hardly believe my eyes. They keep walking by. Tan, young, fit... Oh man. As I was walking to this bench where I am sitting, a group of people sitting in front of a record store yell my name and point. People on the street all stop and stare at me. I put my head down and keep walking along. I don't like being picked out in public. I don't like the straight world. It's ugly, violent and cruel. They try to make it so nice looking. They don't fool me.

Fifteen minutes later: I just finished talking to a girl who sat down next to me and tried to give me a

LOS ANGELES, CA / 8.31.85 (*ED COLVER*)

Black Flag flyer. I saw her earlier. She stood out from the crowd. She had a cruel, beautiful German face and platinum blonde hair. I watched her pass me. Minutes later, she's sitting next to me asking me what kind of music I like. We talked for a while. She has been living here for two years undergoing rehabilitation for heroin addiction. She told me how junk robbed her of all feeling for other people. She said that the men in this town are real lame and that they don't do much except cocaine. As we are talking, a man comes up requesting a light from her cigarette. He lights up a joint with it and walks away. She said that the drug rehab and psychotherapy make her feel depressed. She has a two o'clock curfew that she has to obey. She's saving her money so she can leave this town. She does not know where she will go, but she says, "I have to get out of here or I'll tweak." She leaves to go to the clothes store where she works. "I hate it there. The people and the clothes are so plastic. I hate it there. Five more weeks and I'm gone." I don't think I could last a week here. She and I both agreed that this place is great for paranoia. Her perfume made me sick. I can still smell it. I should walk around more, but I don't think that I want to. I feel too out in the open here on these streets. These bums are looking at me and talking amongst themselves. More hot looking women walk by. A few not so hot looking ones walk by pushing baby carriages. More bums are congregating in front of me. Each asks the other if he has any cash. They all show their hands and shrug. One with an acoustic guitar and a backpack shows the other his beads that he's trying to sell. Hippies, lifestylers and new wavers all walking down the street, not paying each other the slightest bit of mind. Time to go. Find some food.

Later: Found food. The sun sets on Santa Cruz. I'm at the club. "Mommy's Condo." That's what keeps going through my head every time I see these kids on the street. I walk around — my mind going at a furious pace. I take in everything and add the parts together. I sit down and try to write and I slow down to the pace of a wounded snail. I ate breakfast at a Denny's this morning. I'm sitting at the counter when the phone rings at the cash register. Fran, the waitress, picks up the phone. I can hear her distinctly. "Hello, Denny's. Yes, a man with long dark hair and tattoos? Yes, okay." She turns to me, "The phone's for you." I pick it up. Some kind of crank call. Fine. But at Denny's?

In a few days I'll be in Los Angeles. LA is "home". Not really though. I no longer know the meaning of the word. No place like home? I imagine. We crossed into California the other night. 99 days on the road. We came in silently and unnoticed. I saw the skyline of Sacramento from a distance. I felt like a fisherman looking at the lights of Cuba. Outside. That's how I felt. The farther south we go toward LA, the more I find myself not wanting to be there for even one minute. Home is a bunch of people calling me "dude" and asking me when I'm playing next.

I awoke that morning in Sacramento. One of the first things I saw was a highway patrol cruiser. Welcome home to that big shotgun in the front seat. I don't know if I will be able to handle myself around the two or three friends I have in LA. The only person I can relate to is myself and that's getting a little patchy.

After a million questions and constant bantering and abuse, one could find oneself pretty lost. I don't know where I went off the rails, but I went somewhere and I don't know where I am. I have never been so confused in all my life. Inside this confusion, I can still see outside. Maybe I see things more clearly now. I don't know. Maybe I do know. Maybe I'm not confused at all. Maybe I am seeing the true horror. Yes — maybe that's it.

I passed a mirror today as I was walking down the street. I felt subhuman, dirty and insane. I think I saw myself as they see me. It made me look twice because I didn't recognize the face at first. What happens when the soul goes insane? The outside features remain the same. Except for the eyes, which take on a whole new sharpness and gleam. Inside, the soul is electrified, writhing with jolts of pain and unrestrained joy. Everything is dark and there are no walls. Just the endless spinning and swinging, like a pillar of diamonds hanging from a charged wire. Alive, alive, alive. When the body goes to sleep, the soul gets up and paces the room waiting around for the body to get up. Sometimes it doesn't. This happens to me. I will be exhausted but unable to sleep. Last night, I tried to sleep but I didn't do very well. The soul is a madman and the body is a filthy hitchhiker, a parasite — an addict. I am an addict. Where's my fix? What's my fix? Addicted to addiction? Sometimes I think I live for cold turkey. Perhaps the search for the fix yields more than the dose ever could. Crawl, search, destroy, rip limb from limb, chop, bite, chew... annihilate.

9.17.85 TUCSON AZ: The tour ended two weeks ago. I haven't started on my talking tour. I couldn't write during my two week stay in LA. I don't do so well there. Now I'm in the desert in Arizona and it's only now that I can see. I find it almost impossible to be in one place for a long time.

That night in Santa Cruz was one fucked up experience. During our set, a girl took off her spiked bracelet and started punching guys in the crowd. I took the bracelet from the girl and threw it to someone on the side of the stage. Her friend came up to me and punched me in the balls. No problem there. I'm used to stuff like that. I did nothing to retaliate. I don't know what to do in situations when a female hits me. You're not supposed to hit them. I don't. Whatever. After the show, the promoter came up to me and told me that the cops wanted to talk to me outside. That bitch had called the pigs on me. I went outside in just my shorts — no shoes or anything. The pigs were outside waiting for me. One with black leather gloves came up to me and said, "Let's go across the street so no one can see us." I knew that I was going to get my ass kicked. Two more pigs were waiting for us across the street. They started asking questions. The one with the gloves didn't say anything. He just kept staring at me while grinding his knuckles into his palms. I did my best to keep in the streetlight so if the pig started whaling on me, some people might be able to see it go down. I somehow talked my way out of it. They let me go. I went back across the street to the club. That bitch and her friends were standing there laughing at me. The bad guys help the bad guys. That's how it always goes. That pig wanted to hit me so bad I think he would have paid me. Fuck pigs. Kill them so I can have something to laugh at.

Later that night, we were staying at this guy's house and the bitch came over. She didn't know that we were staying there. I dumped my mineral water on her and then I spat in her face. She said that she was going to call the police again because I had blinded her. The guy we were staying with was a dealer and he was shitting himself with that idea. People are so fucked. Women are so fucked. I hope she and all the Santa Cruz pigs die. That pig-calling witch...

The next night was San Francisco. We pulled in around 2 or 3. I immediately called Diamanda Galas. She lives about eight blocks away from where we were playing. I went over there and we hung out. It was great to see her. She looked great. She is working hard on her next record. She took me out to dinner. It was great as well. She told me about how she heard a woman get strangled to Death in the house next door to where she lives. We talked about a lot of stuff. None of which I remember because my brain is spent. Diamanda really liked the show. I'm glad that she got to see us play. I have so much to say, but it's so hard to put it down on paper.

By next morning, I was in LA. We landed at Ratman's place. We had a show that night in LA so almost everybody stayed at Ratman's. Staci came and picked me up and took me to the Ginns'. It was strange walking in there. Pettibon was in his usual place — so was Ms. Ginn. Felt good to be back in the shed. I didn't spend much time there as I had to go down to the show. Our show in LA was a free one. We found a place in a deserted section of downtown. We arranged the whole thing ahead of time. Flyers were put out saying that it was a free show and all, so about 600 people showed up. Our set got shut down about three songs from the end by the pigs. I don't like playing in LA much. People in the crowd telling me I'm a rock star. I asked them to get their sisters to suck my cock.

I went to the shed that night. I can't remember that night at all. My brain was so spent at that point that I couldn't even remember where we played the week before. I woke up the next morning and left with Staci to go down to San Diego for the last show of the tour. I don't remember much of that day. During the set, there were a few males in the crowd hitting people for no reason. I just watched them as I played. I didn't care at all. I tried to help some people out in Santa Cruz and I learned my lesson. Never again. If it's not one of our people in there, I'm going to let it go.

During "Louie, Louie", the last song in the set — I did a whole thing about Kira since it was her last show with Black Flag. I did some raps about getting rid of cancer and what a rancid bitch she was. Then just like that, the tour was over. I can remember sitting in the dressing room feeling real down. The tour becomes more than just a bunch of shows. It becomes a part of you.

After 105 days on the road, I totally forgot any other way of life besides the tour. I felt lonely, like a friend was going away and never coming back.

I caught a ride back to the Ginns' with Dave Chandler, the guitar player in Saint Vitus. I sat in the shed, still damp from the show. I felt confused and frustrated. I had no way to wind down. I didn't sleep except for a few hours. Couldn't relax. I could think of no one I wanted to talk to or see. I didn't want to leave the shed. I just wanted to sit in there until the next tour started. The next day, I just sat in the back yard and spent some time unpacking and playing tapes that I hadn't heard in months. I didn't want to go outside of the back yard.

This always happens after tours. It becomes very difficult for me to decompress. The phone started ringing. People wanted to see how I was and how the tour went. I just answered in one and two word replies. There is no way to explain. I never felt so alienated from people as I do now. I cannot identify with anyone except for someone in our crew.

A girl was flying out to stay with me in a couple of days and I was very nervous about it. I didn't know if I was going to be able to talk to her at all. There's nothing wrong with her. The problem is with me. I am no longer human. I am no longer a sane person. I can't identify anymore. I was afraid that it was go-

(ED COLV

ing to be awful. I thought I was going to scare her or alienate her totally. She came and stayed with me for a week. That was the fastest week I have ever lived in my life. I cannot see where it went. One day I'm in some stinking club with a bunch of people yelling at me and then I'm on a deserted beach under a sunny blue sky with a beautiful blonde in a bikini. Maybe it was a dream. Thinking back on it now — it was one great week.

I did my best to explain where I was coming from. I don't think I did very well. Like right now, I feel like throwing this book out the window. I feel like I am writing behind a wall of cotton. I couldn't even face my mail when I got home. There was a large box of it waiting for me in the shed. I didn't have the uumph to open it up. The two weeks in LA were quite exasperating. I couldn't relax at all. I think I have forgotten how to do it. Even with the girl there, I couldn't relax. There is nothing in this town for me at all. One thing I can remember and that was the constant feeling of disappointment that nothing felt different. I would walk down 21st Street to go to the store and it felt as if I had never left. I felt cheated. Fifteen weeks away and the place swallows me so fast that I cannot even remember ever leaving. I counted the days before I left again. Home is bad. Home robs me of me. I could stay there forever and have my brain wiped clean. I knew I had to get out of there. So here I am in the desert, starting a solo tour that will stretch to near the end of October. I feel relief. I feel free.

I saw John Lee Hooker at McCabe's for the second time while I was in LA. He was great. He played "Rock Me Baby", "Crawling King Snake", "Boom Boom Boom" and "I Cover the Waterfront". He told some great stories. I saw the Grateful Dead two days ago down in Chula Vista. They were amazing. That was one of the best shows I've seen in a while. Man, can they play. That was the best sound system I have ever heard. They played a long time. It was great. I'd go see them again in a second. The cop cars there were all plastered with Dead stickers and the pigs were throwing frisbees and laughing and almost acting kind of human. One pig said to me, "Nice tattoos. If you ever get bored, you can read yourself!" Yeah fine, pig. It would have been great to have laughed back and then to have pulled out a gun and shot him in the head.

Davo and I left the show and drove into the desert to go to sleep. We crossed into Arizona. It was beautiful out there. Clear skies, stars everywhere. We parked in a rest area in the middle of nowhere. We slept with the side doors open. Our view out the door was desert, mountains and stars. I felt so lucky to be out there. I walked into the desert for a short distance. I wanted to keep walking. I wanted to disappear into the night. I stood there — in the dark, alone, bathed in warm desert air. I have dreams of that place. The desert night is the endless perfect night.

9.18.85 LUBBOCK TX: Last night was real good. People were real cool. I'm looking forward to the rest of these shows. It's strange doing shows like this outside of California. Slept in the van last night at a rest stop. I have not eaten yet. This is Lubbock, Texas.

9.26.85 ATHENS GA: I have not written in this book for about a week. Much has happened, but I have no real desire to relate. The shows have been going well. I have been pretty consistent. A few days ago I was in Houston, Texas. A girl that Davo and I were staying with took us out to eat at the Mexican restaurant where she worked. She told us how cool the place was and how great the clientele was. She told me that an older couple would be joining us at the table. She went on and on about how great these two were.

We get to the restaurant, the parking lot was full of very expensive cars. Fine. We go in. We sit down. The place was packed with loud, rich people. They were walking, sitting, going over to each other's tables and shaking hands. I remember that — a lot of handshaking going on. I don't really go in for that crap. We're sitting there with this girl who's chattering away about how great everybody is. All of her friends who work there were all coming up to the table. "Is this the famous one? So glad to meet you!" Fuck... Get me out of here! The din was growing louder by the minute. The couple still had not arrived yet. I totally tuned myself out and concentrated on the candle that lit our table. Finally, the couple came in. I couldn't believe I was being put through this bullshit. They were going to different tables, shaking hands and hugging. The man was a lawyer and the woman was an "artist". The man and I talked for a while. He said to me, "Henry, I don't mean to patronize you. But I have to tell you. A long time ago when I was in college, I was out with my friends having a few beers and we heard about a rodeo across town. Anyone could ride if they signed up. Well, I had some experience with rodeo and I was feeling the beer so I went over and signed up. I'll never forget sitting in that gate with the bull. That bull was a bundle of energy. He seemed ready to bust out of that gate whether it was lifted up or not. You remind me of that bull."

He made me nervous. He was transparent and as easy to read as the Sunday papers. Sure he was successful and rich. So was every male in the place. He was terrifying. A person motivated by money — living for money. I imagined a long train of grinning cowboys, each with his arm extended, burying a knife into the back of the cowboy in front of him. He said, "Henry, if lightning struck this place on a Thursday night, all the beautiful people in Houston would be dead." No shit. Our host just loved the place. I looked around. What I saw made me want to rip right out of there. They were no longer humans. I saw goats and pigs in suits and dresses. The grunting and squealing hit an unbearable pitch. Ugly stinking things. I realized that the lawyer guy would do anything he could to get over on someone. The kind of guy who would smile, look you in the eyes, rip your balls out, feed them to you, pull out his card, shake your hand and say, "If there's anything I can ever do for you, just let me know."

Death machines: They shook hands. I could hear the metal grind as their palms met. Their eyes flickered. Their mouths opened. Business cards came out. Each reached over and extracted the card from the other's mouth.

Later on, the girl told me that she really didn't like them that much, but they were good connections to other things. Too bad that girl wants to be part of that world. She was almost cool. That's what happens in the straight world. You get sucked in, given a knife and you get pointed to the ladder of bodies that you must climb to "get to the top." That's not my life. I am free of that chain gang mentality. Suck ass so maybe someday someone will suck yours. Come on, one more big mouthful of shit. You can do it. Good dog...

10.1.85 NEW BRUNSWICK NJ: I am supposed to do a show in this place tonight. The promoter didn't do any advertising. This bar didn't even know that I was coming. So I was fucked over by the promoter. Isn't that a kick in the ass? Nothing like this to make you feel like a piece of shit. I felt like a fucking idiot asking the guy behind the bar where I was supposed to set up. He looked at me and said I could do it anywhere I wanted. He was pretty fucking funny. The promoter — what a waste of food.

10.5.85 NEW YORK NY: In the Danceteria waiting to do my thing. Waiting, waiting, waiting. Insane.

10.9.85 DETROIT MI: I am sitting outside the club waiting for someone to let me in. It's almost five. I flew in from Newark, New Jersey this afternoon. I had to take a cab here. Called all the Detroit numbers I had, but no one was home.

Later: In the club. Fluorescent lights. Cold in here. I feel like a small man. I'm listening to the people in here. Not my scene. The 24-hour store across the street has a wall of bulletproof glass in front of the cashier. You hand him money through a little chute at the bottom of the window where the counter meets the glass. It's cold outside and cold inside. Since the last time I wrote in here, I have passed through South Carolina, Washington DC, New York, Boston and Connecticut. A lot has happened. It has been hard for me to write in my journal the last few weeks. Every time I try, I get choked up. Doing these shows almost every night is hard. In a lot of ways, it's harder than playing in Black Flag. There is very little physical release, just standing there with the mic in my hand. The shows are driving me into myself like a nail being driven into a rock. I am sitting on a stairwell at the rear of the club. It's the only place I can find where I don't have to see anyone. I have another week of shows and then I will be in LA for a few days then up to Seattle for a show then back to LA for a while.

The cab driver was cool today — reeking of booze. When I put my bag in his trunk, I saw his bottle. Saw Deadheads at the airport today in Newark. I think the Dead will be there soon.

There's no place to go here in Detroit. Tomorrow is Madison. They have a good coffee place. I feel cold and folded inward.

10.10.85 En route to Madison WI: Last night was cool. Not the greatest show I ever did, but not that bad. I got paid very little. That's okay. They gave me what they could and that's great. This plane ride cost me more than I made last night and that's a drag, but that's the way it goes. When I land in Madison, I will take a cab to this coffee place I always go to, then I will have a meal at this real good vegetarian restaurant. That is... if this plane doesn't crash. I lived through the flight yesterday so I'm feeling a bit cocky I must admit. Five more rides until I land at LAX. The plane has landed. I'm in Milwaukee. The plane leaves for Madison in 15 minutes. I can't wait to get off this plane. Fuck it! This existence, that existence. I don't want mere existence, thank you. I look around me and what I see makes me want to run, catch a boat on the Nile and sail up river until my teeth fall out.

There are so many hammocks to catch you if you fall, so many laws to keep you from experience. All these cities I have been in the last few weeks make me fully understand the cozy, stifling state in which most people pass through life. I don't want to pass through life like a smooth plane ride. All you do is get to breathe and copulate and finally die. I don't want to go with smooth skin and calm brow. I hope I end up a blithering idiot cursing at the sun — hallucinating, screaming, giving obscene and insane lectures on street corners and public parks. People will walk by and say, "Look at that drooling idiot. What a basket case." I will turn and say to them, "It is you who are the basket case. For every moment you hated your job, cursed your wife and sold yourself to dream that you didn't even conceive. For the times your soul screamed yes and you said no. For all of that. Your self-torture. I see the glowing eyes of the sun! The air talks to me! I am at all times!" And maybe, the passers by will drop a coin into my cup.

Later: The plane didn't crash. I got to the lobby and called a cab. Minutes later, a cab pulls up and a woman driver gets out and says, "Cab for Henry." I say, "That's me." She says, "I am supposed to ask you if you are *the* Henry Rollins and if you are, would you sign three autographs for the guys at the station." She dropped me off at the coffee shop that I like. So that's where I am right now. Today's featured coffee is Mexican. It tastes real good. The sun is setting on State Street. The air is clear and cold. Here I am in shorts. What a loser.

I saw the film *Mishima* the other night when I was in Boston. I really liked it. I will go back and see it again when I get the chance. Mishima showed me a few things and solidified ideas that have been pacing around in my head for a long time. Yukio Mishima killed himself in ritual fashion, following ancient Japanese tradition. He thought that a man should kill himself at the peak of his physical life so he would not have to die in a pathetic, withering state. There's something very perfect and self-respecting about such a violent act. I need to go check this guy out. I'll try to find someone who knows his books so I can get some advice on which one to read first.

MEET

Henry Rollins

Signing His New Book
Polio Flesh

Friday, October 11   5:00 p.m.
BE THERE

BARBARA'S BOOKSTORE
2907 N. Broadway
477-0411

10.12.85 EN ROUTE TO KANSAS CITY: I played in Chicago last night. It was cool. I also did an in-store appearance at Barbara's Bookstore. That place was real cool. I found two books that I wanted — *In the Belly of the Beast* by Jack Henry Abbott and a book of Comte de Leutreamont's miscellaneous notes and letters. When I got to the bookstore that morning, I cringed. The front window was covered with posters saying "Henry Rollins here at 5:00 p.m. signing his new book *Polio Flesh*. Be there." That shit always freaks me out. Who do I think I am? When no one shows up, can I skulk out the back door dragging my sorry box of books? The place packed out luckily. People there were real cool. By the end of the night, I was pretty well spent. Two hours of talking at the store, one and a half hours at the club and then another hour and a half afterwards doing interviews. Burnout to burnout. My wounds are closing. I'm drying up and turning brittle. Scrape me out and add water.

10.16.85 SHED: The other night I was in Kansas City. I finished the show and left the club — a place called the Fool Killer. We're heading toward the parking lot and we heard screams. A guy is dealing on some woman. I yell at the guy to leave her alone. The guy says okay and gets into his car and drives about ten yards from us. He stops and starts yelling shit out of the window. I could have ignored him. I didn't. I smiled and motioned for him to come back. His reverse lights went on and he sped backwards, hitting a parked car. He got out and started talking shit. I listened to him for a minute or so, but all the time I am sizing him up and seeing the first place to hit him. I wanted him to fuck with me. I wanted it. He kept talking so finally I just spat in his face. He came at me. I wanted him to. It felt like we were being sucked together. I felt like I was going at sixty miles an hour without moving. I didn't remember what happened as it was happening. But now, I can see the whole thing very clearly, blow for blow. I live for that mindlessness, for the times when the mind shuts off and something else turns on. Like ultimate sex. The feeling is indescribable because at that time, no feeling exists. I remember now. My left hand coming forward, smashing him in the eyes. I punched him in the face several times. I remember taking his head and smashing it into the trunk of his car over and over. Where was I during all this? I put him in a headlock and worked on his face. I felt his nose break under my fist. Breaking a nose always feels same. It's like grabbing the brass ring or something. I hit him again. I felt his cheekbone cave in. I kept beating his face in. I had no mind. The world around us didn't exist anymore. We moved inside a vacuum chamber. I beat the man until he crawled into his car and balled up into the fetal position. I walked around to the front of the car — a pain in my left hand sends my brain back into action. I looked at my hand in the headlights. My thumb was sticking out perpendicularly from my hand. I wrenched it back in place. I saw blue dots in my eyes. I spit on the man and left before the pigs came. At the time, it seemed like the right thing to do. I almost wanted to thank him. I wanted it and he let me have it. I sat in bed that night and closed my eyes. It all came back to me in perfectly sequenced slow motion. It's in the vibrating, shrieking house of the soul that infinity is realized. That fight could have been an hour or two minutes. When the mind shuts off and the soul comes forward, all time explodes and everything loses its definition, allowing everything to be everything and nothing at the same time.

10.19.85 SHED: Friday night. The Bad Brains are playing in Long Beach tonight. Yesterday I was all hot to go. This afternoon I was thinking about tonight's show and I decided not to go. A packed house of punkers diving off a small stage sounded like a good thing to avoid — so I did. About two weeks ago, I saw them in Washington DC at the 9:30 Club and it was one of the best nights I've had for a long time.

Earlier this summer, I heard that the Bad Brains were reforming. The band had been broken up for almost two years. When they called it quits, I really missed them.

The Bad Brains are from the same town I'm from. The Bad Brains were one of the first bands that I ever saw up-close. I guess the first time I saw them was in 1979. They changed my idea of music completely. The band's singer, HR, was my idea of how a singer should be. I used to watch him and think to myself, "If I was in a band, that's how I would do it." One night HR came up to me and said, "You got to be a singer, man!" I said, "No way." He laughed and pointed his finger at me and said, "Oh yeah! You are gonna be a singer. You gotta get a band!" That really made me spin. I had always wanted to be in a band. I was a roadie for a DC band called the Teen Idles. At the time, I would watch them play and wish that I was the singer for a night.

HR would make me sing with the Bad Brains every once in a while. He would drag me up onstage and I would do a song. Ian, Black Flag and the Bad Brains are my largest influences and inspiration in music so when I heard that they were getting back together, I was excited.

So I was in Washington DC on a day off and the Bad Brains were playing at the 9:30 Club. Black Flag has played the 9:30 Club several times and I used to go there a lot back when I lived there. I got to the club early so I could say hello to the guys. It had been a long time since I saw them. They were there. I talked with Gary, the guitar player. I told him that I was real glad that they were back together again. I told him that I couldn't wait for the set. He laughed and said he was ready to play. I was so excited. Hours later, the band hit stage. I felt so strange. The time got all fucked up in my head. I looked up onstage. There were the Bad Brains. I looked around me. I saw several faces that I recognized from the old days. I felt like I walked into a time warp. When HR said the titles of the songs, I felt electrified. I thought I was going to jump through the ceiling or something. They played a tune called "I", my favorite Bad Brains song of all time. It was so weird to hear those songs again in that club — in that town. Too much. I thought it was 1980 again. With every familiar note, I was going crazy. They were great. Some of the old Bad Brains' friends came out to the show. One guy named Blue, I had not seen him for years. I remember he came to a Bad Brains show all wasted on angel dust and started wrecking the place. HR physically removed his dusted ass from the place. All this was hitting me at once. The people, the music, the familiarity of the club. What a show. They

HENRY AND H.R. OF THE BAD BRAINS / 1982 *(GLEN E. FRIEDMAN)*

were great. They played a handful of new songs which were real good — "Re-Ignition", "Realize", "She's Calling You" and a couple of others that I didn't get the titles of. Great. I taped the show. Came out sounding good.

Earlier that evening, I was down in the dressing room talking with HR. He made me feel bad. He said, "You play too much. You have forgotten where you come from! Yes, homeboy! You should come and hang out in DC with your homeboys! You have forgotten us, rock star! Hey, can you get us some naked babies for after the show?" I just stared at the ground. Made me feel like shit. A person who told me to be a singer — a person who inspired me to play as hard as I could no matter what — now he was putting me down. Telling me to come home and sit on the front porch! Homeboy? He said, "You should take some time off. Slow down and hang out with your friends. California has turned you into a different person. Come home!" I told him that my schedule didn't permit hanging out. I told him that I had just finished 93 shows in 105 days with Black Flag. He looked around the room and called to his friends and said, "Did you hear that? Oh my goodness, Henry!" Yeah. He lit up a big old joint and said, "Come on Henry, smoke. I dare you. I bet you're scared! Someday I'm going to tie you up, put a gas mask on you and pump you full of pot! Then turn you loose on a stage and watch you go really crazy!" I felt pretty crummy after all that. I don't think his rasta brethren liked my white ass much. I left and went upstairs. Whenever someone gives me the "you've forgotten us" rap it makes me mad. I felt like playing 105 shows in 93 days next time. Makes me feel more resolved to NEVER stop. Fuck these people. They would never be able to deal with the shit that I do — flat out. All we would have to do is play a few weeks on the road and then we would see some shit.

I am never going to stop. I go to DC — the same people are doing the same things. I come back to LA,

I walk into the Ginns' and everything is the same — frozen. I realize that I must keep moving like a river. A river running by statues. I can't stop. I am afraid that if I ever sat down or looked back, I would become paralyzed like when a rabbit freezes in the glare of an oncoming car's headlights. The rabbit would never know what hit him. My lungs would fill with dirt and I would slowly sit down and turn to marble. The river would run dry and I would build my own house on the dry riverbed. A house with a real nice front porch and then I would sit down and watch the sun set forever.

I hear the voices as if they were coming from far away. *Come here. Sit down. Come home where you belong.* It's so true. You can't go home — not all the way. Once you leave, home picks up quotation marks, looks like "home" forever after. I left the club feeling exhilarated and confused. HR hurt my feelings. It's the people you look up to that let you down. I still know he's the man. I couldn't go tonight. I didn't want to cheapen my experience.

I think my thumb must be broken. It hurts a lot. I have to eat aspirin just to push this pen. If I broke my thumb on that guy's face, I wonder how he's looking now.

I read all the mail that gets sent to me. I don't answer all of it. I do answer some. I get a lot of nasty letters now. I never got this much before. A girl wrote that she identified with me and felt a lot like I do and then she told me that I was just a jerk. I don't understand. I read an article in Alternate Routes about me. They said that I don't know what I'm doing — my answers are vague and that I am a total contradiction. I guess they mean "vague" when I say that I'm not a poet and I perform because I like to do it. I guess plain stuff is not very cool for their armchair mentality. It's so hard not to look like an idiot when the questions try to accuse you of something and if you don't answer them their way and escape their "conviction" then they really bum out and call you this and that. Here's some more vague shit from me — Fuck you and your reviews. Fuck you and your letters. I don't care if you like what I do or not. Either stop me or shut the fuck up.

When you laugh at the lightweight, lard-ass armchair warrior, he gets very uptight because the bullshit game is not being played by both parties. The armchair warrior realizes that he is "playing with himself." This suits him fine. He knows you better than you do anyway. Hey, if you don't go outside then you have to try and convince everybody that inside is cooler. What a prison that is. Boy, do they get mad when you beat the rap and laugh at them from outside the gates. These people are so lightweight. They bitch and moan, but they don't know shit about going out there and really trying to make something happen. Then there's me. Some wiseass in his twenties telling them something. It pisses them off. I know that I don't know a lot. But at least I'm going for it. Which is a lot more than any of these people are doing.

10.20.85 SEATTLE WA: Flew in a few hours ago. I did a talking show at the Lhasa Club last night. I took all my clothes off before I went onstage. Felt great walking onstage naked in front of all those people. I said hello, dressed and did my thing for about an hour and forty-five minutes. I think I did pretty good.

Now in Seattle. It's cold and raining. I'm in a coffee place waiting until it's time to hit it. I would rather be in the shed alone with the lights off. There's nothing wrong with Seattle. I think the people at our shows here are real cool. The problem is with me. I don't feel good. I don't feel sick or anything. I just feel like I want to be in a dark room. Across from me, a girl sits with her father.

"You should try to see them every once in a while," he says to her.

"I don't know them. I don't want to associate with them. They make me sick!" she replies.

He says, "You should try to give them half a chance, really."

"Yeah right. I gotta go!" she shoots back and gets up quickly and leaves.

She's almost out the door. The father stands up and yells "Tina!" and she turns around. "Say hello to your mother." Tina leaves.

She returns moments later in a car. Tina jumps out of the car, comes back into the restaurant, drops a small box on the table and says, "Here, I don't want this!"

Dad says, "Honey, I'll let you pick it out yourself. I'll send you a check next week. I'll call you too."

"I don't want anything from you!" she yells and leaves.

The whole place gets very quiet for a few seconds and then there's a small burst of nervous laughter. The father and I look at each other briefly. He looks a bit down. No wonder. Probably going home to a small place where he lives alone. What a shitty fucking night to be involved with.

The pilot on the plane today didn't talk to us passengers once today. Made me nervous. It's always nice to hear the pilot cut in when you are cruising miles above the clouds. Pilots always sound so calm and cool. "Hello, ladies and gentlemen. This is your captain, Lawrence Fullerton. We're cruising at approximately 40 billion feet. Weather below is fair and I'll be back to you when we get a score on the Dodgers game down on the ground. Thank you." Click. Whew! All's cool, did you hear him? Sounds

Henry and Ian, DC Space, Washington DC / October 1985

like he's driving the plane from a hammock. Well, that's fine with me. If he can kick back then so can I. But today, no little messages from up front. What's the matter, Captain? DT's? An impending nervous breakdown? C'mon, Cap! Sound off! Say something! Make something up! Please! If man was meant to fly, he would have been born with a boarding pass.

10.21.85: Yes, I am tempting the hand of fate again. I am on a plane to LA. I hope I make it. One of the engines sure is wobbling on the wing. Looks like it's fixing to drop off any second. They say that these babies can fly with only one engine operating, but I don't believe it for a second. I hate planes. Here I am, strapped in with a bunch of strangers in the middle of nowhere. What an asshole I am! Man was not meant to fly! This is absurd. Why am I here in this thing? Because I wanted to do the show in Seattle.

Last night was real cool. The audience was great. I have learned that with these spoken performances, you can only be as good as the audience will let you be. If they talk and give you shit then you can't lay into it real hard. But usually, the audiences are great.

The tour I just finished showed me how cool people can be. I like Seattle. I like playing there with Black Flag — always a good show. So now I'm just waiting to land. Please land at LAX. I just checked my watch — 38 minutes in. I always click on the stopwatch on my watch as soon as we take off. Oh shit! Turbulence. I'm looking out the window at that engine. Hold baby! You can do it! 63 minutes to go!

I read another magazine that runs me down again. Well shit, I must really be a terrible person — the worst. Oh well, I'll just have to live with it.

Much later: Now in the shed. The plane landed safely. Got here — everything just as I left it. Cold in the old shed tonight. I feel like staying in here for about a year. I've had my fill of people — up to the gills. I don't want to hear the telephone again. This always happens. I read a bunch of nasty shit about me in a magazine. I waste a few minutes trying to figure it out. I combine that with thoughts of walking down the street and seeing people stare at me and then I think to myself, "Fuck, man. I need this shit like a hole in the head." I would just like to go away. I feel like an idiot for ever having done anything in public. Makes me regret the three books, the seven or eight albums, answered letters, hundreds of shows and all the pain and trouble and hard time it took to do all that. It makes me feel so stupid for ever giving anything to anyone. I deserve any criticism I get. If I was smart, I would just leave all of this shit behind and stop being someone that others see. I don't need anyone to make me feel good about myself. But it always takes one besides myself to bring me down. I get put down by humans for being human. I get praised for the same.

I don't get it. I'd probably be better off if I put myself in a bottle and threw myself into the sea. The mainland got a little smaller today, I am slipping away. To a new land? I hope so.

10.25.85 SHED: Yesterday was cool. I talked to Nick Cave, Blixa Bargeld and Diamanda Galas all in one day. Nick sounded good and said he'd call when he hit town. Blixa wanted Diamanda's phone number and then hung up. Diamanda called me from San Francisco.

Oh man, it sure will be a gloomy crowd at the Palace when the Bad Seeds play there tonight. Doom laden, Melrose Ave. locals hanging tough. Well, hanging right in there. Those types always make me smile. Tonight is the night. Hell, I bought a ticket. I'm in. I'm no idiot. This is going to be great.

10.27.85 3:20 A.M. SHED: I feel like a fly drowning in a glass of water. The fly struggles frantically, legs and wings kick and beat furiously. The fly stops to rest for a moment and then starts up again. The fly will eventually take in water and that will be the poor bastard's end. That's me — drowning in a little glass of water trying to convince myself that I'm struggling in a raging ocean. Trying to make an epic battle out of simple frustration. The fly's struggle is more real than mine. Several ideas hang in front of me. They shine like diamonds. They sit like apples on the highest branch. The ones farthest away look the best. Makes sense, they're the hardest ones to get to. Doesn't stop you from being hungry for and attracted to what looks good and sits out of reach.

I was thinking of Greg Ginn tonight. These days I call him "the Washing Machine Man". Every morning, Greg gets up and enters the washing machine. All day long, he's agitated and spun around. At the end of the day, he is against the wall — wrinkled, wrung and damp. There is a lot of pressure right now. Black Flag has no bass player. We have been evicted from our office and practice place. We have about six days to get out. This shit sits neatly on Greg's shoulders. He is put through the machine every day. He's a bit wrinkled, but he's clean and I respect and admire him. I don't think he'll ever know how much.

I have been having funny things happen with my left eye. Several times a day I'll turn around because I thought I saw something out of the corner of my eye. Sometimes it looks like a black snake, sometimes it looks like a rat or something.

My broken thumb is healing crooked. At the base is a big lump where the thumb broke. I kind of like it. My thumb is now permanently jammed in a downward position. Mutilation has always been fine.

Tonight I saw a picture of myself with fresh cuts on my ribs and stomach. The picture was taken in Amsterdam, Holland on my birthday 2.13.83. I ran my hand under my shirt and rubbed the scars. Self-mutilation. The mutilation of thought. The mutilation of mind. There is blood in the water, but I won't turn the channel.

Today a guy asked me why I don't drink. I told him, "I don't want anything to disturb the signal." For me, there is no such thing as "drunken joy". That's an illusion.

Spent most of the day with Staci and Nick Cave. We went and xeroxed some stuff. He xeroxed his novel *And The Ass Saw The Angel* for me. The book is only partly done and already at about 200 pages or so. The Bad Seeds were great the other night. Might be the best time I've ever seen them. They opened with "Tupelo" and went from there. Talked to Tony Alva for a while before the show started. He seems to be doing real good. Tony is a cool guy.

Living a life of mutilation and mutation. Wondering if I will grow another head one of these days. It's never too late to mutate.

Blixa played a new Einsturzende Neubauten project for me yesterday. Sounded great. The Bad Seeds lineup was Nick Cave on vocals and harmonica, Barry Adamson on bass, Mick Harvey on guitar and keyboards, Blixa on guitar and Thomas from Die Haut on drums. Damn was that guy good. Barry was brilliant last night — the whole band. The sound was good, lots of clean low end. Didn't get much of a chance to talk to Nick. Maybe next time — in about 14 months or something.

It's now 4:30 in the morning and I cannot sleep. Thoughts assail me. I am one confused young man. I cannot get myself far enough away. Nothing I can find gives me any distance. Whenever I interact with people, I just get turned off. Those flaky people hanging out at the Bad Seeds hotel room, just there to sell the band drugs and get high. People waste their time. They don't even know the music. They get on the guest list, get in and head for the bathrooms. Sometimes I feel that I'm going to have to leave. I am just going to have to leave and go far away. I don't think I am doing too well here. I mistake my desperation for creativity.

I cannot stop running from the incendiary wave that follows me. Sometimes I feel like I'm running on a railroad track. The train is close on my heels. I am not driven. I am chased. I run. I can't turn around. I can't bear to see the face of the conductor. I bet his face looks like mine.

11 hours later: There is a winter sun in the back yard today. Looks pale and sickly. Makes me wonder if there is a sun that's pulled out for Sunday use only. It's the afternoon. I feel like going away right now.

I woke up early this morning and lay still for a couple of hours, thinking. I saw myself walking down the side of a mountain. I was zigzagging down the slope, avoiding the large rocks. I came to an oblong hole in the ground. I walked right into it. Sitting here now thinking about it, I can remember exactly where that mountain is. It's in a park where I used to live near in Washington DC. At the base of the mountain was a small river. When I was young, I used to poke around in the woods there. One time, I found a small pile of clothes — a girl's clothes — socks, shoes, dress, underwear and bra. It scared me. I never told anybody about that. Damn this place. I fell into a hole. Got lost in a cold neighborhood. Wondered how, wondered why. I disgust myself regularly. Sun's going down. I was going to fly to San Francisco to see Diamanda perform tonight. I am not going. I looked at my finances and they are too low for such fun. I want to go so bad but I cannot afford to.

12.23.85 SHED: This morning, Ms. Ginn woke me up. She came into the shed and said, "Henry, something terrible has happened. D. Boon has been killed!" I just sat there for about five minutes or so. I couldn't believe it. Apparently, he, his girlfriend and her sister were driving in his van in the early morning. Linda, D.'s girlfriend, fell asleep at the wheel. She is okay, her sister is in critical condition. D. was thrown out of the van and killed. I spent most of today thinking about him. I called a few people so they wouldn't have to hear it down the line.

12.31.85 SHED: The last few days, I don't know. I remember all of it, but no parts in particular. We played a party in the Valley the other night. The first time the band has played live in front of people since the last show of the *Loose Nut* tour. Let's see. Friday night, I couldn't sleep. I did doze off between six and seven, I think. I had a short dream. I was in bed with a girl. I guess we were going to fuck or something. I was right about to jump on her when she sat up and pulled out an envelope, stuck her hand in and pulled out a handful of receipts. She started to do some kind of bookkeeping and I helped her. End of dream. I played that party on no sleep. I don't remember a whole lot of it — the playing I mean. Most of the time I thought that I was going to throw up.

I got home around 4:30 a.m. I slept three or four hours. Sunday — I don't remember it. All I know is I didn't practice. I didn't have a voice. Sunday night — no sleep again. I am an enemy of my brain. Makes me mad and scared. I thought I was one, but right now, I am two. I hate that number, the number two. There's only one real number: the number one. Perfect strength. True force. I am an enemy of my brain. Destroying me — driving me insane. Inside turning on the inside. Destroying on the inside. Napalm. Extermination. Jungle calling... ghetto calling... lover calling. Almighty, almighty, almighty.

I just turned against her in my mind. Knives pointed at her. Laughing hyenas at the window of loneliness. So far away. Never, never. I'm sitting alone. Whenever I write, I start to hyperventilate.

Now it's early a.m. Tuesday. No sleep again. Practiced tonight. Leaving for San Francisco in a few hours. Playing January 2 & 3 in San Francisco and Fresno. We canceled some shows so we could be in LA for D. Boon's funeral on the 4th. I think about D. Boon's body lying in a freezer in the Phoenix city morgue. It's not D., it's "the body".

Now being down at the practice place was a trip. The phone rang nonstop. Someone wanting to know about D. Boon. It gets to you. On Christmas Day, I was there answering the phones. The normal D. Boon rap — "Yes, it's true... Arizona... Early Sunday morning... I don't know how... Goodbye." After the fifteenth call in a half hour or something, the phone rang and I answered, "Hello, D. Boon hotline." It was Mike Watt. He was upset, didn't say much that I could understand, except for "...no more Minutemen. It's all over..." He hung up mid-sentence. There's no way you could not like D. Boon. He will be missed by anyone who ever knew him. This is the worst.

My favorite D. Boon memory was when we were building the Ginns' house in 1984. At lunch time, he would fall asleep in the shade of this tree across the street. People would walk by and there is this big fat mother, shirtless, all sprawled out snoring. It was fucking hilarious. What a great guy. I won't forget him.

1:40 a.m.: No sleep. I walked out to the post box. The air is moist and charged. On nights like these, I cannot help wanting to run away to my memories. My memories are my friends. I can walk through them anytime I want. Sometimes I hate them. They make me jealous. The me in them is more happy than I am now. All it takes is a few deep swallows of night air and I'm off down memory lane. I have a tremendous headache right now. I cannot remember what I did today. I'm not tired. Exhausted, but not tired. Davo will probably be by here at around five a.m. or so.

The air out tonight was so thick, so cool. I didn't see a single person out there. Fog, street lamps and all the houses with their Christmas lights up. I had an idea to get a lot of lights and twist them into a big swastika. I would put the blinking holiday spirit Swa up in the front window and watch the expressions on the neighbor's faces.

Destruction mind. Suicide, over and over. To the edge and over. Suicide from the inside. Fuming, greasy corpse. Swinging alone in the middle of the apartment. Swinging free, swinging alone. The number one is seen shining high in the sky, burning like the sun. Ulceration. I have not beat off for about twenty-four hours now. I don't feel like it. I just feel like cutting myself up. Almost twenty-five years old and I'm still into that shit. It feels good.

Ghetto lover calling me. Weak smile. Disease spreading. Infestation. Rats running through the ruins of souls. I am an enemy of my brain. Assassin of thought. Assassin of dreams. Piles of dead dreams stacked high like gutted cars in a junkyard — like a pile of bodies at a Death camp. Dead dreams. The Assassin of dreams stands on the carcasses and glares into my eyes — scanning my thoughts, ready to wrench them into an alley and stab them to Death and throw their corpses on the pile. It's not slaughter. It's not murder. It's annihilation. It's extermination.

Walking in an alley of warm meat. Slaughterhouse inside. Slaughterhouse woman. Torture chamber woman. Gas chamber woman. I think of her when I want to hurt myself. I think of her and I want to inflict pain. I use her to destroy myself. The nicer the thoughts, the dearer her pictures become — the more isolated and cancerous I grow. My love for her is a brain tumor that slowly destroys the cells around it. Soon, there will be no more of me. The tumor of her love will consume my mind and take over completely. It's only a matter of time. The tumor takes advantage of every weak moment to grow in size and strength. She feeds off my weakness. Unbeknownst to her, when she consumes my weaknesses, there will be nothing but strength left for her to consume. Maybe the tables will turn. It's my only chance.

He found his escape. He won. He saw what was happening. He knew that her love was taking him over. He took a gun and destroyed the tumor. A real divorce.

La Crosse, Wi / 6.12.86

THE STACK / 1986

*We got a new bass player named C'el (pronounced "sal"). He learned the set very quickly. We rehearsed a little and hit the road for three six-week legs of America. Also on the tour were two other bands, Painted Willie and Greg's instrumental unit, Gone. Our entourage was two vans and a truck. Mitch Bury of Adams, Mass was the tour manager. My friend Joe Cole came out as a road crew member. This ended up being Black Flag's last tour. If you want to get a different slant on the 1986 tour, you should check out Joe's book **Planet Joe**, which contains his journal entries from this tour.*

1.2.86 SAN FRANCISCO CA: Ratman's new PA is set up. It sounds like the sky is falling down. The staff here at the Stone have their attitude already. They're giving us all kinds of petty bullshit. I walked into the dressing room and a few of them were doing coke. You bring in a system to a place and if it's 3 times better than what they got, they get all pissed off.

The Stone staff are really obnoxious. What's the matter, fellas? Not enough cocaine today? Fat, stupid people always seem to get jobs in clubs. No cocaine today, no cocaine tomorrow. I won't be crying when they all start dying.

1.3.86 Shed: We should be playing in Fresno right now. But the show canceled out and we came home. Last night was one of those nights. During the first song, a guy got onstage and knocked into Greg. Greg tried to swing out of his way and he swung his guitar toward me. I swung my head toward Greg. My face collided with his tuning pegs. I got bumps on my head, cheek and jaw. My eyebrow is cut open. I can't open or close my jaw completely either way because of the swelling. All during the set, this one guy kept screaming, "You sold your soul!" over and over while he grabbed the mic cord and shook it so I couldn't get my mouth near it. He would not stop. I asked him over and over to stop. He did not. I was good. I didn't crack him upside his head, now did I? No. It's okay for people to do this. We are not there to play. We are there for people to poke and scream at. I keep forgetting that. That's the way it is. Makes me wonder what they come for. Makes me wonder what I do it for. I didn't like playing last night. People were coming backstage and trying to talk to me. I had nothing to say to them. I just stared at the ground. I used to try and be polite, but now I see where that got me. If I say nothing, it gets the same reaction. That's no big deal. That's just the way it is. Honesty is the best revenge.

The shows are starting again. It only takes a few days on the road to make me remember everything — the halls, the dressing rooms, the smells, the lack of privacy and the people. Two weeks from now, I will hate the sound of my name. I will hate the fact that any asshole who wants to, will be able to fuck with me. If I stand up for myself, I will be given boatloads of shit by band and audience. My head hurts just thinking about it.

My ship will sail into the sun and burn. No abortions in the lake of fire. No promises in the company of alone. The number one heals, strengthens and illuminates.

1.4.86 Shed: D. Boon's funeral went down today. I didn't go. I couldn't find a reason. D. Boon is gone. Why go watch a body get buried in the ground? I asked Ms. Ginn what she thought. She said that she agreed with me and added that after seeing so many dead bodies, blown apart corpses and TB victims in WWII, she thinks it's ridiculous to have any kind of funeral ceremony whatsoever. I got to thinking. It's selfish to have a funeral for someone. You get to say what you want about a person whom you only knew in life. You don't know that corpse. Funerals make people feel better about themselves. Why can't they enjoy the memories of the living? When I think of D. Boon, I can only think of him living. I can only imagine what his dead body looks like. D. Boon will always be alive and well in my thoughts. I'm sure he wouldn't want anyone to cry for him.

1.14.86 Tucson AZ: Drove all night from Huntington Beach, CA to get here. The show last night was really bad. I felt that we should have refunded those people. I played as hard as I could, that's all I know. There are so many great things about going on tour. Far too many to mention here. One of the great things is leaving town and getting away. I was hoping that Huntington Beach was far enough away but I was wrong. After we had finished our shitty set, the place cleared except for a few.

This woman named Pleasant Gehman and her ugly, fat chick cohorts picked Huntington Beach instead of their normal Hollywood bullshit scene. Pleasant and her nowhere band, the Screamin' Sirens were all there. Drunk and rolling all over the floor with their cheesy, goofy boyfriends. There is nothing wrong with drunks rolling on the floor, but after a shitty set and at the starting end of an all night drive, who the fuck wants to have to listen to a bunch of stupid Hollywood nowhere stylers carry on at one of our shows. We must be losing our edge. I thought what we did alienated fuckheads like the Club Lingerie

HUNTINGTON BEACH, CA / 1.13.86 *(NAOMI PETERSEN)*

crowd. Oh well. All good things come to an end.

Before we left for the desert, we had to follow C'el back to his friend's house in East LA to return the car he borrowed.

C'el was so drunk that one of the people in the van had to get out and take the wheel and finish the drive. Great, it's only the first night of the tour.

It's always interesting to watch a tour take shape. Everyone is different. They have a life of their own. I doubt that C'el is very much into this trip. He will have to do a lot to prove to me that he feels otherwise.

Did an in-store yesterday. No one told me that we had one. It's hard to do those things sometimes. The people are always very cool. But when you spread yourself too thin, you feel it. I have nothing to say to anyone. Nothing at all. That's the way I feel. I don't want to do interviews, in-stores or anything close to it. I want to play and be left alone. Maybe in a few months my mind will change. You never know.

1.15.86 EL PASO TX: We're in some factory district. The place we are playing is a broken down warehouse. The place reeks of stale liquor. There's trash all over the place. Graffiti covers almost every inch of wall space. Lots of biker graffiti and the usual punk rock shit. This place is depressing as hell. Once you're here, there's nowhere to go. You could walk miles before you would find something that wasn't some kind of factory or storage place. The Jimi Hendrix quote, "There ain't no life nowhere," comes to mind as I sit here. The smell of the toilets is now rolling in. All the band graffiti on the walls, which were obviously written by the bands, tells you how great they are. What a bunch of desperate idiots. Places like this are always destroyed by their patrons. They destroy the bathrooms, knock out the walls and get the place busted by the cops for hanging around outside the place with open containers of alcohol. Then they bitch and moan and wonder why they have no place to go.

The show last night was good. I like playing in Tucson. The place wasn't very big and we couldn't bring in the entire system. This dump here is not a whole lot bigger. But it's built differently and we can fit the whole PA, so we're setting it all up and it's going to be very, very loud. That's one way to insulate yourself. Places like this bum me out. A lot of the South is like this.

Later: I walked down a Texas street for a few miles. Railroad tracks, factories and beer and wine bottles on the sidewalk. I watched all these guys getting off work. They came out of the buildings like they were being hatched out of an egg. All the windows were covered with smoke, grease or paint. What a drag. Almost like working in a coal mine. When the sun went down, all I could see were neon and crime lights. I walked for about a half hour without seeing another person.

1.19.86 SCOTT LA: Left Houston at around eight o'clock this morning to get here. Highlights from El Paso: A guy walked up to me and said, "You're Henry, right dude?" and I said yeah. He said, "Spit on me dude. It would be a compliment coming from you." So I spat on him, right in his face. He thanked me and walked away. I stood and stared at him for a few minutes. Finally I walked up to him, grabbed him by his arm and dragged him over to me. I said, "Listen, the next time someone spits in your face, you break his jaw." The guy said, "But it's a compliment coming from you." I told him, "That's a compliment from no one. Don't ever degrade yourself like that." He kind of nodded and walked off. I wonder what's in that guy's head.

San Antonio, TX: We played good I thought. The crowd stood very still and watched us. Most of them had their arms crossed. Some girl came to talk to me after the show. She told me that I was God and that she loved me. I straightened her out on a few things.

Houston, TX: Pulled in around 1 p.m. I was told I was to do a video interview at a record store. I told Chuck that I didn't want to do interviews anymore. I did it. Relatively painless. A few hours later, I'm back at the club. We are playing away. A guy gets onstage and the heel of his shoe cracks me in the eye very hard. No sweat — we keep on playing. I think I said some stupid shit about treating others like you would like to be treated. What a waste of time. You can talk, but no one will listen to you. I asked the crowd if they liked paying money to go into a place so they could have someone kick them in the head. One young male volunteered, "The guy who kicked you didn't mean to." I said, "Okay. Say I'm swinging my icepick around and your head just happens to be in the way. I pull it out of your face and I say, 'Hey, it's okay. I didn't mean it.' " Right, so we keep on playing away and another guy gets onstage and his feet kick me in the balls and chest. I lost my temper and smacked him upside his head. When I did that, I rebroke my right wrist. So one week into a tour that lasts into July and I break my wrist on a man who would laugh in my face if he were reading this right now. I'm an idiot.

I sat up until about 4:00 this morning. Sometimes I get very bummed out being in Black Flag. I can't convince myself that I want to do it anymore. That's how I was feeling this morning. Sometimes I think that I have no friends besides Joe. I think that all the time. With each passing day, I feel more distant from people. That makes me feel bad when I think of people I like. Sometimes I don't think that any of them know what I'm about. That makes me feel very cold inside, like I'm not human or something. I don't know. It's very fucked up.

Sometimes I dream of shit like bailing to a small town and just disappearing from sight. I have several different versions of the same trip. I make the trip almost every day now.

1.20.86 BATON ROUGE LA: Have not played yet. Will be going down to the hall soon. Last night was really cool. I thought we played real well and the crowd was really great. Right before we did the encore, a girl came up to me and said, "Do more old stuff. That's what people are here to see. Give the people what they want." I asked her if it was okay to do what we wanted so our expression could be honest. She said, "Do what you want. But do old stuff." I asked her if that was like, "Breathe any way you want. But breathe how I tell you to." She just stared at me. Oh well.

Later: Show done. I thought we played good. The people were cool. A bit strange, but okay. Someone shoved the mic into my mouth. That hurt — still does. The truck is all fucked up and it's still fucked up and it's still parked at the hall. We have two shows tomorrow in New Orleans. I hope I have some voice left. No matter what you play or how hard or how long you play, the trip with the crowd is always the same — they get mad. We finished "Louie, Louie" tonight and while we were leaving the stage, the only things I could hear were requests for more songs and of course — "Fuck you, Henry."

1.22.86 PENSACOLA FL: Got here about an hour ago. We played two sets last night in New Orleans. I thought they were the two best shows of the tour. Hours later. Gig over, getting ready to crash out in the van. Some kid called me outside and asked if I would do something for this fanzine. I said okay. I went outside and there were all these people out there. They asked me questions. Most of it was okay. The kids were sincere and that was cool. Some of them have to deal with some heavy shit. A kid has to come home to his drunk mother. Maybe dad is strung out on coke. Maybe the kid gets beaten when he gets home. Maybe dad beats mom. Maybe the mom's boyfriend abuses the child. The kid has no idea where to turn. He can't tell his friends because he's too embarrassed or ashamed. He won't tell the police or his teachers because he's probably afraid that he'll get it worse. The kid feels he's totally alone with his problem. He has nowhere to turn. He takes all that damage and turns it inside and keeps it inside. He probably doesn't even know that it's probably happening four doors down the street.

From out of nowhere, this guy comes up, pushes his way through the crowd and in a loud voice starts drilling me with questions. He just wanted to fuck with me. "Are you bisexual?... What drugs do you do?... Do you like to play or are you just in this for the money?... Are you a musician or a punk rocker or is there any difference?" I asked him what his trip was. He said, "You're Henry Rollins, the big star. I want to know everything." I amaze myself sometimes. On any other day, I would have dropped him right there on the pavement, but I didn't. I just smiled and wished him luck. I went inside and tried to find a place to sit alone until I played. No matter where I sat, people would come over, sit right down and start in with the interrogation proceedings.

Some gay guy tried to pick me up. He was pretty great.

"Hi, my name is Ivan. What's yours?"

"Henry."

He extended his hand. I just stared at him, I had nothing to say. He looked at his hand and put it down and said, "Um, you must have leprosy. Where are you from?"

"LA."

"My, that's a long way from Florida. What brings you here?"

I just stared at him. "I guess you and I aren't on the same wavelength." I just stared. He shrugged and walked off. People would not stop. I asked politely to not have to talk, my throat was sore as it was. Of course for this, I am a rock star. Don't you know. Doesn't want to talk to the public and shit. They don't

TAMPA, FL / 1.24.86 (*CHRIS BARROWS*)

respect you. They dig at you so they can get their piece and if they don't get it, they get mad. The set was good I thought. People just kind of watched us with their arms folded. A girl kept feeling up my ass. I took her hand and shoved it into my shorts. You might as well get a handful. Now tell the crowd how small it is. Tomorrow is Tallahassee.

1.24.86 TAMPA FL: We're playing at this outdoor place called the Cuban Club. This will be our third time here. This is a pretty hairy neighborhood. The closest food place is a 7-11 about half mile down the road. On the way to the 7-11, there's a long stretch of project housing. One time Davo and I went to the store to get coffee for the crew and when we came out, these black guys were outside talking and I can remember one of them saying, "You know me. I'll drag them out into the woods and kill the motherfuckin' crackers." We got the fuck out of there.

It's only 7:22 p.m. and it's getting pretty cold. By the time we go on, it should be even colder. My right knee is in pain all the time now. It forces me to limp. Climbing stairs is very painful. I had it operated on in 1982 and the pain has been off and on since then. Doesn't hurt when I play though. Nothing does. Afterwards is a much different story. After shows — pounding headaches, right wrist and knee ache plus my left thumb is still broken a bit from dealing on that guy in Kansas City last October.

I hardly talk to any one of the people on tour. I think they are all great. I have no problems with any of them. Greg does not like me much. At least he told me. I can respect that. It makes playing kind of strange sometimes though. Makes me feel on the outside of everybody. Makes me wonder if I have any friends at all. Faith... Shit, that's like standing in a food line that's so long that you can't even see the soup kitchen. You just hope the food will be there. If it's not, you starve. But at least your faith was strong. Faith... What a concept.

"Excuse me, Mr. Rollins? Could you come over here for a second and talk to your fans?" How would you be after a few rounds of that?

I'm sitting on this bench writing. People on the street are watching me through a gate.

"Look, he's got something on his right hand!"

"That's not him"

"It is, too!"

"Look."

"Oh yeah, it is... Fuck!"

A few years from now, no one will be saying these things when I'm around. I guess this is "fame". You know what they say. Enjoy it while it lasts. Wow, that's some trip.

This trip is hard. It's harder than I am. I can see what it's doing to me. At first when I noticed my face starting to change, it tripped me out. I look at pictures of myself from two years ago and I can see a difference. Kind of scary, but it's in the cards. A few people I know have also noticed it. I guess that's what happens. What a trip. What a war.

1.25.86 MIAMI FL: At a Denny's. Drove all night to get here. Last night, I watched skinheads beat people up through the first two bands. The rented security made no attempt whatsoever to stop them. Later on, our set starts. It's cold outside and we're all in sweatpants and shit. We're playing away and everything seems to be going fine. That didn't last long. People started grabbing me and trying to pull me in. One guy kept punching me in the knees. I let him keep it up for a while and then I clipped him in the head with the mic. Not hard, but just hard enough to make him notice that he's wearing me out. He keeps it up so I wound up and belted him with my fist and the mic. His nose broke and his face was all bloody. Another guy started in on me and I kicked him in the face. Steel cap in the face. Felt like kicking a melon. People keep getting onstage and Ratman and Joe keep throwing them off. I start to notice that people are getting onstage for the direct purpose of fucking with Joe and Rat. They were trying to pull them in. The guy whose nose I broke is now standing in the middle of the crowd with his arms outstretched so he looks like he's nailed to a cross. His headband looked like a crown of thorns. The blood trickling from right below his eye looks great. Old JC is alive and well in Tampa.

During the second to last song of the set, some skinheads pulled the cords from the stage right monitors. Ratman went to go see what was wrong and they got him. From what he says, they got him down and started to kick him in the head. He told me that he was trying to crawl up the stairs to the stage and they kept dragging him back down and kicking him. I didn't see anything except for Rat getting back onstage with his face all mangled.

We stopped playing. The insults started in seconds. I could feel balls of spit pelt me from all over. People started to chant "Bullshit" over and over. I just sat down behind the amps and listened to them. "Black Flag sucks!" — "Fuck you Henry, you pussy!" — "We want our money's worth!" — "Play more, you faggots." — "Henry, you suck! I want my money back!" — "Rock stars!" — "Take the money and run!"

After the show was over, the pigs came and all they did was stand around and tell us to hurry up with the load-out. The skinhead guys were just standing around, right out of reach, laughing. Rat swung at one of them and a pig told him to cool it or he would take him in. Rat looked so bad. His eyes were shutting and his lips were split. It didn't even look real.

They are pieces of shit. They can't hurt me. They just make me stronger. If they all die tomor-

JOE COLE, HENRY AND GREG, TAMPA, FL / 1.24.86 *(CHRIS BARROWS)*

AFTER SKINHEADS BEAT UP RATMAN—TAMPA, FL / 1.24.86 (CHRIS BARROWS)

row, so what. I don't know why they come. I don't know why we come. They bitch and insult and try to hurt me. That's cool. They make me what I am. Everything all those journalist pigs say about me is true. I didn't make the shit up, I learned it from them. If they get all mad when they get it back — when they get themselves mirrored back at them, they won't have anyone to blame but themselves and that's when I start smiling. From now on, I don't trust any of them — not in any town, any country — they're all the same. They are capable of fucking me up. I would like to see some bad things happen to them too.

1.27.86 GAINESVILLE FL: Today is a day off — kind of. It's about 8:30 p.m. and my day off started about an hour and a half ago. I got myself a single hotel room. I wanted to check in about eight and a half hours ago, but I had to wait for everyone to go do their thing. That's the way it is when you travel in a group. The show in Miami was okay — about 900 people came. After we finished the set, I wanted to start from the top and do it all over again. We won't be back there for a long time. The next night (last night) was Orlando, FL — our first time there. About an hour after the doors opened, Joe and some of the others said they recognized some of the fuckers that kicked Ratman's head in the other night in Tampa. We knew they were not there to see Black Flag. We all got ready. I was happy they were there. I was hoping they would start something so I could crack one of their skulls open. Joe was happy — he wanted a piece of one of them too.

Joe and I were at the soundboard, keeping an eye on things. I turned around and they were all standing right there. I just stared at them. I couldn't help but start laughing. I wanted to kill them so bad I could barely keep my seat. I just stared at them and eventually they went away. By then the security was hip to what was going on. They wanted a piece of them too. A Cuban bouncer came up to me and said, "I hope one of those faggots starts some shit." Then he pulls out this stiletto and flicks the blade in and out. "This is my last night. I don't give a fuck." All the bouncer guys got into it and started to stare at the skinheads. One went up to them and said, "If you start any shit, you're all going to get hurt. Then you're going to get thrown out."

We played our set. They did their normal thing — cheap shot people smaller than they were. They tried to give us shit, but they were too easy to cut down. I did some good one liners like, "Well you know what they always say... If you can't do it yourself, get about ten of your friends to help." Some skin yelled out, "Suck my dick, Henry!"

"Of course I won't do that. I know how you skinhead guys are into boys and shit. I'm different. I like girls. I'm funny that way. But hey man, if you guys like to suck cock, that's great. Good luck and bon appetite."

A few more raps that went along the lines of "Some people here are almost ready for the army. Except in the army, you can't be overweight and you have to work out a lot. I know how that would be a bit of a strain on your Budweiser routine." Some skinhead girls were flipping me off. I just waved and said, "Hiya Fatty!" After people started laughing at them too hard, they just kind of stood there. Except, of course, for the occasional cheap shot.

Some guy yelled, "Disappointment big time, Henry! I want a refund!" That made me think. If the crowd disappoints me, I should charge admission for them to get out.

Well, that's Orlando. The skinheads were lucky to have the sense to go home. I don't think they knew what they were in for. All of us had hammers, pipes, etc. If you fuck with one of us, the wheel comes around. No, I would have no problem crushing one or five of their skulls. Their lives are meaningless. I would enjoy watching them twitch.

More and more I start to question why I am doing what I am doing. Greg does not like me at all and thinks that I have ill feelings toward him. There's no convincing him otherwise. I respect Greg more than anyone I know. He's incredible. All of us in the crew are constantly amazed by his playing and his presence. He's totally nonstop. He makes me and Dukowski look like bums — no shit. I think that Black Flag is his second string project, Gone being his first. I think the other members of Gone know that. You can see it when they deal with the rest of Black Flag. It does not bother me. They are incredible musicians. I think they give Greg a run for his money. Gone is the tightest, most together band on this tour. They are always working on their music. I watched Greg play bass for almost five hours straight the other day. C'el doesn't even look at a bass until it's time to play and it shows too. It embarrasses me sometimes. I don't know what I can do. What am I going to say? "Hey C'el, what the fuck? Don't you like playing?" It's hard to find people who really want to go out and do it. C'el is a fucking cool guy, but I don't know if he's cutting it. I hope he comes around. I don't think he will. That's just what I think. I would love nothing more than to be proven wrong. I think his woman in LA is giving him lots of shit about being on tour. I had that happen once. One time I was in England and I called this girl I was going out with at the time. She hung up on me from six thousand miles away. I fooled around with different girls all the way back to LA.

It is becoming very important that I keep to myself around the others. I'm a jerk when I enter into their conversations. I'm not human anymore. When they spit on me — when they grab at me, they aren't hurting me. They're just gouging and defiling my flesh. When I push out and mangle the flesh of another, it's falling so short of what I really want to do to them.

1.30.86 Savannah GA: Played in Gainesville FL last night. I thought it was cool. Did the show and crashed at some girl's house. Used a curtain and a quilt for cover. Slept okay. Crowd here in Savannah were a pretty calm bunch. A few of the military boys were there pushing people around. An okay set, but nothing to rave about. We are going to stay overnight at this place. It's a "teen center". I'm going to sleep under a pool table upstairs. Should be all right. Cold as shit outside. Nothing on my mind. Would like to get some sleep. Tomorrow night is Athens, Georgia.

2.3.86 Charlotte NC: Feeling very rundown today. Last few days have been good. The sets are starting to sound better every night. The shows in Athens were real good. We did a weekend at the Uptown Lounge. The first night, Michael Stipe came up and said hello. He suggested that we get together the next day and go hang out. Sounded like a good idea. The set went real good that night. During the encore, I collided with Greg's guitar. The tip of the tuning board caught me in the right eye. I almost vomited onstage. Head shots make me do that. I finished the set okay I think. I really don't remember. Oh yeah — earlier in the set some woman poured beer on me. I went offstage, grabbed her and spat in her face. Disrespect is a two-way street. Right after that, someone put a wrapped present onstage for me. I didn't touch it. Might have been a bomb for all I knew. Some kid said, "Open it Henry!" I told him that he could open it. Let it blow up in his face.

The next day we did a photo session for Interview. I probably looked wonderful with my right eye swollen shut. Michael came and got me at the club at around 2 p.m. We went here and there and basically hung out for about six or seven hours. We talked about all kinds of shit. Michael is definitely one of the coolest people I have ever met.

That night, we did our second night at the Uptown Lounge. I thought it was good. I spent the night at Michael's house.

Last night was Columbia, SC. Two sets. First set went real good. The second set was good also. At the beginning of the second set, some guy in the crowd was giving me a load of shit. "Get to work, Mr. Rollins. I want my money's worth." Between songs, he said, "That was okay. Now it's time to get to work, Mr. Rollins."

A few hours ago, I was sitting out in front of the club and the owner came up to me and asked me a few questions about the band. He told me that apparently two gangs of skinheads from different towns are meeting here tonight to beat each other up. Why at our gig? Why not in an abandoned parking lot where no one will be there to stop it. The fact that they need to do it at a show tells me a lot about them. They don't have the guts to do it where they won't be stopped. They need an audience. I thought they were supposed to be tough guys.

Right knee is giving me more and more trouble. Today I woke up and everything was hurting — knee, eye, wrist. What a drag.

They annihilate time. They ask questions. They don't care about the answer. They want a piece of your time so they can acknowledge themselves. They do their trip on you. It's not communication, it's something else. It wears me down. It makes me hate. It makes me feel so old sometimes. Some girl came up to me last night and said, "Oh, your greatness. Can I have the privilege of having a piece of paper signed by you?" I told her, "I'm sorry, I have no pen. There is no way I can be of any service to you." I just stared at her until she walked away. I've got nothing to say to that shit. Every time someone gives me a line like that, I feel very stupid that I have put myself in a place where people feel the need to approach me in this manner. They'll never get me. That's my problem. I've heard and seen it so many times that sometimes I think I'm a mind reader. I think what it really is — is that people are pretty much the same all over. What a burnout treadmill assfuck trip they want for me. Years ago, I didn't understand. Now I think I do.

2.4.86 GREENSBORO NC: Last night's show was good. Lots of people. Seemed to be a good crowd. I was told later that at one point in the set, a beer can went whizzing by my head. After the show, these heavy metal women were sticking around. Of course, C'el and Anthony started talking to them. As I loaded out the equipment, my ears were battered by some of the most vacant conversation imaginable. Anthony will talk to any female who sits still. He will talk about anything no matter how boring it is. I guess he doesn't find it boring.

We loaded out and went to this hotel and got a room so everyone could shower. C'el kept trying to squeeze money out of Mitch so he could get a room for his pickup. C'el is well overextended on his pay so Mitch cheerfully refused. Those girls had such loud mouths! I thought they were going to get us busted.

I took a shower and slept in the van. Woke up around 11:00 and read part of the movie screenplay that Nick Cave sent. It's about prison, *Ghosts of the Civil Dead*.

I talked to Staci on the phone a few hours ago. She gave me some news. One thing that I thought was interesting. A few days ago a boy killed himself. His death made news because apparently the boy killed himself after playing a bunch of Ozzy records. It seems that the guy was also a big fan of Nick's. The Australian papers picked it up and are laying into Nick pretty hard. Evan English from Australia sent me news clippings. That's real gross. I bet Nick feels pretty awful about that one. What a drag.

We are playing at an armory. We are surrounded by army vehicles and barbed wire. The sound is terrible — all cement and steel, the echo never stops. What a depressing place to play. There's no place to go eat or anything. Men in fatigues are everywhere, milling around like cattle. No place to go. No place to escape Painted Willie's soundcheck. They are one of the most boring bands I have ever heard in my life. Sitting through their soundcheck and their set is cruel and unusual punishment as far as I'm concerned.

Last night some man came up to me and told me that me, John (Lennon) and Johnny (Rotten) were his favorites. I said I hoped that I lived longer than Lennon. The guy got all offended and walked off in a huff.

Feeling rundown and low spirited again today. Same as yesterday. Getting harder for me to be around people. Sometimes no matter what they say to me, it bums me out. It's take, take, take, and rarely is it the other way around. People who give you something always want something in return and I never seem to be ready when it's payback time. Nowadays I am suspicious of anyone who wants to give me anything. I would rather give anytime. I am probably a much better giver than receiver anyway. One of the best parts of yesterday was when this kid came backstage, eyed a plate of fruit that we had and left. He came back about five minutes later. He came up to me and said, "Are you Henry?" I said, "Yeah." He said, "Can I have an apple?" I gave him an apple. He gave me a big grin and said, "Thanks!" That was one of the only parts of yesterday that I want to remember.

ATLANTA, GA / 2.8.86

Later: Sitting in the mess hall. Going on in about forty minutes. On the way back from the latrine, some guy got me to sign his 7-11 smock. I see those all the time now. Sometimes I am sorry that I ever wrote that thing for Spin. I hate talking about shit I did nine months ago. Anyway, I drew a swastika in one of the red circles. Let him wear that one to work.

2.14.86 TULSA OK: Last night was a trip. We played this very straight place. You never know where Dukowski will drop you down next. The set was good. The crowd was fairly friendly. So we finish the set, everybody is leaving and they all need to have autographs and stuff and I'm serving them as best I can. In the meantime, I'm looking around for my clothes so I can get dressed. I go to my backpack and I look for my shirts. They are gone. In their place is a shitty punker shirt. I guess the scenario went as such. Thieving fuckup punker goes up to Henry's shit and says, "Fuck, I'll rip off that asshole Rollins." He takes the shirts then something pops into his vacant brain. "I know. I'll take these two shirts that don't belong to me, being the low prick that I am. And in return, I'll put my shitty punker shirt in their place!" He walks off into the moist Little Rock night.

The next trip was this huge woman who bought me flowers — it being my birthday and all. She comes up to me and says, "Do you remember me? I'm the girl who gave you flowers." I remember her. "That negro over there (she points to one of the cleanup guys). He's been hounding me all night. I hear that they like big women. He just came up to me and said, 'Who do you go with?' and I pointed at you. He says he wants to arm-wrestle you to try and get me away from you." Thanks a lot lady. I walked away from her and sat down on a piece of equipment. Sure enough, the man comes up to me and asks me to arm-wrestle him. I say to him, "Man, I know why you want to arm-wrestle me. That fat lady told you that she's with me. Well she's not. I've never seen her before tonight. She's full of shit." He says, "I hear you man. Check this out." He lifts up his sleeve and flexes his arm. His biceps kept getting bigger and bigger. Finally, he twisted his wrist and this golf ball size muscle popped out on top. Looked kind of sick to me. I said, "That's wonderful. You're more than a match for me." He grinned and walked away.

Minutes later, this real tough looking woman comes up to me and points to my cock and then to her mouth. I just smile. She gestures with her hands as to the size of my cock. I take my thumb and index finger and indicate a length of about three quarters of an inch. She comes over and extends her hand and says, "Let's go." I look at her closely. Man, what a tough looking broad! She sits down in my lap and says, "Come on, let's go. Just lay back and enjoy it." I ask her name. "Peach Melba." I say, "Peach, my dear. I want to tell you that you have the nicest ass of anyone here tonight. But I can't go with you." Peach asks why. I say, "Peach, you're a man! Now there are certain things that I won't do. I don't want some guy sucking my cock. But shit honey, thanks anyway." *He* asked me if I would have gone for it if I hadn't been able to tell. I skip the answer and comment on his vivid green pantyhose. I said that I had a Madonna record that had a picture of her on it wearing the same shade. We both agreed that Madonna was awesome. He told me how he scammed on C'el and even danced with him. We talked for a while and he told me that his real name was Tim. I told him that I liked Tim much better. Fuck, that guy had about an inch of makeup on his face. I told him that he shouldn't shave for about three days and then go out in drag with all that stubble.

Tim said that he would give it a try. He got up and split.

Thieves. No one is to be completely trusted besides yourself. To trust someone else is an unfair demand on that person. Black Flag "fans" are not to be trusted in the least. Last night, they stole from me. I will never trust any of them again. If someone gives me something, I will ask what that person wants in return and if that person says that he wants nothing in return, I will return the gift. No trust. They always want something in return at some point. I hate having my back turned when they come to collect. None of them are to be trusted. They cheer while you play and then when you don't play

MITCH BURY / 1986

what they wanted to hear, they hurl insults at you. I learned something from that shit. I learned that it's all the same — praise, damnation, love, hate — all the same. No one can tell me different. I expect nothing from everyone. I am rarely let down. I am occasionally pleasantly surprised. No one. I will not trust anyone completely outside of myself, except Joe. I hope for the same from others. Complete trust is stupid. Complete trust is for fools. It's right up there with "faith".

2.17.86 DALLAS TX: Day off. Played here last night. Last few days, the shows have been good and with little incident. The Tulsa show was okay until the pigs showed up around the second to last song. After having crew members hauled to jail in Knoxville, we shut it down immediately. I tried to get to the bathroom right before the set. I went in and there was this kid all fucked up, staring at his face in the mirror while he ran his hands through the water coming out of the faucet. A young girl whose name I forget, sat at my feet and hugged my ankle while I stood at the soundboard. I tried to talk to her. She didn't say much. She just looked at me with these big doe eyes. I asked her what she wanted from me. "Just to be near you, that's all." Great. No matter how much I told her I was just another grimy slob, she just shook her head and rested her head on my calf.

The next night in Norman was okay. We played in a good hall. The PA sounded good in there. During our set, a guy came up and kept punching the air with his fists. He would not stop. Eventually he hit me in the mouth and knees enough times that I hit him back. I cracked him in the face with the mic. He started to bleed. His friend got all mad at me. Now do you think that I cared? I bet you don't. Good. Their flesh.

They murder mine and they get so steamed up when someone walks toward them on the street of disrespect. Love, hate... it's all the same to me now. No shit.

Last night was Dallas. Good show, good crowd.

Robert Palmer understood what Greg was trying to do a lot more than 99% of the other journalists that reviewed the band's music. Critics like Robert Palmer and Billboard's Chris Morris understood that Ginn was only after one thing — MUSIC.

BLACK FLAG ADDS A SOUPCON
OF SOPHISTICATION TO PUNK ROCK
Written by Robert Palmer for The New York Times, *2.23.86*

Black Flag, formed as a rock band in Los Angeles in the late 1970's, has been growing with leaps and bounds lately with every new record release — growing *musically*, and that's perhaps the hardest thing for a rock band to do.

While some punk rockers develop minimal competence on an instrument principally so they can participate in the life style and make a lot of noise, others have genuine musical talent, and a decent musician will improve, even without trying. And it is at this point that the basic punk rock bands and the die-hard punk audience reach a crisis point. Some bands are going to want to keep banging out those two or three chord in lock-step forever; other bands are going to evolve. The trick is persuading their listeners to come along for the ride.

Throughout a stormy career, Black Flag has done the latter, while contending with problems that would have wrecked other bands. For one thing, there was frequent turnover in personnel. In addition, volatile audiences at the band's early shows earned it a reputation for violence.

But through it all, Greg Ginn, Black Flag's guitarist and only remaining original member, persevered in his vision of what Black Flag could be. He helped form the independent record label SST to insure that the band would retain complete artistic control. He found new, like-minded musicians when others left.

Early Black Flag albums like "Damaged" were classic punk rock, chronicles of spiritual decay behind southern California's prim suburban facade, ironic comments on the punk life style that compassionately traced its causes, often to parental and societal neglect, without ever glamorizing it or pretending it could be anything but a dead-end street.

Things began to change when Black Flag brought in Henry Rollins, a powerfully physical stage performer, as its new lead singer. For all his apparent ferocity, Mr. Rollins proved to be a thoughtful and resourceful lyricist, adept at describing inner turmoil and the hidden wounds that can result from power games and interpersonal relationships. He has now published several books of stories and poetry, and his lyrics have given the band's songs a sharper focus and added emotional punch. They are angry and direct; angry at least partly because Mr. Rollins sees so many of his contemporaries — the lock-step pre-meds and the lock-step punks — reacting to the transition from schooldays to adulthood by shutting off their feelings and no longer thinking for themselves. For Mr. Rollins, not *feeling* is the ultimate obscenity. "I smash my fists/into my face/I can feel it/this is good," he sang on a recent Black Flag release.

There was always a certain musical tension between Greg Ginn's rhythm playing — his ability to fashion guitar riffs into the backbones for songs makes him a kind of latter-day Keith Richards — and the wilder, tumbling chaos of his solo breaks. What he needed was a sturdy but adaptable rhythm section, and after many failed attempts he has found it in the bassist Kira, a willowy young woman whose playing is a model of firmness and strength, and the fine drummer Bill Stevenson. But the group chemistry didn't sort itself out overnight.

Black Flag fans began to wonder what was happening to the band when at least three successive albums — "My War", "Family Man" and "Slip It In" — betrayed considerable confusion as to direction, capturing what was essentially a new band in the process of sorting itself out. Last year's "Loose Nut" was an improvement. There were still plenty of problems, but the music had began to cohere in a different sort of way. Still, nothing on that album prepared the listener for Black Flag's two new releases — "In My Head", the band's most consistently inventive and invigorating album in years, and "The Process of Weeding Out", a four-song, all-instrumental recording by Black Flag minus Mr. Rollins.

On "In My Head", Black Flag's music is intriguingly, sometimes dazzlingly fresh and sophisticated, but the band hasn't had to sacrifice an iota of the raw intensity and directness that are punk's spiritual center. Instead of saving his more fanciful, prolix and anarchic musical inspirations for brief guitar breaks, Mr. Ginn and his team players have used these to build up the structures of the songs. The title tune, for example, is part waltz, part old-time blues shuffle, but one doesn't hear the components, one hears a song, and a sound. Other tunes use multiple and mixed meters, tempos that speed up and slow down both abruptly and gradually, stacked chords that obliterate any sense of key center. And hearing the polyphony of shifting shapes that is the principal guitar motif in the brilliant "White Hot" is like listening to the once-revolutionary guitar break from the Yardbirds' mid-60's hit "Shapes of Things" wild one's turntable goes up in flames.

Yet for all its sophistication, this is jagged, abrasive rock and roll, music hard and direct enough to appeal to any punk or hard-rock fan. How was this alchemy accomplished? The secret is in the way Mr. Ginn's guitar parts, Kira's bass, and Mr. Stevenson's drums cohere in the middle and lower range frequency spectrum, fusing into an immense, dark, primal sound that months of practicing, recording and touring, not to mention exceptional musicianship, have leavened with responsiveness and flexibility.

"In My Head" is the sound of heavy metal rock as it could be but almost never is, metal without the posturing, the pointless displays of fretboard prowess, the bashing rhythm sections and banal lyrics that have become endemic to the idiom. "The Process of Weeding Out," Black Flag instrumental EP, is what jazz-rock could have become if the best of the musicians who first crossbred jazz improvising with rock's sonic fire power had followed their most creative impulses. In a sense, this Black Flag disk takes up where, ground-breaking jazz-rock albums like John McLaughlin's "Devotion" and Tony Williams' "Emergency" left off in the early 70's.

Most of the jazz rock albums made since those two disks have concentrated on efficient ensemble virtuosity, with solos as exercises in ego gratification. Many jazz musicians seem to have forgotten that improvisation, the heart of jazz, is more than just noodling and display. In the best jazz, it tells a story, but now it is the punk rockers, rather than the jazz rockers, who most successfully create atmosphere and convey feelings and ideas in their improvisations.

This exactly the sort of thing Mr. Ginn is after on "The Process of Weeding Out," and with the help of Kira and Mr. Stevenson he achieves it, especially on the 10-minute title track. He begins with a thematic launching pad, a set of vaguely Eastern melodic figures that he examines, develops, twists and mutates, proceeding in a manner reminiscent of the processes at work in Ornette Coleman's music. As the piece picks up steam, the three musicians weave the original thematic threads into its onrushing momentum. The end result is an exciting, genre-stretching performance with an overall direction, coherence and unity.

Generic labels are never very precise, and their uses are limited; when music like this comes along, they should be dispensed with altogether. It would be ludicrous to suggest that this is progressive post-punk jazz rock, or something of the sort. The jazz great Charlie Parker insisted that there are only two kinds of music anyway, good and bad. Black Flag's "In My Head" and "The Process of Weeding Out" are good music.

BLACK FLAG / 1986. L-R: HENRY, C'EL, ANTHONY, GREG. (ED COLVER)

3.27.86 TUCSON AZ: Been about a month or so since I wrote in this book. That month was spent in LA. Time spent home rarely has anything worth writing about. I'm back on tour. It feels so good to be back out here again. It's to the point now that after a week back in LA, I start to lose sleep. My brain dulls. Home is bad. It kills. Home makes me soft — makes me weak. The road is the only thing that keeps me sharp. I spent a lot of time in the back yard and in the shed. Sometimes I like to take my chair outside and sit in front of the shed door. I sit and look at the back yard. The trees are so thick that the neighbors would have a hard time looking in. The pine tree, the hummingbirds, the offshore breeze, the sun. It makes me know that these days are numbered.

You should see that view in the early part of the evening. Incredible. The way the sun comes through the avocado tree makes it look like the tree is performing some kind of slow, erotic fire dance. The floor of the yard is covered with pine needles. The needles of a giant pine tree that stands on the northern edge of the yard. There is nothing in the yard that can injure bare feet. The back yard is a very safe place. Sun, trees, birds, quiet — it's like a sunny womb. Every time I'm in there, I feel worlds away from the streets. Sometimes I don't venture out into the streets for two or three days straight. I won't set foot out of the front door. When I emerge onto the streets days later, I feel I've lost the language. It's so easy to forget. That's why I'm always glad to leave there, nice as it is. Numbered as the days are. When I leave the streets, I want to leave forever. The jumping in and out of the fire is too strenuous.

When I want to get gone, I want to get all the way gone. In the back yard, the spell can be so easily broken by the ring of the telephone. From out of nowhere I have to be with them again. Makes me think that a man with obligations is a fool. I have obligations all over the place. I am spreading myself too thin. I learned that when I was last back there. If I'm not careful, I could throw all my cards in. Not enough time in one lifetime. Must make more time for myself. Only one me for me.

4.2.86 TRENTON NJ: Last night we played in Charlottesville, VA. The show was okay. Some people in the crowd were a bit antagonistic, flipping me off and shit. One young man who was flipping me and Greg off doused me with water during "Louie, Louie". Joe went up and grabbed him and told him that was a really shitty thing to do. I went off the stage to have a word with him myself. He saw me coming and ran out of the club. Joe and I took off after him. Caught him in the parking lot. He started telling me how he had all our records... blah blah blah. I punched him a couple of times and chucked a bottle at his head. The bottle missed. Disrespect is a two-way street. Finished the show, loaded out and drove all night to Trenton, NJ.

Now we're in Trenton. We're playing with Venom tonight. Joe, C'el and I drew big pentagrams on our hands and every time we see these metal guys, we flash our palms and say, "Hail Satan." Good fun.

The Venom boys aren't here yet. Last night in Atlanta, they refused to play their gig. They missed their flight to Trenton. We're waiting around to play.

Called Ian about twenty minutes ago. He just got back from England and he said he had a cool time. He did some recording with Jeff over there. He said his band Embrace is breaking up tonight. Oh well... Hopefully I'll see him on Saturday.

Got very little sleep last night and I'm feeling it now. This is an early show. We'll be done with our set by about 8:30. The only drag is that Venom is using our PA so we have to wait around until they're done.

4.3.86 MORGANTOWN WV: Played that show with Venom last night. I thought we played real good. When I came out onstage, I did some Satan raps and shit. The best one was "Give me an 'S'!... Give me an 'A'!...

etc. What does that spell?... Satan!!" It was hot. The crowd was into it. I said, "Hail Satan! Party hearty and surf naked!" We dedicated a few numbers to Satan and had a wicked good time.

Venom took almost an hour to get onstage. They had roadies tuning their guitars and shit. Finally, they hit stage. They were hilarious. It was like seeing Spinal Tap. The drummer had a guy that held an electric fan next to him and kept him high and dry. The singer/bass player was named Kronos. He had some great raps. He got the crowd to chant what I thought was "Black Funky Metal" over and over which I thought was pretty cool and then I thought that maybe I was wrong about these guys. I found out later that it was "Black Fucking Metal." Oh, excuse me. I expected them to go into "Sex Farm Woman" at any second. The guitar player was so bad it was painful. I had a great time. Joe, C'el and I were hanging in back saying "Hail Satan" to people and prancing around like idiots. What a night. The bass player was hilarious. He would wiggle his tongue and roll his eyes. But he also would fix his hair every fifteen seconds or so.

After an hour of "I can't fucking hear you!" they said, "Good fucking night, New fucking Jersey!" and ran for the dressing room.

As Kronos was going to his motel destined ride, Joe jumped in front of him and laid a "Hail Satan" on his ass. The drummer came into our dressing room and asked Anthony if he knew who was responsible for the drums being all fucked up. He also said they were having problems with their wardrobe.

Load-out was great. All the Venom management and roadies were there and we were staring at them — laughing and doing Spinal Tap/Venom raps. They bummed out real bad, but they didn't say anything. I have a feeling that there will be Venom raps going around our camp for a long time now.

Venom is weak. Everything about them was weak. They can't even play. They had a bunch of roadies to do everything. Weak, weak, weak. I would love to play with fucking "heavy metal" bands more often. It was fun crushing them. It's all lights and makeup. What bullshit. Venom suck. They are so full of shit. What a bad joke. They don't sweat and they probably don't even fuck.

Got up early this morning and drove to Morgantown. I don't have much voice and we got two sets tonight plus an eight hour drive to New York afterwards.

4.8.86 BALTIMORE MD: Pulled into Baltimore about one or two hours ago. The place is a battered store-front. Graffiti all over the walls. I'm sitting next to the trash can. It stinks of beer and food in various states of decay. All the Black Flag flyers on the walls have our faces scratched out. This punker girl told me that skinheads are going to beat me up after the show. The van just got broken into and Davo's backpack containing all his savings was taken.

The show in Morgantown was good. We left the place and headed for New York. We got there around lunch time. We loaded in and got some food. I called Michael Gira to see if he was

RATMAN AND DAVO

coming down to the show. He had just gotten back from England a couple of days before. He said that the Swans had done some recording while they were there. Can't wait to hear that stuff.

We went on very late. The place was full. More people than I've ever seen in that place for us. During the second song in the set, I collided with some people who were onstage. Knocked me out. I remember getting up and falling down again. I got up a second time and sat on the drum riser. People in the crowd were yelling at me to hurry up with the next song — telling me to get up off my ass. I got up and we went into the next song and finished the set although I really don't remember it very well.

After everything was loaded out, we headed south to Washington DC. I don't remember what time we got there — around noon, I think. My head was giving me a lot of trouble and my left eye had started to swell.

Hung out with Ian that afternoon. There wasn't really time to do a whole lot.

I hardly recognized anybody at the show. I don't think I should at this point. The whole trip has changed so much since I was around. All these people kept after me for autographs. One guy kept getting in my face and yelling at me, asking me all these stupid questions and shit. I answered the first few questions and then I asked him to cool out a bit. He kept on me so I grabbed him by his hair and pulled his head over the soundboard and asked him again. He got all mad. Disrespect is a two-way street.

Later the guy comes into the dressing room and I notice he has his arm in a cast. He sits down next to me and asks me why I'm such a rock star and all that kind of shit. I said, "I'm a rock star and you're just one more drunk asshole in my face." I got up and threw him and his chair over. He bummed out and left. During the set, he flipped me off with his good hand. Good thing he didn't have a cast on each arm. What the fuck would he have done then?

I thought we played real well. I couldn't get close to the edge of the stage because I kept getting hit by people climbing on. I am tired of getting hit by people's boots. I stayed back by the drums and did the set from there. Didn't have a good time. DC isn't such a hot place to play anymore for me. I can find nothing wrong with the place or the people. It just wasn't happening. After the show, Ian and I left. We took Guy home and then Ian dropped me off.

The next day we took off for Richmond, Virginia. Two sets. We got there and found out that the club was up a flight of stairs. Makes load-in a bit of an ordeal. We handled it, no sweat.

I went down the street to the Safeway to get some fruit. These kids were outside. They were hanging out waiting for the show to start I guess. I had to sign all these autographs for them. Finally, I got inside. Kids were in there. They saw me and then I'm signing all this other shit. That kind of thing makes me feel very vulnerable. Anyone who recognizes me can go right up to me and do their trip and I have to deal with whatever it is that they want to throw my way. This is not the way a smart person runs his life. No one who is smart or in his right mind would want to be a moving target on the street.

The sets were good, especially the second set. This one guy was screaming at me, "You're God! You're the Devil!" over and over. I don't remember much about that set. I do remember sitting on a small stairwell behind the PA system. I was hiding out, waiting for people to leave so I could go to the dressing room without having to shake a bunch of hands that belong to people I don't know and write my name on slips of paper. I was sitting behind the PA system, trying to get my mind together and people started coming back there to talk to me. It's always the same.

"Hey man, I need to talk to you."

"I'm really tired. I don't want to talk, okay?"

IAN AND HENRY / 1986

"Yeah, okay, but one thing…" They don't care. Why should they? I don't expect them to know how it feels to have played two sets and want to just sit quietly for a short while. None of them are my friends and that's okay with me. All they care is that they paid real money to see the show and since they did that, it proved they are into it. The band owes them something besides playing the music. I owe them my time, anytime they say I do. If I am tired or want to be left alone, during the time they want to talk to me, then I am what you call a rock star. I understand that. I understand people's inability to put themselves in someone else's shoes. I see it in myself all the time.

The next day was a day off in Washington. I didn't do much. Hung out with Ian. Couldn't get to sleep until about 4:00 in the morning. I felt like I wanted to leave everything. I feel like that a lot these days. I like the playing. But having to be on other people's time all the time is very hard. I am constantly "in debt". I have to pay back the "debts" with time spent away from myself. I am not a selfless person. I'm not the guy in U2. I don't want to "bring people together" or any of that shit. People are big boys and girls. They can stand on their own two feet just fine. They certainly don't need to talk to themselves with me in front of them.

4.9.86 TRENTON NJ: Drove here from the show in Baltimore. Got here about 4 a.m. Show in Baltimore was okay. At one point, the PA on Greg's side fell over. Nearly squashed Greg. I saw the lights go down first. I thought, "Fuck man, shouldn't those lights be up higher?" Seconds later, there were PA cabinets tumbling across the stage. I'm no fool. I got the hell out of there. After a while, we got the PA back up and finished the set. I got kicked in the chest and in the teeth. After the show, some stripper asked me if I wanted to smoke a joint. No skinheads came to provide me with my beating for the night. Although I heard later that they cheered when the PA fell over. We loaded the truck and got out of Baltimore.

Later: In Dover, NJ at a club called the Show Place. I blew it this time. I'm really in America now. We played here last year. Ugly strippers are dancing like cows in front of some Bruce Springsteen clones. Whenever we open the loading door, a stripper comes from around the bar and yells, "Close the fuckin' door!" Once Ratman came in and a stripper grabbed him and pushed him out the door.

I went to the market across the street and got some food. I came back out and was walking back when I heard a car horn. I turned around and there was this guy getting out of his car and talking some shit to a guy in another car. The guy in the car was saying, "Hey, I was just trying to see if the horn worked. I wasn't beeping at you!" Shit… Testy people.

All these guys are yelling at the stripper telling her to take it off, yelling at her to "Go for it." They're begging. Last night in Baltimore when that stripper girl saw me looking at her tits that were falling out of her shirt, she said, "What's the matter? Haven't you ever seen a tit before?" I think that says it best. From all the way across the club, the men and the music together sound like dogs barking to a synth beat.

4.10.86 HOBOKEN NJ: Sitting at the club in Hoboken. Ratman and C'el flipped the truck en route to the gig. Both are okay. Tonight we are using the house PA and Gone's in-store equipment. This will be about a tenth as loud as we are used to playing so tonight should be interesting. About the damage done to the truck and equipment — who knows. Needless to say, tomorrow will be a busy day for us.

I have to go on either a radio station or to a video place to do a thing about drinking and driving. I don't remember which. That's the only interview type thing I have agreed to do. The other day in New York, I was approached by interviewers for the Village Voice and NME. I have nothing to say to those people, especially the Voice.

I'm glad Rat and C'el are okay. I wonder how much it's going to cost to put the truck back on the road. Tomorrow's show canceled so that gives us some time to get it together.

4.11.86 NEWARK NJ: Here at the video place, did some ID's for the station and for the video I did for the song "Drinking and Driving". It's 7 p.m. now. Some day off. Spent a few hours driving through the ghettos of New Jersey to get to this place. Bad time. Nice toilet in this place though. Cold as shit outside. Dark, cold New Jersey. What a drag.

4.14.86 BOSTON MA: At a Greyhound bus station in Boston. Rest of the crew is up in Adams. I stayed to do a video ID thing. Pure bullshit. Now I have to take a bus to meet the others — three hours. Last night was real cool. We played at Brandeis. The place held about 900 so it got sold out pretty quick. The show was good. The only thing that bugged me was the people who kept flying onstage with their boots in close proximity to my head and my nuts. One guy got me in the knee real good — still hurts. Have mercy... Been waiting for the bus all day.

4.16.86 POUGHKEEPSIE NY: Sitting in the truck outside the record store where Gone was supposed to do an in-store. Gone will not do the in-store on account of Greg's guitar getting stolen within minutes of the van pulling up to the front of the store. The guitar was stolen through the open window on the passenger's side. Mitch was in the back of the van and saw an arm reach in and grab it. He figured it was one of the crew. Greg went off to find a new guitar somewhere.

It's raining, it's cold and we're in the middle of a shitty neighborhood. What a day. The record store is one of those gross head shop places with overpriced bootlegs, jewelry and other assorted shit. Balding, creepy stoners behind the counter watching your every move. I got out of there. In front of the place, a kid almost got run over by a car. People were yelling at the driver. Joe started yelling at the kid.

Later: In the place — just some hall in a black activities building. All these heavy guys watching us load in. What a shitty town this is. I have no idea where we are playing tomorrow night. That doesn't really matter right now. We have to get through this one first.

4.19.86 PHILADELPHIA PA: Survived the last few nights without incident. The Poughkeepsie show was real cool as was Providence, RI and Enfield, CT. The Philly show is going to be one to remember. The show

PROVIDENCE, RI / 4.17.86 (JILL HEATH)

is in a burned out building. Most of the floor is wet dirt. The roof leaks. There's no toilet and no power. A generator had to be brought in. It looks like an old warehouse or something. What a drag. Tomorrow is Trenton, NJ, then down to Washington DC. I'm sitting outside on a curb. The time is 5:06 p.m. The sun is hot. Pig cars on either side of the street. I think this show is going to be a bust. Pigs now going into the hole/ hall. One has a flashlight, probably going in to inspect the place. There's a woman outside with two of them. She's looking at the promoter and shaking her head. She just got in her car and said, "I'll be right back." She left. Kids down the street telling Flag stories. The woman just came back with an old man — her husband! I can't hear what she's saying, but it doesn't sound very friendly. Neighbors are starting to gather. Seeing the police cars, a third pig car has just pulled up. Mitch is out talking with the pig. Now he's talking with the lady. A police van has just pulled up. I'm out of here.

Later: In Trenton. The show was a bust. We loaded in and loaded out. What a waste of a day. The promoter jerk just stood there as the cops read him up and down. He looked like he didn't have a clue. Promoters like that should be taken out and dumped in the river.

4.26.86 PITTSBURGH PA: The shows have been going real good. All bands playing consistent. The drives have been cool. Not much to report.

Last night we played in Buffalo NY. The promoters oversold the place. There were about 700-800 people packed into a place that could reasonably hold about 500. The temperature in that place was insane. Sweat city. I hardly remember any of the set, I just tried to find air to breathe. The floor had no rug and I kept making puddles all over the place. Nearly broke my ass a few times. People grabbing at my face nonstop. People yanking my hair, taking their shirts and soaking up my sweat, taking the towels. What a trip. After the show, the guys who owned the hall freaked out and started chasing people around with bats and clubs. One guy nearly hit Andrew from Gone with a nightstick. They came busting into the dressing room glowering and talking all tough and shit. Here are these guys running around with weapons, waving them at a bunch of guys putting clothes on or loading out equipment. What a joke. Anyone with a weapon in their hand is a little man using a cannon for a microphone. It was hilarious. "We're trying to load out.

GONE (L-R: SIM CAIN, GREG GINN, ANDREW WEISS)

Excuse me, could you get that bat out of my face so I could get this cabinet into the truck. Thank you very much." Slept in the van last night. Went to sleep with a headache and a knee ache. Right knee is giving me all kinds of problems — hurts more all the time. Sometimes I can't even load out the equipment into the truck because I can't walk up the ramp with the hand truck.

People bug me with the autograph and star trips they run on me all the time. None of that shit weakens me anymore. In years past, the crowds used to wear me out and dry me up. That's not the way it is anymore. Every day makes me stronger. Every experience teaches me something. The fan shit still bugs me. I mean fuck, man. I'm not very social and I'm not going to pretend to be something I'm not. That doesn't mean that every person who wants to meet me or talk to me is some asshole. Not at all. But I'm sure not going to pretend that I love meeting strangers.

Later: Walked out onto the floor to see Gone play for a while. People started walking up to me and trying to talk while the music's going full blast. The way one guy introduces himself is by shoving me or poking me in the ribs. "Oh, hi! So nice to meet you too!" Right. On the sixth or seventh poke, I turned around and poked back. It was a very frail, young girl and I jabbed her in her breast. Her eyes bugged out a little. She put her hand on the wounded tit and said, "I've always wanted to meet you." I sure felt bad about that one. I went back into the dressing room. I don't mix well with people.

4.30.86 KENTUCKY: I have had some bad luck. Two days ago, we played at Penn State. We finished the show and I retreated to a small space behind the drum riser to wait for people to leave. As I walked into the space, I felt a small stinging sensation on my left foot. I thought I had stepped on a splinter. I felt around on the floor but could find nothing. About six hours later, I woke up in the van with my left foot in great pain. It was all swollen and red. I checked my foot closely. There were two little red dots at the center of the swelling. I guess I got bit by a spider.

By that afternoon, my foot looked like a red potato. I didn't think I was going to be able to play that night. Hours later, it was time to play. My entire body was aching and I was having hot and cold sweats. I pulled off the set — barely. During one part when the band was jamming, I crawled offstage and lay on the floor. I could hardly move. I felt so bad. But I got up and finished the set. I don't really remember it very well. That was last night.

Tonight, I don't know. The swelling is worse and it's spreading up my leg. I can barely walk. I just sit. I took some aspirin about an hour ago. Can't feel any difference. That spider juice is some strong shit. I do remember one thing from last night. The short time I spent on the floor during the set, my body aching and hot, I could feel the poison in me. I could feel it in my joints. I started to like it. I felt like a spirit. Lighter than air. The pain and the heat made me start to laugh out loud. I felt like I was made of hot steel. Nothing will stop me except Death. The spider bite is just another rite of passage — another test. Something that's showing me something about myself.

I am walking down the trail. My body is exposed to the elements — air, sun, poisonous animals, killers. The elements put me here and they'll take me away as well. The elements are like a blacksmith's hammer — shaping me, altering my form — defining me. I'm sure as fuck not walking down marble halls. The hot pain that's presently occupying my leg tells me what I need to know. I'm loving every minute of it.

DAVO

Every day I feel stronger. My soul becomes more tempered. My carcass becomes more like armor. Every moment I render myself to the elements I grow stronger. The soft white underbelly becomes scarred and hardened. My sight becomes more keen. My awareness sharpens. Each day is a pass at the whetstone.

5.3.86 ST. LOUIS MO: Finished show in St. Louis about an hour ago. Spider bite on foot still hurts. Foot swollen and discolored. Right knee hurting all day. Nearly fell down in an intersection yesterday. During sets, knee causes great pain — makes me unable to move around much. The constant pain of left foot and right knee drains me and makes me very withdrawn. Show tonight was good. Played hard — lots of people and all that good shit.

Last night, C'el dropped acid before he went on. He fucked up a lot of songs because of it. What bullshit. What a slap in the face to the rest of the band. He fucks up left and right.

The other night, this guy spat at me twice while I was playing. He tried to split, but I sent Joe after him. Joe reeled him in and had him by the side of the stage for later. The show ended and I grabbed the guy by his arm and took him into the dressing room. At this point, I was very crazed from playing and having one of those pricks you can never get your hands on right there in front of me. I grabbed his head and bashed his skull into the wall a couple of times. It felt very good to do that. Then I grabbed him by his armpits and started slamming him into the wall. I decked him one and then I grabbed his head, brought it to me and spat into his eyes until I had no more spit in my mouth. I took his shirt and ground the spit into his face then I told him to get the fuck out before I got started again. He split. I turned around and a few of the band and crew were there. They looked pretty tripped out. Greg was there. He looked bummed out about it. I bum him out a lot anyway it seems, so what the fuck.

Tonight was our 14th straight show. There are seven or so left on this leg. There are no days off. I guess we'll be up to 21 or 22 shows straight. Fuck... No sweat. Every night I get stronger. Every jerk in my face with nothing to say, but saying it anyway, makes me stronger. Every mile driven, every waking moment on this trail makes me stronger.

5.7.86 TOPEKA KS: Last few days have been a little rough. The other night in Champaign, IL, I collided with Joe onstage, resulting in a swollen nose and a small shiner for me. The next night in Carbondale, IL, a guy spat on me a couple of times and then got on the PA to jump off. I punched him off the stack. He ate shit on the floor and I broke his nose. He called the police on me. The filthy little prick called the pigs. I was loading out and all of a sudden there's a fucking pig in my face. That's great. They can do what they want because if it gets too heavy for them, they can always call their baby sitter to come and arrest the big bad wolf. I didn't get arrested though. The pig took all my info and said he had to "file a report." I'd like to see that guy get arrested and jailed for spitting on me and wasting my time.

Last night was Columbia, MO. I thought we played real good. The crowd was cool. Some of the people in front kept pounding on my feet. When someone would hit the left one, the pain would make me forget the words to the song.

After the show, I went to the soundboard to get my clothes and my pants were gone along with about $125 and some stuff I wrote. They pay money to come see you play. They walk up to you and say, "Can I have your autograph? You guys are great!" and all that shit. They run into each other and yell and scream and cheer. And then they steal from you. They steal. None of them can be trusted. None of you can be trusted. I always have to watch out because you spit on me and you steal from me. You are only concerned with yourself and what you can get. I don't trust anyone except myself. Someone is sitting there laughing his ass off at what a good haul he made off that jerk who was too busy playing his ass off to notice. Fuck you. You all are potential thieves. It could be anyone of you at anytime. What a drag. Go to these places to do a show and have someone rip you off. That's the way it goes. Taught me a thing or two.

Now I'm sitting in the hall in Topeka watching all the people file in. Last time we were here was pretty strange. There seems to be more people this time. I see this guy to my right. He's waiting to talk to me. If I take my eyes off this book, I know he'll start in with his thing. I have no choice in the matter. Everyday I get smarter and stronger.

5.26.86 SAN FRANCISCO CA: Playing tonight at the On Broadway. I think this will be our 14th or 15th time at this place. The last time we played here was almost two years ago.

Last night was Guernville, CA. Show went well. I liked our playing a lot more than the show in San Diego.

DAVO, JOE COLE, HENRY / 1986

The show in San Diego was a drag. Nonstop punkers on the stage. Finally, I got tired of getting run into and I grabbed one guy and dumped him off the back of the stage. Joe dropped some guy pretty hard.

We finished the show. I walked around looking for the girl I was with. I couldn't find her anywhere. She was out by the van. A girl beat her up during the set. I don't really understand what happened. I think some girl just had it out for her because she saw her with me. Her eye was fucked up and she had some cuts on her chin.

We are on the final six week leg of this tour. We had a ten day break. I did two talking shows that I thought went well. I didn't do much except for playing and fucking. That was good enough for me.

I'm starting to get sick of the shed. Maybe this is due to the fact that I never spend much time in there these days. I feel like an outsider there. It's time to move. But that will happen soon enough. The next door neighbors have taken the fence down between the two back yards. What a drag. It used to be you could go out there and not see anyone. Now the guy's dog comes in to the shed if the door is left open. It really doesn't matter. I'm gone from there anyway.

I'm always relieved to be back on the road. In the shed, there's no challenge — just the days ticking by until we hit the road again. It's a frustrating feeling. The ten days off were good. My body needed the rest.

5.27.86 SACRAMENTO CA: Got here a few hours ago. Show last night okay. A girl in the crowd pulled out a can of Desenex and was going to throw some of it on me. I stared at her and she put it back in her pocket.

Pain in my legs is giving me trouble. Could hardly load out last night. Feel very stiff. Right knee is feeling like it's starting to come apart. I don't know how much longer I can keep doing this.

Slept on the floor of someone's room last night — cold and damp. Managed to get a good night's sleep though.

Sacramento is a strange place. The sky is blue, the grass is green and all the buildings are very nice. But there are trash and bums and bikers all over the place. Pretty great. See some nice woman coming out of some bullshit office. Watch her have to step those nice legs over a bum who's sleeping in the doorway. Watch her walk down the sidewalk with the trash blowing over her nice shoes. She pretends that she cannot see. What a lie. What a joke. It's like "everything is beautiful if you don't look down." I like it when I see the trash on the streets of California. Rats running wild in Beverly Hills. That's great. It's cool to watch these straight people deal with the trash right at their doorstep.

5.28.86 MEDFORD OR: Did the show in Sacto. During the set, people up front wouldn't leave me alone. One guy grabbed my ankle and tried to pull my leg out from under me. I kicked him in the head with my

SAN DIEGO, CA / 1986 *(SHANNON WAGSTAFF)*

other foot. A guy directly in front of me pounded my feet and jabbed his finger at my eye all night. One time I did it back to him and he got real mad. He said, "I want my money's worth, Henry! Come on!" and pounded my feet some more. A girl kept clawing my legs. We jammed out "Kicking and Sticking" and I looked at these people — these little mohawk guys, skinheads, all these tough looking girls. I kept repeating, "Planes coming over your city. Dropping fire. You come running out of the house screaming. Your house on fire. Your hair on fire. Your body on fire. The hills are on fire. Smell your flesh as it burns. Your body on fire. Bodies on fire. Your world on fire." That's all I could say. I looked at them and I could see their bodies on fire. Sometimes I think I'm stupid as shit for putting myself in the same country as them. It seems like the last thing they care about is the music.

After the show, I went into the bathroom to wash my feet and put on my shoes and socks. I walked in and the stench was overpowering — ammonia. Blood, paper towels, broken glass, water, piss all over the floor. Shit and bottles crammed into the overflowing toilet. I stood in front of the sink and washed the dirt off my feet. I do this every night. I don't know how many times I've seen a sink filled with blood soaked paper towels. I stood there alone, naked in the middle of it all, smelling the piss and shit. I looked at my face in the mirror — hair all stringy and greasy from sweating. What a joke.

My legs are causing me great pain. No matter how much I warm up my muscles, they tighten back up again. Last night, they were burning.

After I had changed, I went out and sat against the wall. I didn't feel like loading out. Body hurt too much. I sat and listened to the bouncers tell each other about the people they punched. An ambulance came and took one kid away.

That was last night. Tonight we're in Medford OR, a bit north of California. Got to bed last night at 3:30 or so. Up at 7:00. On the road by 8:00. Got to the hall around 3 p.m. Feel pretty tired. Legs ache.

I am up in the loft of the truck. Ratman has installed a light in here so you can see what you're doing after it gets dark. I've been up here for a couple of hours. I don't want to talk to anyone.

I talked to Dukowski on the phone today. He said that assorted Christian organizations have been trying to outlaw live rock music in the state of Washington. They have been harassing the promoters of our upcoming shows in Walla Walla, Spokane and Seattle. They almost shut down the Seattle show, but it's still on since we had a contract signed by the owners of the hall. Chuck said that there will be plainclothes cops at every show. He also said that this may be the last time we play in Washington for a long time. I have to start stretching to get ready to play.

5.29.86 EUGENE OR: Last night's gig in Medford was good. The people were real cool. The cops came in and busted the show about five songs from the end of the set. Someone stole my shorts while I was loading out.

Today was Eugene, OR. We were playing at the University of Oregon at Eugene. We set up outside on the lawn. It was too good to last — it looked too great. There was no charge. There were lots of people and the weather was great. Gone played. They were hot. Painted Willie got off about five songs and then the pigs pulled the plug. End of that dream.

We went to this frat house down the road. The frat guys said we could play there, so we did. It was good. We played in the basement that was used to shoot the Otis Day and the Knights scene in the movie *Animal House*. The people were real cool. Now I'm going to find somewhere to sleep. Knee aching. Makes it hard to fall out.

6.1.86 SPOKANE **WA**: We played Seattle last night. Two sets. Second set interrupted by police.

Tonight was Spokane. While I was
loading in today, my right knee went
out and I nearly fell down a flight of
stairs.

The set was up and down. I caught
a water balloon in the nuts. I saw a boy
ready to throw another one so I got off
the stage and grabbed him. I remember it very clearly. I was trying to rip
his trachea out. I had my fingers
wrapped around it and I was pulling.
It felt good. A mess of people pulled me

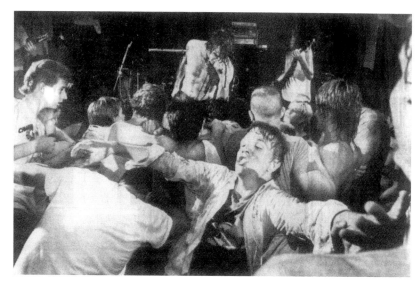

SEATTLE, WA / 5.31.86 *(ANDY NELSON)*

off of him. The rest of the set was spent getting my feet grabbed and my balls squeezed. I had to dodge the
stage dive guys. I sang some too. A girl came up to me and asked if she could kiss me. I said no. A guy gave
me a tape. I threw it away. A guy gave me a book. I threw it away. A girl gave me her address and asked if
I would write her. I told her that I would not. I don't want anything from anyone. It's all water balloons in
the balls to me.

6.10.86 OMAHA **NE**: Have not written for a while. Burned out. Nothing to say. Played a lot of shows here
and there. Last night was Lincoln, Nebraska. I thought we played real well. Crowd was cool.

Human decency is a thing for policemen to remember right before they beat the shit out of someone
for no reason. It's all water balloons in the balls to me. Their flesh is nothing. What do they expect? You
play the game and don't expect to get played back?

The other day in Salt Lake City, I heard this skinhead boy talk about how he was at a gig in Long
Beach, CA. These Samoan bouncers told the skinheads to get out because they were fucking up. The
skinheads tried to get bad so the Samoans took them outside to deal with them. A Samoan put a gun to a
skinhead's head and shot him. I heard this boy telling how he saw parts of the head come clean off. He said
how the Samoans were such dicks. He looked around at us like we're supposed to agree with him. I guess
he couldn't handle the real thing. I thought the skins were supposed to be so tough. I thought that Samoan
bouncers would pose no problems to them. Why was he complaining? Didn't he expect someone, somewhere not to take their shit? It's all the same to me. I won't be crying when they all start dying.

Knee in pain all the time. Nearly fell flat on my face the other night. I don't trust anyone. I don't need
to. I have all the friends I need — Me and Joe.

6.15.86 MILWAUKEE **WI**: Occasional violence and unexpected free food temporarily removes me from my
head. Shows have been good.

Green Bay, Wisconsin parking lot. I'm sitting in the truck playing a tape of Mississippi Fred McDowell
and minding my own fucking business. People come by the truck every few minutes to give me things to
put my name on, to offer me alcohol, to apologize for how low-quality their booze is or for how their town

MINNEAPOLIS, MN / 6.11.86

sucks. "I'm sorry, man. Really. Want to smoke a joint? It's shitty weed, but what the fuck, man. Hey, can you hold on a second, man? I want you to meet my girlfriend. She's over there. She's dying to meet you, but she's scared to Death to come over here. She's lame, but what can I say, man?"

Pudgy lady in fake leather pants that crawl up the crack of her ass talks to a boy in the parking lot. The boy comes up to me and says, "I don't know if this means anything. But this lady just told me that someone is coming to the show tonight to kick your ass. She says he's really big — a wrestler or something..."

It would be great to have a gun. Some wrestler guy comes up to me in a parking lot and says, "I read about you in a magazine. I don't know you really. But like 99% of the human race, I believe everything I read and uh... I'm here to kick your ass." I say, "Yeah right" and blow his head clean off his shoulders and then I get in my limo and ride off into the pulsating sunset.

The Madison show was cool. Friendly people, no big deal. Spent the night at a friend's house.

This morning when we were leaving, the truck would not start for shit. We were parked on an up-grade so Ratman figured he would just roll start the truck in reverse. He went for it. The rear axle snapped. The truck is parked in Madison and it will be there until another axle is brought over. The equipment came to Milwaukee in a Ryder. So here we are...

6.17.86: Very tired. Knee in pain. Last night was Rockford, IL and the night before was Milwaukee, WI.

Milwaukee was good. People were cool. Someone threw a beer mug at the stage and it missed all four of us.

Rockford, IL: The show was good. We played inside a basement-type club. Some people threw stuff and one guy took a swipe at my head, but he didn't get me that bad.

After the show, we drove until 5:00 a.m. to Rock Island, IL. We slept a few hours, until about 9:00, and then went down to this place for a noon show.

Good show. All these people chasing me around for autographs. Gets to be a bit ridiculous. People gotta get the fuck up on their own two feet. It trips me out seeing these people standing in a loose line/ huddle around me with their stuff that they want me to write my name on. Like I said, the people were real cool and we all had a good time.

We loaded out of that place. Well, the other guys loaded out. I didn't load out shit. I'm not much good for that anymore. My knee hurts like fuck when I try to load equipment up the ramp or stairs. I can hardly get my body up much less carrying a piece of equipment.

We drove ten minutes down the road to the other show. I helped load out. Knee fought me all the way. Fucked up. Makes me feel like a useless piece of shit.

Hours later, we play. I thought we played real good. A lot of drunk jocks in the crowd whaling on each other — screaming at me, telling me what songs we should play. Someone threw some chunks of ice at me. They missed. Finished the show. Legs in pain. Went and sat down and some guy walks up and says that he's

ROCK ISLAND, IL / 6.17.86

the biggest asshole in the place because he's coming up and talking to me after I have finished playing and he knows how tired I must be. I tell him that it was really cool to meet the biggest asshole in the place. I told him I admired him because there was a lot of really tough competition out there and that he must really be worn out. He said, "Yeah, it's tough out there." And I said, "You know there was this thing my old man once said to me. He said, 'Son, there's more assholes out there than you can shake a stick at.' " I added that I've had a lot of sticks shaken at me in my time.

We packed out. I sat and watched. We went to some guy's house and we slept. There is no show today. I'm sitting in a room alone. Legs hurt.

6.23.86 LANSING MI: It's almost 8:00 p.m. and the sun is still very high in the sky. I'm sitting in front of the club watching the college girls walk by.

The shows in the past few days have been real good. The people have been real cool. I'm feeling pretty good. Knee hurts, but what the fuck. Today is Monday. The last show is Friday in Detroit. We played Detroit last Saturday as well. During the show, I watched some skinheads try to waste a longhaired guy. I told them to stop or we would. They stopped.

I feel pretty burned out, but I'm still playing good. I just can't remember where we played three days ago without the help of a calendar. We got two sets tomorrow and two sets the day after. That should be pretty raw, but what the fuck.

Later: Sometimes I swear I'm made of wax. This shit can make me feel very low. Dark club, late — hardly anyone around and not a thought in my goddamn head. Feel hollow. I feel like wax. That's how I feel — lifeless, dull and stiff.

I sat for minutes. Not a thing in my head. The music and the voices and the video pinball machines making a solid wall of sound. I am a long dark hallway. No wind — not hot, not cold — not anything at all. Been feeling like this all day.

I walked for hours today up and down the same street. College towns really depress me. Most of the people on the streets are students. They look like they took the Pepsi Challenge seriously. A lot of them are wearing those ridiculous shorts with bright floral and print patterns that come down past the knees. Lots of guys wearing Reebok shoes, riding Hondas and drinking pitchers of Budweiser. Who the fuck put them up to it? I can see it now. "Okay you guys. Now put on these clothes, get in that bar and start knocking them back until you vomit. If I hear any intelligent conversation out of any one of you, you're gonna be sorry."

Now some guy is sitting at my table waiting for me to lift my head so he can engage me in some conversation. What an asshole I am for putting myself in this fix. I should hit myself with a brick until I come to my senses. I need to find my senses. I've been walking around senseless for quite sometime now and I'm feeling like a two-legged bovine.

He goes for it. "Do you know where Tangerine Dream is playing?" And I say, "Yeah, over there in the corner," and I point to the neon Budweiser sign. He leaves. Another dissatisfied customer.

6.26.86 ANN ARBOR MI: Two sets last night, two sets the night before. I think they went real good. Last night, the night crowd in Mt. Pleasant was real drunk. There were a handful of jocks who were doing a lot of stupid shit. But they always do, so what the fuck.

Today we're in Ann Arbor, MI. Playing the same place as we did last year — some kind of gay disco. I'm sitting at a table in back and I'm listening to one of the waiter guys talk about some guy who chased him around the club grabbing at his tits. The waiter guy tried to get him thrown out. But the manager just told him to mellow out and only come back to him if the man grabbed his balls.

The tour ends tomorrow night in Detroit. Two more sets then it's all over with for now. Seems strange. Feels like it just started. I can't remember the beginning at all. The idea that we have been on this trip for the last seven months seems impossible.

7.12.86 SHED: Been here about two weeks. I've been doing okay. Feels strange being in one place for so long.

When the tour ended, I felt like I had stepped off a fast moving train. You look behind you and it's over. It's so over with, it's as if it didn't even happen. So much for glory.

I feel somehow cheated in a way. It's hard to explain. It's just over. *You did your time – now get the fuck out of here*. I don't think I can explain. I feel empty, restless and out of place. I have had a hard time sleeping. I can manage only a few hours at a time. You figure there's going to be some movie type of ending to the whole thing, some big climax, but there's not. It's just over and everyone goes home and promises to keep in touch, but never does.

I have been doing some writing and reading. I did two shows of my own — one at Bebop Records, another at UCLA. I thought they went real well.

The door to the shed had a seven foot pot plant growing next to it when I got back. Thanks Pettibon. That's all I need. Funny guy.

Fuck it. I don't feel like writing anything. Life has slowed down to a crawl. Without the tour, I don't know what to do with myself. I feel like getting in a fight or slicing myself up some.

HENRY, GREG, ANTHONY, C'EL / 1986 *(ED COLVER)*

Rollins, Los Angeles / January 1987 (*Suzan Carson*)

A F T E R W O R D

At some point in August 1986, I was in Washington DC when Greg called me. He told me that he was quitting the band. I thought that was strange considering it was his band and all. So in one short phone call, it was all over.

In a way, it was a relief. I don't think any more good music would have come from the band, seeing how we didn't get along anymore. Looking back at it, it was a good time to stop. It was time to do something else.

By April 1987, the Rollins Band was on tour. Since then, I have not stopped touring and recording.

Since Black Flag was around, the music world has become a smaller place — more calculated and mechanical. Bands don't live like we did. They don't have to. They don't have to put up with the same kind of shit. Many reach platinum record sales on their first album. It might be interesting to see which bands of today would still be around three years after their inception if they went the Flag route. It doesn't matter. I know some things they'll never know.

While I was editing this book, it was hard for me not to become angry every few minutes. I had forgotten how cruel people were to us at times during the band's existence. All the scathing reviews, the lies. The petty shit that the pigs and some of the people at the shows got away with. The disrespect and grief that Greg Ginn and Chuck Dukowski endured to keep the whole thing running, when they knew that what they had come up with was completely brilliant. I know what I know from seeing it. I've had it done to me by people. I have the scars to prove it.

To this day, it is extremely difficult for me to be at ease around people. I do the best I can, but sometimes it's a struggle. If no one ever showed up to one of my gigs ever again starting tomorrow, I would not be surprised in the least. People get tired of what you're doing and they go somewhere else. That's my relationship with people. They are the ones that might change their minds and attack me at any moment. I rarely equate loyalty with people. I foolishly give interviewers the truth and so many times, I have been burned. Imagine being compromised by one of those guys. If we were in the jungle, they would be in the pot and I'd be stirring — that's for fucking sure.

I don't mean to be negative, but this is the truth. I want you to know. Here's some more. I don't know you. But I like you. When I see you at the shows year after year it makes life worth hanging around for. I've been doing this for thirteen years now. This is not my hobby until I go to college. This is what I do. This is who I am. I am a guy who used to work at an ice cream store in Washington DC. I am of average intelligence. There's nothing special about me. If I can get this far, I would be very surprised if you couldn't get at least twice as far. Fuck them. Keep your blood clean, your body lean and your mind sharp.

H. ROLLINS
JUNE 1994
LOS ANGELES, CALIFORNIA

BLACK FLAG LINEUPS / TOUR DATES

1981

GREG GINN: GUITAR
CHUCK DUKOWSKI: BASS
DEZ CADENA: GUITAR
ROBO: DRUMS
HENRY ROLLINS: VOCALS

AUGUST
?? Huntington Beach CA
21 Huntington Beach CA
22 Boston MA
?? San Diego CA
26 Huntington Beach CA

SEPTEMBER
11 Northridge CA (Devonshire Downs, CSUN)

OCTOBER
09 San Diego CA
10 San Francisco CA
11 San Francisco CA
20 San Pedro CA
21 Huntington Beach CA
31 San Francisco CA

NOVEMBER
06 Tucson AZ
07 Phoenix AZ
14 Westchester, CA (dorm party)
15 Hemet CA (party)
19 San Francisco CA
20 San Francisco CA
21 Riverside CA
27 Houston TX
28 Austin TX

DECEMBER
01 Greensboro NC
03 Washington DC (2 sets)
06 London UK
10 Manchester UK
12 London UK
15 London UK
16 Colwyn Bay Wales
17 Preston UK
20 Leeds UK

GREG GINN: GUITAR
CHUCK DUKOWSKI: BASS
BILL STEVENSON: DRUMS
HENRY ROLLINS: VOCALS

23 New York NY
25 Passiac NJ
26 Boston MA (2 sets)
27 New York NY
28 Pittsburgh PA
29 Chicago IL (2 sets)
31 Los Angeles CA

1982

GREG GINN: GUITAR
CHUCK DUKOWSKI: BASS
DEZ CADENA: GUITAR
EMIL: DRUMS
HENRY ROLLINS: VOCALS

MAY
08 Austin TX
10 Oklahoma City OK
11 Tulsa OK
12 Dallas TX
14 Houston TX
15 Houston TX
16 New Orleans LA
17 New Orleans LA
18 Atlanta GA
19 Orlando FL
20 Miami FL
21 Tampa FL
22 Daytona Beach FL
23 Chapel Hill NC
25 Raleigh NC
26 Richmond VA
27 Asbury Park NJ
28 Hartford CT
29 Providence RI
30 Mt. Vernon NY
31 Long Island NY

JUNE
01 Passiac NJ
02 Albany NY
03 Worcester MA
04 Philadelphia PA
06 Baltimore MD
07 Trenton NJ
08 Pittsburgh PA
09 Pittsburgh PA
10 Buffalo NY
12 Ottawa Canada
13 Ottawa Canada
14 Quebec Canada
15 Montreal Canada
16 Toronto Canada
17 Detroit MI (2 sets)
18 Kalamazoo MI (2 sets)
19 Chicago IL (2 sets)
20 Milwaukee WI
21 Madison WI
24 Salt Lake City UT
25 Lawrence KS
28 Denver CO (2 sets)
29 Denver CO
30 Portland OR

JULY
01 Victoria BC
03 Vancouver Canada
04 Seattle WA
06 San Luis Obispo CA
09 Monterey CA

1983

GREG GINN: GUITAR
CHUCK DUKOWSKI: BASS
DEZ CADENA: GUITAR
CHUCK BISCUITS: DRUMS
HENRY ROLLINS: VOCALS

GREG GINN: GUITAR
CHUCK DUKOWSKI: BASS
DEZ CADENA: GUITAR
BILL STEVENSON: DRUMS
HENRY ROLLINS: VOCALS

15 Tucson AZ
16 Phoenix AZ
17 Los Angeles CA
22 Sacramento CA
23 San Francisco CA
24 San Francisco CA
26 San Francisco CA
30 San Pedro CA
31 Hemet CA (party)

AUGUST
06 San Pedro CA
07 Los Angeles CA
12 San Francisco CA
19 San Antonio TX
20 Austin TX
21 Houston TX
22 New Orleans LA
25 Memphis TN
26 Memphis TN
30 Richmond VA

SEPTEMBER
01 New York NY
02 New Jersey
03 Detroit MI
04 New London Canada
05 Ohio
06 Ohio
07 Champaign IL
09 St Louis MO
11 Bridgeport CT
12 Montreal Canada

OCTOBER
13 Redondo Beach CA (party)
19 Valencia CA (Cal Arts) & W. Covina CA (party)
21 Palm Springs CA

DECEMBER
02 Phoenix AZ
03 Tucson AZ
04 Nogales CA (party)
10 Los Angeles CA
19 San Francisco CA
20 San Francisco CA

JANUARY
07 Santa Barbara CA
08 San Francisco CA
14 Torrance CA
21 San Francisco CA
22 San Francisco CA
29 Long Island NY
30 Boston MA

FEBRUARY
02 New Haven CT
03 Washington DC (2 sets)
04 Baltimore MD
05 Philadelphia PA
10 London UK
12 Amsterdam Holland
13 Hanover Germany
14 Hamburg Germany
16 Köln Germany
17 Osnabrück Germany
18 Berlin Germany
19 Munich Germany
20 Vienna Austria
22 Milan Italy
23 Geneva Switzerland
27 Osnabrück Germany
28 Copenhagen Denmark

MARCH
01 Aarhus Denmark
04 Brixton UK
10 Brooklyn NY
11 Baltimore MD
12 Cleveland OH
13 New York NY
14 New York NY
15 Binghampton NY
16 Detroit MI
17 Chicago IL (2 sets)
18 Minneapolis MN (2 sets)
20 Denver CO

APRIL
14 Sacramento CA
22 Stockton CA
23 Berkeley CA
26 Los Angeles CA
29 San Diego CA
30 Santa Monica CA

1984

MAY
07 Hermosa Beach CA (party)
13 Tucson AZ
14 Phoenix AZ
18 Los Angeles CA
26 San Luis Obispo CA
27 San Francisco CA
28 San Francisco CA
29 Arcata CA

JUNE
11 Santa Monica CA

JULY
04 Los Angeles, CA

AUGUST
05 Portland OR
06 Eugene OR
07 Seattle WA
08 Vancouver Canada
20 Los Angeles CA
21 Los Angeles CA

DECEMBER
29 Torrance CA (party)

FEBRUARY
23 Los Angeles CA

MARCH
03 Malibu CA (party)
09 Santa Monica CA
19 Venice CA
24 Phoenix AZ
25 Tucson AZ
27 Norman OK
28 San Antonio TX
29 Austin TX
30 Dallas TX
31 Houston TX

APRIL
01 New Orleans LA
02 Baton Rouge LA
03 Birmingham AL
04 Atlanta GA
05 Columbia SC
06 Washington DC
07 Philadelphia PA
08 Baltimore MD (two sets)
09 Richmond VA
11 Pittsburgh PA
12 Harrisburg PA
13 New York NY & New Haven CT
14 Boston MA
16 Providence RI
17 Syracuse NY
19 Toronto Canada
20 Detroit MI
21 Milwaukee WI
22 Minneapolis MN (2 sets)
24 Kansas City KY
25 Denver CO
26 Salt Lake City UT
27 Seattle WA
28 Portland OR
29 Victoria Canada
30 Vancouver Canada

MAY
02 Eugene WA
04 San Francisco CA
05 Los Angeles CA
14 London UK
16 Birmingham UK
17 Glasgow Scotland
18 Redford UK
19 Leeds UK
20 Stevenage UK
21 Manchester UK
22 Nottingham UK
24 Folkstone UK
25 Rotterdam Holland
26 Hengelo Holland
27 Venlo Holland
28 Nijmegan Holland

29 Groningen Holland
31 Stockholm Sweden

JUNE
01 Karlshamn Sweden
02 Göteborg Sweden
03 Jönköping Sweden
04 Malmö Sweden
08 Bremen Germany
09 Hanover Germany
10 Berlin Germany
11 Berlin Germany
12 Hamburg Germany
13 Bochum Germany
30 Lawndale CA (party)

JULY
06 Los Angeles CA
07 San Diego CA
08 Phoenix AZ
14 Berkeley CA
15 Monterey CA
22 Santa Monica CA
25 Chicago IL
26 St Louis MO
27 Kentucky KY
28 Columbus OH (2 sets)
29 Cleveland OH
30 Toronto Canada
31 Montreal Canada

AUGUST
01 Ottawa Canada
02 Adams MA
03 Marlborough NJ
04 Southgate NJ
05 Trenton NJ (2 sets)
06 Washington DC
07 New York NY
08 Bridgeport CT
09 New York NY
11 Tampa FL
12 Miami FL
25 Sacramento CA
26 San Francisco CA

SEPTEMBER
01 Manhattan Beach CA
14 Tijuana Mexico
22 Guernville CA
23 Portland OR
24 Olympia WA
25 Seattle WA
27 Salt Lake City UT
28 Denver CO
29 Lawrence KS
30 Omaha NE

OCTOBER
01 Columbia MO
02 Lincoln NE
03 Minneapolis MN
04 Oshkosh WI
05 Milwaukee WI

06 Madison WI
08 St Louis MO
09 Cincinnati OH
10 Flint MI
11 Kalamazoo MI
12 Madison WI
13 Kent OH (2 sets)
15 Pittsburgh PA (2 sets)
16 Harrisburg PA
17 Storrs CT
18 Washington DC
19 Trenton NJ (2 sets)
20 Providence RI (2 sets)
21 Boston MA
22 Worcester MA
24 Philadelphia PA
25 Baltimore MD
26 Raleigh NC
27 Columbia SC
28 Charlotte NC
30 Tallahassee FL (2 sets)
31 Miami FL

NOVEMBER
01 Tampa FL
02 Atlanta GA (2 sets)
03 New Orleans LA
05 Baton Rouge LA
06 Lafayette LA
07 San Antonio TX
08 Austin TX
10 Dallas TX
11 Houston TX
12 El Paso TX
15 Phoenix AZ
16 San Francisco CA
17 Los Angeles CA
21 Las Vegas NV
23 Bakersfield CA

DECEMBER
02 Tucson AZ
03 Albuquerque NM
04 Albuquerque NM
05 Santa Fe NM
06 Oklahoma City OK (2 sets)
07 Tulsa OK
08 Memphis TN
09 Nashville TN
10 Birmingham AL
11 Knoxville TN
13 New York NY
14 Adams MA
15 Amherst MA
16 Syracuse NY
17 Quebec Canada
18 Montreal Canada
19 Toronto Canada
20 New London Canada
21 Chicago IL
23 Winnipeg Canada
26 Edmonton Canada
27 Calgary Canada
29 Vancouver Canada

1985

JANUARY
25 Long Beach CA (Instrumental gig, Rollins sings on one song)

FEBRUARY
03 Los Angeles CA (Instrumental gig, Rollins sings on one song)
08 Los Angeles CA (Instrumental gig)
09 Los Angeles CA (Instrumental gig)

MARCH
16 Los Angeles CA (Instrumental gig)
22 Santa Monica CA (Instrumental, Rollins sings on 3 songs)

APRIL
20 Los Angeles CA (Instrumental gig)

GREG GINN: GUITAR
KIRA ROESSLER: BASS
ANTHONY MARTINEZ: DRUMS
HENRY ROLLINS: VOCALS

MAY
19 Phoenix AZ
20 Tucson AZ
22 Salt Lake City UT
24 Denver CO
25 Albuquerque NM
27 Lubbock TX
28 Oklahoma City OK (two sets)
29 Tulsa OK
30 Austin TX
31 Dallas TX

JUNE
01 Houston TX (two sets)
02 San Antonio TX (two sets)
04 Lafayette LA
05 Baton Rouge LA
06 New Orleans LA
07 Memphis TN
08 Nashville TN
09 Knoxville TN
10 Athens GA
11 Birmingham AL
12 Atlanta GA (two sets)
13 St. Petersburg FL
14 Miami FL
15 Tampa FL
16 Tallahassee FL
18 Columbia SC
19 Charlotte NC
20 Raleigh NC (two sets)
21 Richmond VA (two sets)
22 Morgantown WV
25 Washington DC
26 Washington DC

28 Dover NJ
29 New York NY
30 Boston MA

JULY
01 Providence RI
02 Katausqua PA (two sets)
03 Enfield CT
07 Trenton NJ
08 Baltimore MD
10 Bennington VT
11 Rochester NY
12 Albany NY
13 Buffalo NY
14 Syracuse NY
16 Flint MI
17 Ann Arbor MI
18 Mt. Pleasant MI (two sets)
19 Detroit MI (two sets)
20 Cleveland OH
21 Columbus OH
22 Kentucky KY
23 Kokomo IN
24 Kalamazoo MI
25 Lansing MI
26 Chicago IL
27 Madison WI
28 Milwaukee WI
30 Champaign IL
31 St Louis MO

AUGUST
02 Columbia MO
03 Kansas City KS
04 Topeka KS
06 Lincoln NE
08 Omaha NE
10 Minneapolis MN (two sets)
12 Winnipeg Canada
14 Calgary Canada
15 Edmonton Canada
17 Vancouver Canada
18 Victoria Canada
20 Seattle WA (two sets)
21 Spokane WA
22 Walla Walla WA
23 Portland OR
24 Eugene OR
26 Sacramento CA
27 Reno NV
28 Palo Alto CA
29 Santa Cruz CA
30 San Francisco CA
31 Los Angeles CA

SEPTEMBER
01 San Diego CA

1986

GREG GINN: GUITAR
C'EL: BASS
ANTHONY MARTINEZ: DRUMS
HENRY ROLLINS: VOCALS

JANUARY
02 San Francisco CA
10 San Diego CA
11 Los Angeles CA
12 Long Beach CA (party)
13 Huntington Beach CA
14 Tucson AZ
15 El Paso TX
17 San Antonio TX
18 Houston TX
19 Scott LA
20 Baton Rouge LA
21 New Orleans LA (2 sets)
22 Pensacola FL
23 Tallahassee FL
24 Tampa FL
25 Miami FL
26 Orlando FL
28 Gainesville FL
29 Jacksonville FL
30 Savannah GA
31 Athens GA

FEBRUARY
01 Athens GA
02 Columbia SC (2 sets)
03 Charlotte NC
04 Greensboro NC
05 Raleigh NC
06 Knoxville TN
07 Birmingham AL
08 Atlanta GA (2 sets)
10 Birmingham AL
11 Nashville TN
12 Memphis TN
13 Little Rock AR
14 Tulsa OK
15 Oklahoma City OK
16 Dallas TX
16 Lubbock TX
19 Amarillo TX
23 Phoenix AZ (2 sets)
27 Los Angeles CA
28 Long Beach CA

MARCH
07 Glendale CA
08 Palo Alto CA
12 Los Angeles CA
13 Huntington Beach CA
14 Fresno CA
20 Monrovia CA
21 Los Angeles CA
26 Tucson AZ
27 Tucson AZ

APRIL
02 Charlottesville VA
03 Trenton NJ
04 New York NY
05 Washington DC
06 Richmond VA (two sets)
08 Baltimore MD
09 Dover NJ
10 Hoboken NJ
13 Boston MA
14 Bennington VT
16 Poughkeepsie NY
17 Providence RI
18 Enfield CT
20 Trenton NJ
21 Washington DC
22 Albany NY
23 Binghampton NY
24 Syracuse NY
25 Buffalo NY
26 Pittsburgh PA
27 Cleveland OH
28 Pittsburgh PA
29 Columbus OH
30 Kentucky KY

MAY
02 Indianapolis IN
03 St. Louis MO
04 Champaign IL
05 Carbondale IL
06 Columbia MO
07 Topeka KS
09 Kansas City KS
10 Lawrence KS
11 Fayetteville AR
23 San Diego CA
25 Guernville CA
26 San Francisco CA
27 Sacramento CA
28 Medford OR
29 Eugene OR
30 Portland OR
31 Seattle WA

JUNE
04 Salt Lake City UT
06 Denver CO
09 Lincoln NE
10 Omaha NE
11 Minneapolis MN (2 sets)
12 La Crosse WI
13 Green Bay WI
14 Madison WI
15 Milwaukee WI
16 Rockford IL
17 Rock Island IL & Moline IL
19 Cedar Falls IA
20 Chicago IL
21 Detroit MI
22 Grand Rapids MI
23 Lansing MI
24 Kalamazoo MI (2 sets)
25 Mt. Pleasant MI (2 sets)
26 Ann Arbor MI
27 Detroit MI

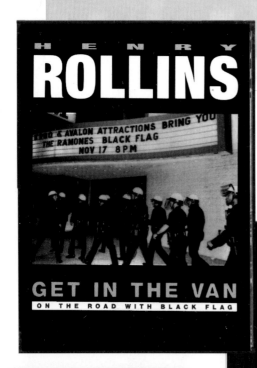
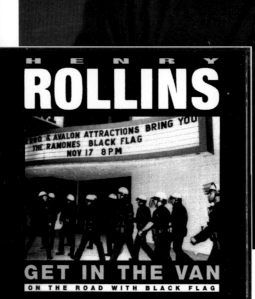